THE DAY WE WON THE WAR

THE DAY WE WON THE WAR

Turning Point at Amiens, 8 August 1918

Charles Messenger

Weidenfeld & Nicolson
LONDON

First published in Great Britain in 2008
by Weidenfeld & Nicolson

3 5 7 9 10 8 6 4 2

© Charles Messenger 2008

A CIP catalogue record for this book
is available from the British Library.

ISBN 978 0 297 85281 0

Typeset by Input Data Services Ltd,
Bridgwater, Somerset

Printed and bound in the UK by
CPI Mackays, Chatham ME5 8TD

The Orion Publishing Group's policy is to use papers that
are natural, renewable and recyclable products and made
from wood grown in sustainable forests. The logging and
manufacturing processes are expected to conform to the
environmental regulations of the country of origin.

Weidenfeld & Nicolson

The Orion Publishing Group Ltd
Orion House
5 Upper Saint Martin's Lane
London, WC2H 9EA
An Hachette Livre UK company

www.orionbooks.co.uk

CONTENTS

ILLUSTRATIONS

MAPS

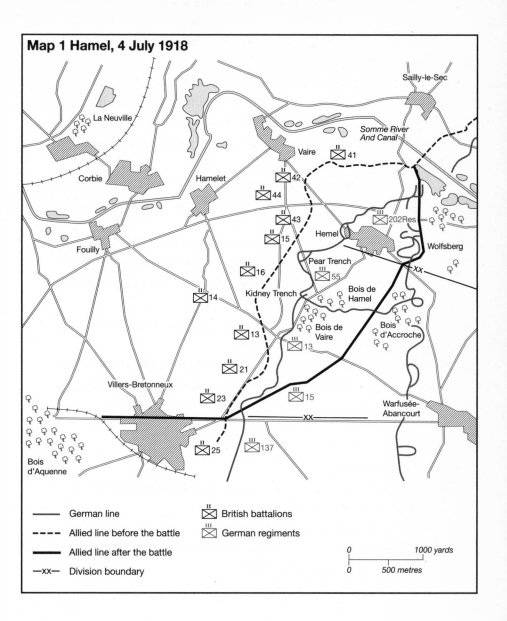

Map 1 Hamel, 4 July 1918

Sailly-le-Sec

La Neuville

Somme River
And Canal

Vaire $\boxtimes$ 41

Corbie Hamelet $\boxtimes$ 42

$\boxtimes$ 44

$\boxtimes$ 43 202Res

$\boxtimes$ 15 Hemel Wolfsberg

Fouilly Pear Trench

$\boxtimes$ 16 $\boxtimes$ 55

Kidney Trench Bois de
Hamel

$\boxtimes$ 14

Bois
d'Accroche

$\boxtimes$ 13 Bois de
Vaire

$\boxtimes$ 13

$\boxtimes$ 21

Villers-Bretonneux

$\boxtimes$ 23 $\boxtimes$ 15

Warfusée-
Abancourt

$\boxtimes$ 25 $\boxtimes$ 137

Bois
d'Aquenne

——— German line $\boxtimes$ British battalions

- - - - Allied line before the battle $\boxtimes$ German regiments

——— Allied line after the battle

0   1000 yards

—xx— Division boundary

0   500 metres

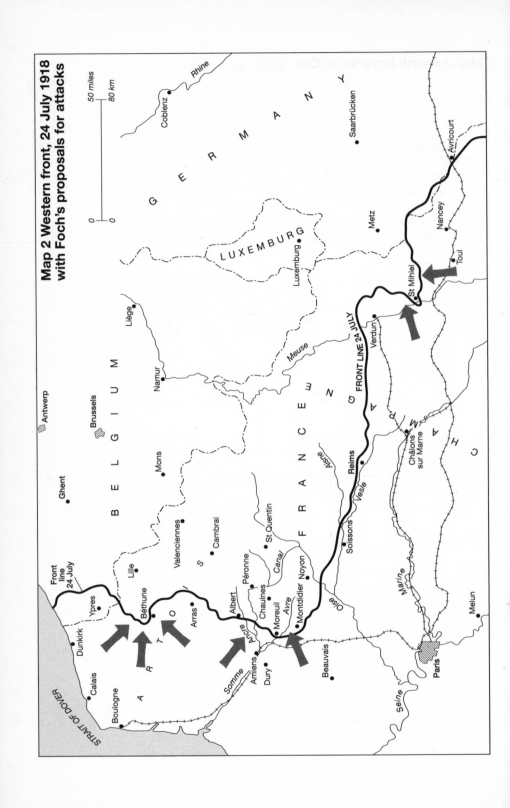

Map 2 Western front, 24 July 1918 with Foch's proposals for attacks

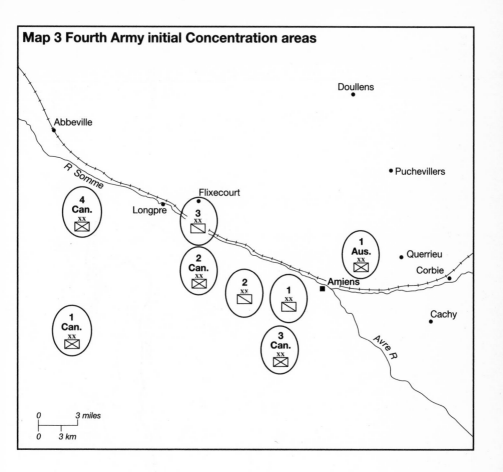

Map 3 Fourth Army initial Concentration areas

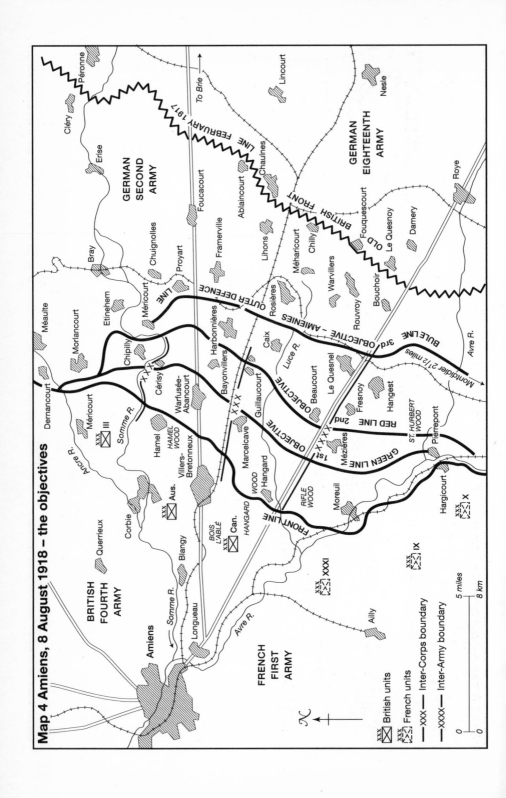

Map 4 Amiens, 8 August 1918 – the objectives

BRITISH FOURTH ARMY

FRENCH FIRST ARMY

GERMAN SECOND ARMY

GERMAN EIGHTEENTH ARMY

LINE FEBRUARY 1917

OLD BRITISH FRONT

OUTER DEFENCE LINE

AMIENS – OBJECTIVE

BLUE LINE

RED LINE

GREEN LINE

FRONT LINE

3rd OBJECTIVE

2nd OBJECTIVE

1st OBJECTIVE

Péronne
Cléry
Erise
Bray
Morlancourt
Méaulte
Dernancourt
Méricourt
Hamel
HAMEL WOOD
Warfusée-Abancourt
Villers-Bretonneux
Corbie
Querrieux
Blangy
Longueau
Amiens
Ailly
BOIS L'ABLÉ
HANGARD WOOD
Marcelcave
Hangard
RIFLE WOOD
Moreuil
Hargicourt
Pierrepont
ST. HUBERT WOOD
Mézières
Fresnoy
Hangest
Le Quesnel
Beaucourt
Guillaucourt
Bayonvillers
Harbonnières
Caix
Rosières
Lihons
Méharicourt
Chilly
Warvillers
Rouvroy
Bouchoir
Damery
Le Quesnoy
Fouquescourt
Roye
Chaulnes
Ablaincourt
Framerville
Proyat
Méricourt
Chuignolles
Etinehem
Chipilly
Cérisy
Foucaucourt
Chuignes
Lincourt
Nesle
To Brie

Luce R.
Somme R.
Somme R.
Somme R.
Avre R.
Avre R.
Ancre R.

III
Aus.
Can.
XXXI
IX
X

Mondidier 2½ miles

N

British units
French units
Inter-Corps boundary
Inter-Army boundary

0   5 miles
0   8 km

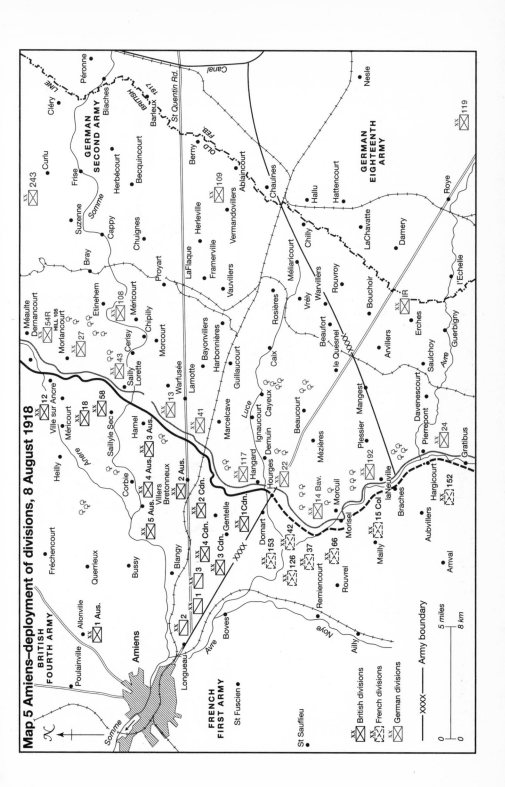

Map 5 Amiens–deployment of divisions, 8 August 1918

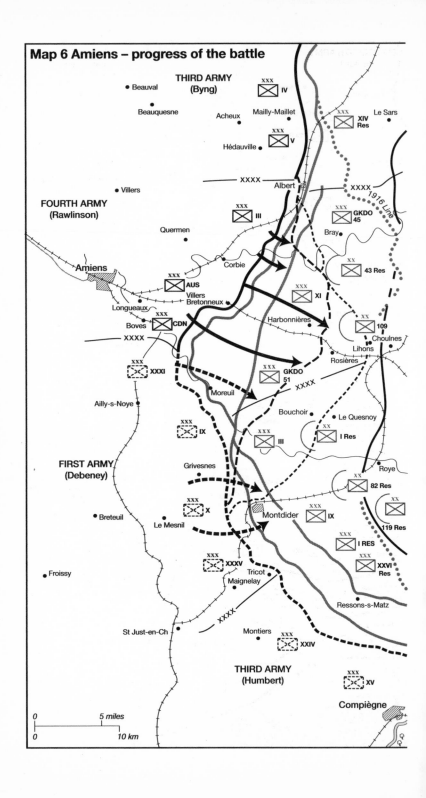

Map 6 Amiens – progress of the battle

THIRD ARMY (Byng)

Beauval

Beauquesne

Acheux

Mailly-Maillet

Hédauville

XXX IV

XXX XIV Res

Le Sars

XXX V

Villers

XXXX

Albert

XXXX

1916 Line

FOURTH ARMY (Rawlinson)

Quermen

XXX III

XXX GKDO 45

Bray

XX 43 Res

Amiens

Corbie

XXX AUS

Villers Bretonneux

XXX XI

XX 109

Longueaux

XXX CDN

Boves

Harbonnières

Choulnes

Lihons

XXXX

Rosières

XXX XXXI

XXX GKDO 51

Moreuil

XXXX

Ailly-s-Noye

Bouchoir

Le Quesnoy

XXX IX

III

XX I Res

FIRST ARMY (Debeney)

Grivesnes

Roye

Breteuil

Le Mesnil

XXX X

Montdidier

XX 82 Res

XXX IX

XX 119 Res

Froissy

XXX XXXV

Tricot

Maignelay

XXX I RES

XXX XXVI Res

Ressons-s-Matz

St Just-en-Ch

Montiers

XXX XXIV

XXXX

THIRD ARMY (Humbert)

XXX XV

Compiègne

0   5 miles

0   10 km

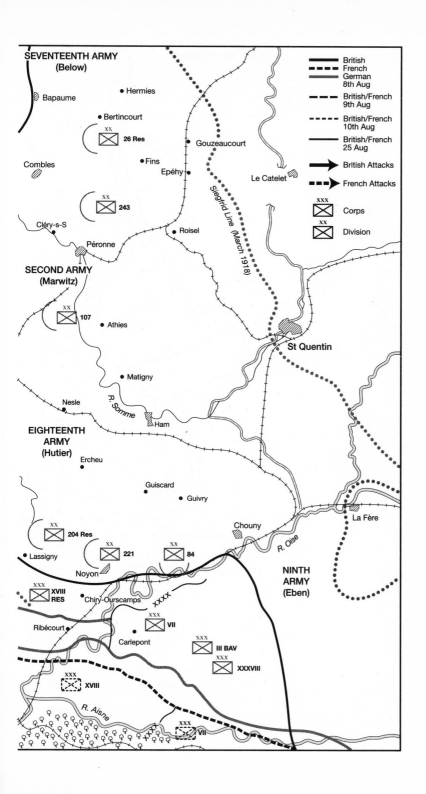

SEVENTEENTH ARMY
(Below)

Bapaume

• Hermies

• Bertincourt

XX
26 Res

• Gouzeaucourt

• Fins

Epéhy •

Combles

XX
243

Le Catelet

Cléry-s-S •

• Roisel

Péronne

SECOND ARMY
(Marwitz)

XX
107

• Athies

St Quentin

• Matigny

Nesle

R. Somme

Ham

EIGHTEENTH
ARMY
(Hutier)

Ercheu

• Guiscard

• Guivry

Chouny

La Fère

XX
204 Res

XX
221

XX
84

R. Oise

NINTH
ARMY
(Eben)

• Lassigny

Noyon

XVIII
RES

Chiry-Ourscamps

XXXX

Ribécourt •

XXX
VII

Carlepont

XXX
III BAV

XXX
XXXVIII

XXX
XVIII

R. Aisne

XXX
VII

Legend:

	British
	French
	German 8th Aug
	British/French 9th Aug
	British/French 10th Aug
	British/French 25 Aug
→	British Attacks
⇢	French Attacks
XXX ⊠	Corps
XX ⊠	Division

Siegfried Line (March 1918)

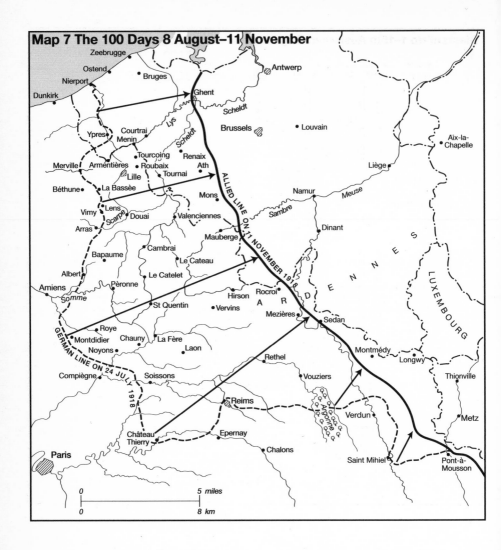

Map 7 The 100 Days 8 August–11 November

Zeebrugge
Ostend
Nierport
Dunkirk
Bruges
Antwerp
Ghent
Scheldt
Courtrai
Menin
Ypres
Lys
Scheldt
Brussels
Louvain
Aix-la-Chapelle
Merville
Armentières
Tourcoing
Roubaix
Lille
Renaix
Ath
Tournai
Liège
Béthune
La Bassèe
Mons
Namur
Meuse
Vimy
Lens
Douai
Arras
Scarpe
Valenciennes
Sambre
Dinant
Bapaume
Cambrai
Mauberge
ALLIED LINE ON 11 NOVEMBER 1918
Albert
Le Cateau
Le Catelet
A R D E N N E S
LUXEMBOURG
Amiens
Somme
Pèronne
St Quentin
Hirson
Rocroi
Vervins
Mezières
Sedan
Roye
Chauny
La Fère
Laon
Montmédy
Longwy
Montdidier
Noyons
GERMAN LINE ON 24 JULY 1918
Rethel
Thionville
Compiègne
Soissons
Vouziers
Argonne
Verdun
Metz
Reims
Château
Thierry
Epernay
Chalons
Saint Mihiel
Pont-à-Mousson
Paris

0   5 miles
0   8 km

Diagram No 1–15th Australian Brigade attack formation, 8 August 1918

Scouts
Tanks

59th Battalion

57th Battalion

| Section 13th Light Horse | Bn.☐ Headquarters | Section 1st Cyclist Battalion | Section 13th Light Horse | Bn.☐ Headquarters | Section 1st Cyclist Battalion |

Section 14th Field Company

Section 14th Field Company

15th Light Trench Mortar Battery

58th Battalion

60th Battalion

| Section 13th Light Horse | Bn.☐ Headquarters | Section 1st Cyclist Battalion | Section of 13th Light Horse | Bn.☐ Headquarters | Section 1st Cyclist Battalion |

15th Machine Gun Company

Hotchkiss Gun Section of 13th Light Horse (Anti-Aircraft)

Exploiting Detachment in Mark V* tanks

○ ○ ○ ○ Supply Tanks

INTRODUCTION

The Butchers and Bunglers School of the study of the British contribution to the war on the Western Front 1914–18 was started by David Lloyd George when he wrote his memoirs, and was carried on by a wave of 1960s historians. It still has a large following, often encouraged by the media, who believe that this is what the general public wants to hear. This school believes that either the war in the West ended on 1 July 1916, the first day of the Battle of the Somme, when the British Army suffered more casualties in a single day than before or since, or amid the mud of Passchendaele Ridge fifteen months later. If it does consider 1918 it is merely to point out the near defeat of the Army in March 1918 or that Germany was beaten by the naval blockade. It is a school that ignores the fact that both the French and the Germans also suffered heavy casualties to little avail – the Germans at Verdun in 1916 and the French at Chemin des Dames in April 1917, to give but two examples.

In the last forty years or so a growing group of serious historians have sought to restore the balance. The pioneer of the School of Revisionism was the late John Terraine, whose writings in the 1960s and 1970s, notably *Haig The Educated Soldier*, were initially those of a lone voice in the wilderness and he endured numerous brickbats for his trouble. He faced these unflinchingly and gradually others were encouraged by him to re-examine the war on the Western Front and to recognize that the conditions in which it was waged were such that the commanders had to relearn their craft. That they did, and in such a short time, albeit at a fearful cost in human life on both sides of No Man's Land, is to their credit. That they were not afraid to embrace emerging technology is another feather in their caps.

For the British, in particular the Australian and Canadian Corps that played the dominant part, the attack at Amiens on 8 August 1918 was a culmination of the hard lessons of the previous years. Erich Ludendorff, the German Quartermaster General and so influential in the conduct of the war, would call it 'the Black Day for the German Army' and so it was. For the attack at Amiens marked the beginning of the so-called Hundred Days which brought about ultimate victory in the West. In this the 90th anniversary of the year in which the Great War finally came to an end, it is fitting that we should remember Amiens and the contribution made by those who fought in the battle. More especially it needs demonstrating what a long way the British Army, and indeed that of the French, had come since the killing fields of 1915–17, as well as the reverses they had suffered earlier in 1918. Perhaps, too, as we come to 11 November 2008, more of us might come to rethink the achievements of the Allied armies during those last and epic months and recognize the spirit that brought the fighting to an end so much earlier than most, especially the politicians, believed possible.

One cannot write a book like this in isolation and my gratitude goes out to a number of people. First, I would like to thank Ian Drury, former Editorial Director of Weidenfeld & Nicolson for commissioning it and for suggesting its rather provocative title. The staffs of the National Archives, Kew and the West Hill Lending Library, Wandsworth, London, sadly now closed, for their unfailing courtesy and willingness to help. The same thanks go as well to the Churchill Archives Centre, Cambridge. My friends and colleagues in the British Commission for Military History have, as usual, given me numerous leads in the course of discussions, usually propping up bars with drinks in hand. I must, not for the first time, also pay tribute to Chris Baker and his Long, Long Trail website and, in particular, its extraordinary Great War Forum, which at the time of writing has over 17,000 members worldwide and who are always so willing to share their knowledge. Indeed, today, as I write this, I posted two last minute queries and received informative replies within the space of ninety minutes.

There are, too, some other individuals to whom I would like to express my heartfelt thanks. David Fletcher, Librarian at the Tank Museum, Bovington and an old friend, did his best to answer some of my more obtuse questions, especially on anti-tank mines and antidotes to the internal tank fumes. In Australia Chris Roberts not only sent me copies of relevant chapters from his collection of Australian unit histories but also carried out research on my behalf into personal accounts of and articles on the battle at the Australian War Memorial, Canberra. Through Chris I would also like to thank Ian Smith of the Australian War Memorial for his help in identifying relevant material. Andrew Pittaway, the City of Fremantle archivist, also very generously sent me copies of chapters of his equally extensive collection of Australian unit histories. In Illinois, Chris McDonald sent me information on the 33rd US Division, while in Canada Brian Curragh provided some most useful material on the part played by the Royal Canadian Dragoons and Ed Bainton on the 78th Battalion. Dwight Mercer of the Canadian Expeditionary Force Study Group also very kindly sent me the Group's very extensive list of relevant websites. Andrew Spooner, Cartographer of the Western Front Association, provided me with copies of 1917 1:40,000 map coverage of the battlefield, without which it would have been very difficult to make sense of the battle. Finally, I must express my deepest gratitude, as well as profound apologies, to Keith Lowe, my editor at Weidenfeld, for his unfailing courtesy, especially in the context of an overdue manuscript and a very tight publication date to meet.

Charles Messenger
London
February 2008

CHAPTER ONE

SETTING THE SCENE

The beginning of July 1918 witnessed a brief lull on the Western Front. While the combatants wondered what the immediate future held they could also look back on the events of the last eight months, a period that had seen the initiative pass from the Allies to the Germans. It had also marked a change in tactics by both sides, tactics that provided the prospect of the restoration of manoeuvre warfare which had been so absent since the early days of the war in the West.

On 20 November 1917, and spearheaded by over 300 tanks, six British infantry divisions broke through the formidable defences of the Hindenburg Line to the south-west of Cambrai. It was the first time that tanks had been used *en masse* and that the artillery had not compromised surprise by registering its guns prior to the attack. Coming immediately after the grim stalemate in the mud of the Third Battle of Ypres the assault at Cambrai provided a ray of hope that the deadlock on the Western Front could finally be broken. Church bells in Britain, which had been silent since the outbreak of war, were rung in celebration. This proved to be premature. Subsequent days saw the German defences harden as reinforcements were deployed, and the British Third Army, which was conducting the attack, lacked sufficient reserves. The offensive was therefore closed down. Then, on 30 November, the Germans mounted a counter-attack which regained most of the ground that had been captured. It was a portent of things to come and would mean that the tank attack at Cambrai would be the last significant offensive action that the Allies would take for almost nine months.

Two major factors caused the Germans to switch to the offensive in the West in early 1918. The first was the October 1917 revolution in Russia. The Bolsheviks' initial priority was to take their country out of the war and although the Treaty of Brest-Litovsk, which formally brought this about, was not signed until March 1918, the Germans were able to begin switching troops westwards almost as soon as the revolution took place. Indeed, some of the divisions sent to Cambrai came from the Eastern Front. This was allied to the fact that they were very conscious of the arrival of Americans troops in France and knew that the time would come when the Western Allies would achieve overwhelming strength. There was, too, the question of the Allied blockade which within Germany was fostering growing discontent with the war. Consequently the German High Command resolved to strike in the West. Von Hindenburg and his staff concluded that the sector running from Arras in the north to the River Oise offered the best possibility for a breakthrough. This was held by the British Third and Fifth Armies.

As the British had at Cambrai, the Germans enjoyed the bonus of fog when they attacked on 21 March 1918. This suited the infiltration tactics that they had used at Cambrai and enabled them to break through General Sir Hubert Gough's Fifth Army, which had only recently taken over an additional 25 miles of front from the French, and to peel back the right wing of Sir Julian Byng's Third Army. The latter, however, managed to hold the two northern German armies, the Seventeenth and Second, but von Hutier's Eighteenth Army reached the River Somme on the third day of the offensive and almost shattered Gough's army. It continued to advance and began to threaten the vital communications centre of Amiens. French reinforcements came up from the south, but in order to better co-ordinate operations, on 26 March the Allies finally appointed a generalissimo, Ferdinand Foch. The German advance now began to slow. The assaulting troops were tired and they were now amid the old 1916 Somme battlefield, whose broken terrain restricted mobility, especially in terms of the supporting artillery and supplies. By 5 April the Germans had been brought to a halt at Villers Bretonneux, just

10 miles from Amiens. The salient they had created extended to a depth of 50 miles on a base of 60 miles, but they had failed to achieve a decisive breakthrough. Even so, Erich Ludendorff had prepared another offensive which was now ready to go.

On 9 April Operation Georgette, an offensive south of Armentières, opened. This time the aim was to capture the Channel ports through which the supplies and reinforcements for the British Expeditionary Force (BEF) passed. Success would also enable the Germans to bombard southern England with their heavy artillery. Fog once again came to the aid of the attackers and the main blow was struck against the weak Portuguese Corps, which broke immediately. However, wet weather prior to the attack had not only hampered air reconnaissance but also reduced many of the roads to a quagmire. It meant that progress was not as fast as it had been during the early days of the Michael offensive of the previous month. Nevertheless, the attack did make progress and steadily pushed back Sir Hubert Plumer's Second Army. Foch deployed French reinforcements but initially was not willing to allow them to become embroiled because of a build-up of German forces which appeared to threaten Paris. The Germans saw Kemmel Hill as the vital ground and brought in Alpine troops to capture it. It eventually fell on 25 April, but by this time the Germans were exhausted and, with little further progress made, Georgette was closed down at the end of the month. Further south, and to dissuade the French from sending reinforcements to Flanders, the Germans had attacked at Villers Bretonneux on 24 April.* They took the village, but it was quickly recaptured by British and Australian troops.

In spite of the failure of its two offensives to achieve a decisive breakthrough the German High Command was by no means finished. There were losses in manpower, general fatigue, and a

---

* This day also marked the first ever tank versus tank action when three British Mark IV tanks engaged three German A7Vs. Two of the Mark IVs (females armed with just machine guns) were damaged, but the other, a male tank armed with 6pdr guns, caused one of the A7Vs to overturn and forced the crew of another to abandon it.

lowering of morale among the troops, but Ludendorff was determined to maintain the pressure on the Allies. Von Hindenburg still
saw Flanders as the decisive sector, but there was a need to remove
the French reinforcements from there. He and Ludendorff therefore
decided that the next attack should fall on the French sector. They
selected the Chemin des Dames sector to the west of Rheims and
scene of the abortive French offensive of spring 1917. The French
Sixth Army's defences were weak there and it had its back to the
River Aisne. Consequently when the Germans attacked on 25 May
they had little difficulty in penetrating and getting across the river. It
was an irony that four British divisions sent to this sector to recuperate after the earlier German offensives found themselves caught up
in the attack and suffered severely. By 30 May the Germans had
reached the Marne and were less than 60 miles from Paris, but they
had been surprised by their success and had committed more troops
than they had intended. The French had deployed reserves and were
able to hold the Germans on the Marne. This was also the first action
for the Americans, who had two divisions involved. Frustrated once
more the Germans launched yet another attack, this time between
Noyon and Montdidier, on 9 June. Again they enjoyed initial success,
but Henri Pétain, commander-in-chief of the French Army, had now
learned how to deal with the German offensive, by holding his
reserves until the moment was right. As the Germans attempted to
cross the River Matz, they were hit in the flank, bringing the offensive
to an immediate halt.

The remainder of June gave both sides an opportunity to draw
breath. Both were very tired and the prospect of an early end to the
war seemed remote. The Germans were becoming desperate. Not
only had their offensives in the West failed, but their Austro-Hun-
garian ally's major offensive across the River Piave in northern Italy
had also been brought to a halt: the Italians, with British and French
troops under command, were now counter-attacking. As for Germany's other allies, the Ottoman Empire was crumbling in the face
of the largely British campaigns in Iraq and Palestine, and Bulgaria
was beginning to waver.

Meanwhile, the situation in Germany itself was growing ever more grim. Severe food rationing was in force, with Berliners limited to just one pound of potatoes per week, and starvation was beginning to threaten. War weariness was gripping the nation, which remained largely apathetic to the recent victories in the West. There was also a creeping Socialist influence, invigorated by the Russian Revolution, which was beginning to call for the overthrow of the Kaiser and an end to the war. Some soldiers who had fought on the Eastern Front had also become influenced by Bolshevik ideas. Germany's industrial base was suffering, with raw materials becoming ever harder to come by, thanks to the Allied blockade. The manpower barrel was also becoming ever more bare. In the spring of 1918 the Class of 1920, which was composed of 17-year-olds, was called up two and a half years ahead of its due date. Average battalion strengths had fallen from more than 800 men to under 700 men during the period February–May 1918 alone. Discipline, too, was not what it was. Both von Hindenburg and Ludendorff commented on the propensity of the troops during the recent attacks to fall off the line of march and loot well-stocked Allied dumps and canteens which they found in their path. This was another reason why the momentum of the advance had slowed. It also added to the growing disillusionment because the troops had been told that the Allies were suffering equally from shortages. General Georg von der Marwitz, who was commanding the German Second Army in the Somme sector, was very concerned by the decline in discipline. On 7 June 1918 he issued an order decrying the tendency of commanders to shield their officers and men by giving them only light punishments or none at all for infractions of discipline and military regulations. Eleven days later, he commented in a further order on the subject: 'Cases of soldiers openly refusing to obey orders are increasing to an alarming extent.'[1]

Across the other side of No Man's Land the Allies, apart from the Americans, were also suffering manpower problems. General Pétain had estimated that he would need just over a million men to maintain the strength of the French Army during 1918 and that there would be a shortfall of nearly 200,000. In the event, and even by calling up the

1919 draft in spring 1918, he would receive only some 750,000 men. Furthermore, he had made no allowance for the high level of casualties that the French Army suffered as a result of the German offensives – 340,000 alone during the period 21 March – 2 May. Morale, too, was still a tender plant. In the aftermath of the disastrous spring 1917 offensive and the resultant mutinies within the French Army Pétain had been brought in to restore its spirits, which he did through providing more leave and better recreational facilities, as well as keeping the Army on the defensive. The German offensives had a bad effect on morale. Apart from heavy casualties, the more open style of warfare meant that supplies often could not keep up and mail became irregular. Leave was also stopped. The war seemed to be never ending and by early June there was once more deep pessimism within the ranks. As one French soldier wrote in a letter: 'The Germans will soon be in Paris. I would rather live as a German than die as a Frenchman.'[2] Yet the *poilus* still defended with tenacity. They were also encouraged by the ever greater number of US troops in France and the frequent visits made to the front by their prime minister Georges Clemenceau, who was more than living up to his nickname of the Tiger.

British manpower problems had become apparent before the end of 1917. The War Office estimated that it would need 600,000 fully fit conscripts during 1918 if the Army was to be kept up to strength, but the monthly total of new recruits of all medical categories was falling off during the last months of 1917, with only 25,000 joining the colours in December. At the beginning of January the Manpower Committee placed the Army low down on the list of priorities. Apart from the government's concern to maintain Britain's industrial base, which also needed manpower, Prime Minister David Lloyd George was concerned not to allow Haig to embark on another costly offensive like Third Ypres. Rather he envisaged the Allies remaining on the defensive during 1918 while the Americans built up their strength in France. The immediate consequence of this was that Haig was forced to reduce each infantry division by three battalions because of his shortfall in strength. This was carried out just six weeks before the

Germans struck for the first time. When they did the heavy casualties they caused during the opening days of the offensive forced the War Office to go back on its rule that no soldier should be sent to a theatre of war until he had reached the age of nineteen.* Now 18½-year-olds were sent out. Even so, by May 1918 some divisions had been reduced to mere cadres. Three of these had to be sent back to Britain to reform and one, the 39th Division, remained in France as a skeleton in a training capacity for the rest of the war.

The only formations in the BEF which had avoided the reduction in the number of battalions per division were the Australians and Canadians. The conscription, although bitterly opposed by Canada's Liberal Party and the French-Canadians, had become law in July 1917, but was not put into effect until the beginning of 1918 and did not supply more than 25,000 men to the Canadian Corps during that year. As it was, the 5th Canadian Division, which was based in Britain, was disbanded in February 1918. The Canadian Corps itself was based in the Arras area and did not become involved in the German offensives. Hence by July 1918 it was reasonably up to strength and well rested. In contrast, the Australian Corps was still reliant on volunteers, since referenda held in the country in October 1916 and December 1917 had shown Australians to be against conscription. The Corps had spent the winter in the sector south of Ypres, but when the Germans struck in March it was sent down to the Somme to help halt the thrust towards Amiens. The 1st Australian Division was then ordered back northwards to protect Hazebrouck in the face of the second German drive and stayed in that area while the remainder of the Corps occupied the right sector of Rawlinson's Fourth Army on the Somme.† When they had turned back the

---

* It should be pointed out that a not insignificant minority of the volunteers of 1914–15 were underage, since they did not have to produce birth certificates on enlistment. See Richard Van Emden *Boy Soldiers of the Great War* Headline, London, 2005.
† The serious defeat of the Italians at Caporetto in autumn 1917 had necessitated HQ Second Army being sent to Italy. Its role in Flanders was taken over by Rawlinson and HQ Fourth Army. In mid March 1918 HQ Second Army returned from Italy and resumed its former role. In the meantime Rawlinson went to Versailles as the British Representative on the

Germans at Villers-Bretonneux in late April the Australians not only began to dominate No Man's Land, but also nibbled away at the German defences through aggressive patrolling, a technique they termed 'peaceful penetration'. The 1st Australian Division used much the same tactics in Flanders.

The morale of the BEF was largely measured by the tone of the letters sent home from the Front. A report dated 12 July and drawn up by the BEF's censorship department noted that morale did take a battering during the German offensives and that there was a significant element of war weariness. A soldier (unit unknown) writing in mid June:

> We are expecting Fritz over any time now. I think the quicker he drives us out of France the better. It is quite time to end it somehow or other ... everybody is fed up with the war out here and don't care who wins so long as we get it over.

There were many grumbles over the lack of home leave, especially that officers obtained leave very much more frequently than the men, an observation that was sadly true. The Australians, too, were getting tired as a result of their active defence of Amiens. A member of the 1st Australian Brigade writing home on 8 June:

> Things are not too good over this side, they are sticking the dirt into the Aussies a treat. Its a barstard [sic] in the line and its a barstard out. A man would be better off in the clinc [sic] doing a couple of years.

Yet, many others were more upbeat. There was a general feeling that the Germans could not continue to endure the level of casualties that they were suffering and that the corner was being

Supreme War Council, but on 28 March replaced Gough as commander of the Fifth Army. This was renamed the Fourth Army five days later. A Reserve Army was designated at the same time and this became Fifth Army on 23 May.

turned. It is best summed up by another Australian writing at the end of June:

> There seems to my mind to be a wave of optimism on our side just now. It was not so pronounced two or three months ago, but as the enemy seems to be held here, really held I mean, and in view of the large influx of Americans – good men too – and now the Italian victory [on the Piave], it has put fresh heart in many of the men, some of whom are really war weary and worn.

All did recognize, though, that hard fighting lay ahead.[3]

Relations between the British and the French in the early summer of 1918 were not at their best. The latter tended to blame Perfidious Albion for failing to halt the German offensives and to suspect that the British government was no longer prepared to make the manpower sacrifices that the French were continuing to have to do. As Clemenceau said to President Raymond Poincaré: 'The British are trying for an excuse to escape efforts and want us to do the same and leave to the Americans the burden of continuing the war. This is also to some extent the tendency of [the French] parliament.'[4] At an Anglo-French meeting on 1 June Foch accused Lloyd George of holding back reinforcements to such an extent that the BEF would be reduced to a mere thirty divisions by the autumn. When Haig reminded Lord Milner, the Secretary of State for War, that the War Office had told him that the figure was likely to be a mere twenty-eight divisions, the two British ministers were discomforted, but invited Foch to send 'an expert' to inspect the manpower figures.[5] Earlier that day, however, the prime ministers, including Vittorio Orlando of Italy, agreed to send an appeal to President Woodrow Wilson for additional American troops. Pointing out that 162 Allied divisions now faced 202 German divisions in France and Flanders and that the French and British were no longer in a position to increase their number of divisions, the prime ministers urged Wilson to deploy no less than

100 divisions at as earlier a date as possible at a suggested rate of 300,000 men per month. The note made clear that ultimate victory against Germany could not be achieved without this step.[6] Thus, there was general acceptance that the war was likely to continue until well into 1919.

As for the American Expeditionary Force (AEF), the basis for deployment was enshrined in the General Organization Project, drawn up by General John Pershing and his staff in July 1917. This called for an Expeditionary Force of one million men to be deployed to Europe by May 1918. This figure was considered 'the smallest unit which in modern war will be a complete, well-balanced and independent fighting organization.' The key word in this statement is 'independent', since Pershing was determined from the outset that the Americans would fight as a distinct entity and not be split up under French and British command. The Project went on to state that, especially in terms of industrial planning, the AEF might be expected to reach a strength of three million in two years.[7] Set against this background, the European Allies' June 1918 request to President Wilson does not seem unreasonable.

Intense pressure was put on Pershing to dissipate his force. The British proposed in early January 1918 that he pass over 150 battalions to them so that they could be absorbed by the British divisions and thus avoid reducing the strength of each by three battalions. Needless to say, this suggestion was quickly dismissed.[8] The Americans were nonetheless conscious that they needed training in trench warfare and that, because their munitions industry was having to develop almost from scratch, they were reliant on the British and French for the supply of much of their weaponry and equipment. As a result it was agreed that units would be attached to the British for training for a period of approximately ten weeks, after which they were to return to their parent US division. A similar arrangement was made with the French, who were also keen to see US units in the line for the sake of morale. In this case entire US divisions were deployed in the line, beginning with the US 1st Division, which relieved the Moroccan Division at the end of January 1918. By the beginning of

July nine divisions had actually deployed in the line in the French sector. One division, the 93rd, which consisted of black troops, was dispersed by regiments to be under command of various French divisions, and five other divisions had entered the line for training, three of them with the British. Of the last named the 33rd Division was under the British Fourth Army, with elements of the 131st and 132nd Regiments under the Australians for instruction.

The Australians themselves were about to embark on a rather more ambitious operation within the context of Peaceful Penetration, an operation which would have a significant influence on the August attack at Amiens. The focus of this operation was the village of Hamel, which lies just south of the Somme and two miles south-south-east of Corbie. (See Map 1) The Germans had captured the village on 4 April and it formed the base of a salient jutting into the Australian line. The high ground around Hamel also gave the Germans excellent observation. Encouraged by the apparent low morale of the Germans facing the Australians, the poor state of their defences, on 18 June Rawlinson asked John Monash, who had recently taken command of the Australian Corps, and Brigadier General Anthony Courage, commanding the 5th Tank Brigade, which was supporting the Fourth Army, to draw up a plan for eradication of the salient. This was to be the Australians' first attack with tanks since the ill-fated assault at Bullecourt in April 1917 when the 4th Australian Division suffered some 3,000 casualties and blamed their reversal on the supporting tanks, almost all of which were victims of German fire or mechanical breakdown. They therefore viewed tanks with suspicion and would need some convincing that they could make a significant contribution.

Weaponry and techniques had, however, changed significantly since the days of Bullecourt. The most prominent development had been the artillery's ability to fire off the map. A number of factors contributed to this. There was a much greater understanding of how the shell behaved in the air after firing and of how barrel wear could affect the accuracy of a gun. Meteorology played its part in the former, with so-called Meteor messages being sent to the guns every four hours giving wind speed and direction and temperature at various altitudes.

Guns were test fired to establish the individual behaviour of the shell in each barrel. Surveying, too, had become very much more accurate and enabled the position of the target in relation to that of the gun to be established on a map with confidence. Counter-battery work was a crucial artillery task in support of an attack. Air photography played a significant part in locating enemy gun positions, but sound ranging was also becoming an effective method (provided the wind was in the right direction). It consisted of a series of microphones established along a base line. These picked up the report of a gun firing and by measuring the time differences between the various microphones detecting the report it was possible to pinpoint the gun's position.

Tanks had also improved since the Mark Is and IIs used at Bullecourt and the Mark IVs at Cambrai. The new Mark V, with which the 5th Tank Brigade was equipped, was much better protected, had a slightly higher speed – 4.6 miles per hour as opposed to the Mark IV's 3.7 mph – and was much simpler to drive, requiring just one man rather than the four on previous models. A larger fuel capacity gave it an increase of 10 miles range over the Mark IV's 15 miles. Even so, the Australians were suspicious of them, especially General Ewan Sinclair-MacLagan, commanding the 4th Australian Division which was to carry out the attack. Nevertheless, Monash and Courage got on with the planning. The Australian commander's main concern was casualties, since his corps was already more than 8,000 men under strength, and if his losses were high there was a very real danger that he would have to disband one of his divisions. He therefore decided that he would employ just two brigades on a 7,000 yard front, relying on his 60 tanks and 600 supporting guns to compensate for the lack of infantry numbers. The objective was strictly limited, involving a penetration of not more than 2,500 yards. The plan itself bore many of the hallmarks of Cambrai – no preliminary bombardment, tanks concentrated, and great stress on security. The original plan called for a rolling barrage fired by the heavy artillery to be laid down 300 yards ahead of the tanks, on the basis that this and the firepower of the tanks themselves would crush any resistance, enabling the following infantry to occupy the ground with the minimum of casualties. But Monash's chief of Staff, Thomas Blamey, and Sinclair-MacLagan were not happy with this and proposed that the field artillery provided the rolling barrage, with the heavies concentrating on likely points of resistance. Monash accepted this, as did Rawlinson.

Airpower was also to play its part. This was built around the RAF's V Brigade, whose four scout squadrons would provide close air support over the battlefield, with three further squadrons from IX Brigade carrying out high altitude patrols. The bulk of the artillery target spotting work was to be carried out by No. 3 Squadron Australian Flying Corps, while No. 9 Squadron was given a novel task, namely the dropping of ammunition to the forward troops once they had achieved their objectives. Rawlinson watched the Squadron in training on 1 July and thought it a good idea, although he noted that the actual drops were very inaccurate.[9] During the nights preceding the attack aircraft flew up and down the Australian sector, the object of this exercise being to mask the noise of the final move up and deployment of the tanks up to Zero Hour.

Secrecy was paramount. Monash insisted on the minimum being committed to paper and the bugs in the plan were ironed out through a series of conferences. The troops taking part were withdrawn from the line. MacLagan's 4th Brigade would take the lead part, with the 11th Brigade (3rd Australian Division) on its left and two battalions from the 2nd Australian Division on the right. In all, ten battalions would be involved, together with a battalion-sized force from the 15th Australian Brigade to protect the northern flank on the other side of the Somme. They underwent rigorous training with the tanks at Vaux-sur-Somme, 12 miles east of Corbie and on the north bank of the river. Rawlinson visited on 30 June and noted with obvious relief: 'I think we have now got the Australians to understand and appreciate the Tanks.' Later that day he attended Monash's final conference and noted that it lasted four hours and 20 minutes.[10] Haig, who visited Monash on the following day, considered him 'a most thorough and capable commander who thinks out every detail and leaves nothing to chance. I was greatly impressed with his arrangements.'[11]

Monash experienced two last minute problems. The first was as a result of a visit by Australian prime minister Billy Hughes on 2 July. After a tour of the Australian sector Hughes commented to Monash on the tired appearance of his men and told the Australian commander that he must rest them. Monash pointed out that he was answerable to Haig, but Hughes reminded him that he was his prime minister and that his orders must be obeyed. He went on:

> If you wish, I can have you removed from your Australian command. This I do not wish to do, but I want you to understand that the welfare of Australia's troops is my first concern. Tell General Haig that unless my request is agreed to, I will withdraw all Australian troops from France.[12]

With the Hamel operation shortly to take place Monash chose to ignore Hughes's threat, but it must have discomforted him all the same.

He was now to be faced by another bombshell. It had struck Rawlinson that it would be a good idea for some of the American troops training with his army to have experience of a set piece attack. He broached the idea to Monash, who was enthusiastic and suggested eight companies' worth. Since an American company consisted of 250 men the extra numbers were a considerable attraction. After obtaining Haig's agreement Rawlinson approached General George W. Read, the commander of the II US Corps, which was administering the divisions being trained by the British. He agreed that a battalion's worth of troops could be made available and ordered Major General George Bell Jr of the 33rd Division to select them. He, in turn, chose two companies each from the 131st and 132nd Infantry Regiments. These belonged to the 66th US Brigade, which was training with the British III Corps, and not to the 65th Brigade, which was already with the Australians. In the meantime, Rawlinson had selected Independence Day, 4 July, for the attack on the grounds that 'it was the first occasion on which American troops had taken part in an actual attack alongside our fellows.'[13] However, Monash had decided that it would be good to have one US company embedded with each of the ten attacking Australian battalions and had been led to believe that these would be forthcoming. Rawlinson and Read visited Haig on 29 June and Read agreed to provide an additional six companies, which were provided by 131st Regiment, with the whole of its 1st and 2nd Battalions now involved. Three days later, on 2 July, General Read informed Rawlinson that Pershing was objecting to the use of American troops in the attack on the grounds that they were insufficiently trained. Rawlinson thought it too late to withdraw them, but contacted General Sir Herbert Lawrence, Haig's chief of staff who was attending the Supreme War council at Versailles with his master, and asked him to speak to Pershing. Haig saw Pershing on the following morning and the latter reiterated his insistence that American troops not be used. When Haig asked him if he would like him to intercede Pershing replied that Rawlinson had the matter in hand. In fact, Rawlinson had agreed with Read that just the additional six companies be withdrawn. The orders to do this were received by the relevant Australian battalions on the morning of 3 July. It meant that they now had to reorganize their attack formations and cope with having considerably less men. There was also great disappointment among the Americans. When the officers of the company attached to the 16th Australian Battalion were told the news:

> ... they were dumbfounded. When they communicated the contents to their men, the latter were inclined to disobey the command. A violent discussion took place among them, and they came over and sat down among the 16th, who were then making their final dispositions. The officer in command of the Americans gave the 16th his men's best wishes and wished the battalion good luck.[14]

The companies then withdrew.* But that was not the end of the matter.

* According to Bean *Official History* Vol 6 p.276 and fn one or two Americans did disguise themselves with Australian tunics and stayed to take part in the attack. He cites a report by

As a result of the discussion between Haig and Pershing Lawrence telephoned Rawlinson to say that no Americans whatsoever were to take part in the attack. Pershing also told Read the same. By now it was 4 p.m. and Rawlinson in turn telephoned Monash to give him the unwelcome news. He then spoke to Sinclair-MacLagan and his brigade commanders, who were aghast. At Monash's request Rawlinson motored to HQ 4th Australian Division and met him there at 5 p.m. Monash told Rawlinson that if the Americans were withdrawn he would have to cancel the attack. He therefore proposed to go ahead with the operation unless Rawlinson expressly forbade him, but the order would have to come before 6.30 p.m. since otherwise it would be too late to stop the deployment of infantry, artillery and tanks. He also said that cancellation might well result in an 'international incident' in the form of a clash between the Diggers and the Yanks. Rawlinson must have felt that a pistol was being pointed at his head and told Monash that although he wanted the attack to go ahead he was risking being sacked from his command if he so blatantly disobeyed an order from GHQ. Monash apparently retorted that good Australian-US relations were more important than the preservation of an army commander. Rawlinson took the point and agreed to speak to Lawrence again and if he did not receive an answer by 6 p.m. the attack would go ahead with the remaining Americans. This deadline was put back to 6.30 p.m. and then 7 p.m. since Haig and Lawrence were on their way back from Versailles and not contactable. Rawlinson did manage to speak to Lawrence, who spoke to Haig just before 7 p.m. The Commander-in-Chief's reaction was: 'The first essential is to improve our position east of Amiens as soon as possible. The attack must therefore be launched as prepared even if a few American detachments cannot be got out before zero hour.' The 'green light' had been given and Americans would take part. The whole episode had put unnecessary pressure on Monash

---

the 42nd Battalion that two Americans with them resorted to this ploy. But this does not make sense since Sanborn *The 131st US Infantry in the World War* p.45 states that its Company C attacked with this battalion.

and his command at a critical juncture. It also left a sour taste in Rawlinson's mouth: 'If Pershing goes on like this we will never win the war.'[15]

The Hamel sector itself was held by elements of two German divisions. Covering the area from the Bray–Corbie road south to and including Hamel was the 43rd Reserve Division, which completed its relief of the 77th Reserve Division only on the night before the attack. Its 202nd Regiment was in the line, with one battalion forward, one in support, and the third resting. The Division itself had taken part in the Lys offensive in April and suffered heavy casualties. It had recently completed a period of recuperation. To its south was the 13th Division, considered first class by British intelligence. True it had 40 per cent casualties during the March offensive, but had been quickly brought up to strength again and served for a short time on the River Avre before being rested. All three of its regiments were in the line, with their battalions deployed in the same way as the 43rd Reserve Division. The defences in the sector varied in quality. Hamel itself and Hamel and Vaire Woods to its south were well fortified and there were also a number of other strongpoints. The actual trenches existed almost only in name. They were shallow and broken, with many of the defenders in the front line occupying mere shell holes. There were no proper dug-outs and no communication trenches. Such were the Australian security measures that an attack was not expected. As for the overall look of the battlefield it was open grass-land, mixed with crops which had grown to waist high.

At 6 p.m. on 3 July the assaulting battalions were informed that Zero Hour would be at 3.10 a.m. Most had moved into the trenches during the previous night, with the remainder going in during the coming hours of darkness. The 60 fighting tanks were made up of three companies from the 8th Tank Battalion and two from the 3rd Tank Battalion. In addition there were 12 supply tanks. These were to carry ammunition and defence stores to deliver to the infantry once they had reached their objectives. The tanks had lain up during the day in the Fouilloy and Hamelet areas, 2 and 1 miles respectively behind the front line. At 10.30 p.m. they began to move forward, with aircraft drowning the noise of their engines, and arrived at their start line, 1,000 yards behind the front line, by 1 a.m. In addition, No. 101 Squadron, with its FE2bs, attacked woods east of Villers Bretonneux with bombs throughout the night. To get the tanks forward to their attack positions ahead of the infantry, harassing fire was put down, beginning eight minutes before Zero Hour. The rolling barrage itself began promptly at Zero Hour, with that of the 18 pdrs, one to every 25 yards of front, initially falling 200 yards in front of the start line. Two hundred yards beyond this was the 4.5-inch barrage and 200 yards beyond that of the 6-inch howitzers. After four minutes the three barrages began to creep forward by 100 yards every three minutes. By this time the tanks were up and ahead of the infantry and advancing right up close to the barrage. This contained an element of smoke and some shrapnel. A noticeable ground mist also made observation difficult for the Germans.

Some of the guns were found to be firing short and both the 15th and 43rd Battalions suffered casualties. A tank was also knocked out. But otherwise the barrage was most impressive. Capt Carroll M. Gale, whose Company C of the US 131st Infantry was with the 43rd Battalion:

> ... the falling shells of the 18-pounders, exploding as they hit the ground, formed an almost straight line from the north edge of the action at the Somme to as far south as we could see ... [the barrage] was laid down so perfectly that we were able to approach it at about seventy-five yards, as ordered, without receiving any casualties from it.[16]

There was, too, hardly any return artillery fire from the Germans, an indication that the counter-battery work by the heavies was effective. The infantry moved forward, with the Germans in front of them firing many red and green distress flares. The inexperienced Americans with the 43rd Battalion actually dashed into the barrage itself and had to be hauled back. One German position had been identified as a strongpoint. This was Pear Trench, which lay to the north of

Vaire Wood. The 15th Battalion, which had already suffered from shells falling short, found itself up against this obstacle. Unfortunately, the tanks which were supporting the battalion had temporarily lost their way in the murk and were not immediately available to deal with the problem. Undaunted, the infantry pushed forward, Lewis gunners firing from the hip through the tall crops to suppress the German machine guns, which were then rushed. Other sub-units managed to get round the flanks of the position and in this way the Germans holding it were forced to surrender. Vaire and Hamel Woods were also expected to give trouble. Their capture was to be the task of the 16th Battalion which was suffering from the fact that its two companies of attached Americans had been withdrawn the previous evening. Its supporting tanks were available and took advantage of the rides through the woods to help suppress the opposition. The comparatively slow advance of the rolling barrage was also of considerable help. The two flanking brigades experienced few problems and, indeed, the tanks got ahead of the infantry and advanced close to the barrage. In this way they were able to destroy machine-gun nests, either by fire or literally running over them, or forcing the crews to take cover and be dealt with by the following infantry.

The final place from which stiff resistance was expected was the village of Hamel. The 43rd Battalion was to be responsible for its capture, with the 44th Battalion, which would operate in two parts, attacking on either side of the village so as to double envelop it. Since this sector represented the deepest advance, half of the available tanks were allocated to it. Opposition was much less than expected and the attack went almost like clockwork. The Germans had been taken totally unawares. The 202nd Reserve Regiment admitted this and that its 3rd Battalion, which was in the line at the time, was annihilated.[17] It was notable that many of its men were wearing gasmasks, fearing that the smoke shells being used in the barrage might contain gas. Many also were found sheltering in deep dug-outs and Cpl Schulte of the 43rd Battalion captured the complete headquarters of the German 3rd Battalion in this way. The attacks on the flanks had also gone according to plan. It had been envisaged that the operation would last 90 minutes; it actually took 93 minutes to secure the final objectives.

In the skies above No. 3 Squadron AFC bore the brunt. Its aircraft flew a total of 79 hours during the day. They assisted in the neutralization of no less than 41 German batteries, dropped over 130 bombs and took 108 photographs at a cost of just one plane lost. The DH4s of No. 205 Squadron carried out a number of bombing raids during the day, mainly against bivouac areas, billets and dumps, and two planes from No. 8 Squadron co-operated with the tanks, noting their positions and identifying those that had been disabled.* The fighter squadrons not only ensured air superiority, but also carried out low flying attacks on the ground. Finally, No. 9 Squadron carried out ammunition dropping with its twelve RE8s. Each aircraft carried two ammunition boxes, which were clipped to the parachutes, which were in containers fitted to modified bomb racks, the normal bomb release gear being used. Each aircraft made four trips from the Squadron's base at Poulainville, some 16 miles from Hamel. They dropped a total of 93 boxes on spots indicated on the ground by N- and V-shaped panels at a cost of two aircraft lost. The dropping was not especially accurate, although one box did land within ten feet of one of the 6th Machine Gun Company's positions. Even so, this method of resupply was found to be useful.† Between 9 and 11 a.m., however, the presence of British aircraft was sharply reduced. The Germans took advantage of this and their planes were soon machine-gunning the Australians in their newly captured positions. When the RAF returned in strength the Germans were driven off.

The tanks had begun to withdraw to their rallying points some 5 miles to the rear at 5.30 a.m. Only five had been disabled – they were

---

* Each disabled tank hoisted a red flag, although these could not be identified from the air above 600 feet.

† According to the 11th Australian Brigade's report on the attack (TNA WO 95/3429) German aircraft delivered food to their men by the same method. Bean *Official History* Vol 6 p.309 collaborates this, but states that it took place on 5 July and was done without parachutes.

all recovered during the next two days – and the casualties were just thirteen crewmen wounded. The Mark V had certainly proved itself to have an infinitely better performance than its predecessors, especially in terms of manoeuvrability. It certainly dispelled the deep suspicion that the Australians had had of them. As the 6th Australian Brigade report on the operation expressed it: 'In this action the tanks showed their value and, having seen them in action, the infantry have a very high opinion of their work, and confidence in the protection they afford during an attack.'[18] One particularly useful innovation was the installation of a bell inside the tank which was connected to an external bell pull, which the infantry could use to attract the tank commander's attention. This meant that co-operation between the two arms was much closer than hitherto. The supply tanks also impressed, especially since they represented a significant saving in manpower in terms of carrying parties.

With the tanks now withdrawn the infantry still faced the prospect of a German counter-attack, something which past experience indicated was likely to be sooner rather than later. News of the capture of Hamel did not reach the headquarters of the 202nd Reserve Regiment until 5.45 a.m. Its 1st Battalion was ordered to move up at 7 a.m. and the 1st Battalion of the 201st Reserve Regiment, north of the Somme, was also ordered to deploy. The move of both battalions was severely hampered by low flying aircraft and they were not in position until 10.45 a.m. The 43rd Reserve Division learned at 8.20 a.m. that Hamel was in Australian hands and ordered its artillery to lay down 'annihilating fire' on it while the 1/202nd Battalion recaptured Wolfsburg, a hill lying just to the east of the village. Once again low flying aircraft proved a major hindrance and not until evening was the attack mounted. The Germans claimed to have cleared most of the hill, albeit after heavy fighting, and to have taken twenty-six Australians prisoner and captured three machine guns. This was true in that they succeeded in occupying some 200 yards of trench held by the 44th Battalion. However, a counter-attack led by bombers drove them out in the early hours of the morning. As for the 13th German Division to the south, news of the Australian penetration of its sector began to be received from 5.20 a.m. onwards. The three resting battalions of the division were alerted and its superior corps headquarters ordered four batteries to be deployed south of Morcourt, together with two battalions of the 448th Infantry Regiment, which was part of the 233rd Division. Otherwise, it would seem that the 13th Division did little, pinning its hopes on its northern neighbour recapturing the Wolfsburg. The initial shock of the Australian attack had been so great that the German efforts to counter-attack had been little more than a whimper.[19]

As for the tangible results of the attack, the Australians captured just under 1,900 Germans and killed or wounded approximately a further 2,000. Their booty included 2 field guns, 26 trench mortars, 171 machine guns and 2 anti-tank rifles. The last named was a new discovery. Manufactured by Mauser it fired a 13mm armour piercing round, but had a very fierce recoil which made the weapon rather inaccurate. The Australians suffered 775 killed and wounded and the Americans 134. Two Victoria Crosses were subsequently awarded to Australians and a Congressional Medal of Honor to an American.* Rawlinson called it 'a good day'. The Supreme War Council was meeting at Versailles at the time and the proceedings were stormy. Lloyd George, always the Easterner, wanted to remove troops from France for an offensive in Palestine. Clemenceau and Foch were vehemently opposed to this, although the former had sanctioned an Allied offensive in Salonika. Matters were smoothed by attendance at a parade of French and American troops in the Place d'Jéna on the morning of 4 July. Maurice Hankey, Secretary to the British War Cabinet, thought the Americans 'as fine a set of ruffians as you

---

* The Congressional Medal of Honor was awarded to Cpl Thomas A. Pope of Company E 131st Regiment for singlehandedly overrunning a machine-gun post. He was also awarded the British Distinguished Conduct Medal and the French Medal Militaire and Croix de Guerre for the same act. He was the longest surviving World War I Medal of Honor winner, dying in 1989 at the age of 94. The Australian VCs were Cpl T. A. Axford of the 16th Battalion (he was also a Military Medal winner) and Pte Harry Dalziel of the 15th Battalion, both again for overcoming machine-gun nests. Dalziel had been wounded in the hand and later in the day suffered a severe head wound, but ultimately survived.

would wish to see fighting for you' and compared their freshness and enthusiasm with the 'war-worn but determined French'.[20] That afternoon the Council had a further session, at which the Australian, Canadian and Newfoundland and New Zealand prime ministers were present for the first time. News of the success at Hamel came through and the latter three asked Billy Hughes if he would pass their congratulations to Monash. Clemenceau began to draft his own message, but then changed his mind and declared that he would congratulate the Australians in person. Accordingly, the following Sunday, 7 July he visited the headquarters of the 4th Australian Division and spoke to a large group in English. He praised their performance and expressed France's gratitude for the contribution they were making to the war. He ended:

> I have come here just for the very purpose of seeing the Australians. I am going back tomorrow to see my countrymen and tell them: 'I have seen the Australians. I have looked into their eyes. I know that these men who have fought great battles beside us in the cause of freedom will fight alongside us again until the cause of freedom for which we are battling is safe for us and our children.'[21]

The opportunity to take part in such a battle would not be long in coming.

CHAPTER TWO

PLANNING

On the day after the capture of Hamel, Haig held a conference of his army commanders. Before it opened he saw Rawlinson alone. The latter was very keen to capitalize on his success and wanted to launch another attack south of the Somme. Haig, however, was not keen 'because it would result (if successful) in extending our line, and also because my present reserves were so small!' Even so, he told Rawlinson to consider the matter further and come up with a plan in the eventuality that the troops could be made available. Haig also spoke to the First Army commander, General Horne, about putting the Canadian Corps back in the line. Subsequently he got Horne and Byng, commanding the Third Army, together and proposed to them that the Canadians, together with 'three or four more divisions with tanks' should be used to recapture a feature to the west of Monchy le Preux near Arras.[1] Canadian insistence that their troops should not be used piecemeal was clearly beginning to frustrate Haig and since, compared to many other divisions, they were comparatively fresh he was keen to take advantage of this.

On 11 July Foch and his chief of staff Maxime Weygand met Haig's chief of staff Herbert Lawrence, Haig himself having gone on leave to England on the 6th. The Generalissimo stated that he was expecting another German attack, this time in the Chateau Thierry–Argonne region, and asked for two British divisions to be deployed as a reserve astride the Anglo-French boundary. Foch also hoped to go over to the attack once this assault had been held and requested that Haig consider an offensive operation.[2] He confirmed this in writing through a letter to Haig the following day, but on the 13th demanded a corps headquarters and a further four divisions. Lawrence had duly arranged for 12th and 18th Divisions to be deployed south of the Somme. However, on his return to France Haig expressed his concern that his reserve was being severely reduced and at a time when the Germans were still posing a major threat to the BEF in Flanders.

Foch's belief that the Germans were about to strike again was totally correct, as was Haig's continuing concern over the northern part of his sector. After the failure of their assault on the Matz in June von Hindenburg and Ludendorff had briefly considered going over to the defensive in the West, but various factors dissuaded them. Morale on the home front had been raised by the recent victories, but such was its fragility that it was likely to decline rapidly if the military initiative was lost. The failure of the Austrian offensive on the River Piave in Italy and Turkey's ever weaker position meant that any decision in Germany's favour could only come in the West. The German High Command was also ever more conscious of the steady American build-up in France. Thus it saw an early resumption of the offensive as the only option. Von Hindenburg and Ludendorff agreed that the best chance of creating a situation whereby the Allies would be forced to negotiate remained a successful attack against the BEF in Flanders, with the same aims as in April – cutting the British off from their cross-Channel supply lines and enabling long range guns to bombard south-east England. They believed that they had been foiled then by the arrival of French reserves, as had also been the case with the March offensive. Consequently, an essential preliminary would again be to attack the French first so as to tie them down to the extent that they would be unable to help their ally. As to where the attack should take place, they decided that it should be on either side of Rheims. Not only would this be certain to draw in the French reserves, but it would also improve the existing limited supply routes into the large salient that the Germans had created west of Rheims during their May and June offensives. The plan was to attack on both sides of the city so as to double envelop it and reach the line Epernay–Châlons-sur-Marne. The attack would take place on 15 July.

The Germans were unable to hide their preparations from the prying eyes of Allied aircraft, but their security was lax in other ways. Prisoners captured by the French divulged the date and area of the attack and it appeared to be common knowledge back in Germany itself. Hence Foch's confident knowledge of the German plans. It also enabled the French armies in the Rheims sector to prepare accordingly. The respective French armies used two different concepts, however. Henri Pétain believed that the way to defeat the German assaults was to adopt a fluid defence, allowing the Germans to come on until they had outstripped their supporting artillery and then counter-attacking them in the flanks. General Henri Gouraud, commander of the French Fourth Army to the east of Rheims, followed the Pétain doctrine and held the bulk of his troops well back out of German artillery range, but his fellow army commanders, General Henri Berthelot of the Fifth and Jean Degoutte of the Sixth Armies, which were positioned to the west of Rheims, stuck to the traditional idea of keeping their forward positions strongly manned. When the Germans did attack, employing fifty-two divisions, they were quickly rebuffed by Gouraud, but succeeded in establishing a bridgehead across the Marne to the south-west of Rheims. It was in this context that Foch and Haig met at lunchtime that day. The Generalissimo assured his ally that the four British divisions he had requested would only be deployed as a last resort and would be returned to Haig if the BEF came under positive threat. Haig, who had delayed sending the additional four divisions until he had seen Foch, now relented. Lawrence had already arranged for Sir Alexander Godley's XXII Corps HQ with the 51st and 62nd Divisions to be deployed and to these were now added the 15th and 34th Divisions.

In Foch's letter to Haig of 12 July he had referred to his Directive No. 3 of 20 May 1918. This had been drawn up three weeks after the end of the German offensive on the Lys and a week before they were to launch the first of their attacks against the French. The underlying theme was that the Allies must become offensive minded once more, even though it was probable that the Germans would attack again. To this end, Foch had laid down some objectives, both between the River Oise and the North Sea. One was the liberation of the coal mines in the Lys sector and Foch suggested a British attack from the line Festubert–Robecq and directed on Estaires combined with the French attack aimed at Mt Kemmel, the objective being to eliminate the salient based on Armentières and hence free the mines. The other called for an attack to remove the threat to the Paris–Amiens railway. (See Map 2.) Foch suggested how this might be done:

> ... in the area between Oise and the Somme, the French attack launched northward from the front Montdidier-Lassigny combined with an Allied offensive launched from the front between Somme and Luce, but later directed southwards, may be expected to produce a sufficiently deep disorganisation of the enemy system between Montdidier and the Somme to free at the same time both Amiens and the railway Paris-Amiens.

Foch directed that both operations be prepared.[3] As it happened, three days before this directive was issued Haig had visited Henry Rawlinson and ordered him to draw up plans, in conjunction with his southern French neighbour, General Marie Eugene Debeney, commanding the First Army, for an attack south of Roye, which precisely echoed Foch's concept in his directive.[4] Thus, the seeds for the attack at Amiens had been sown early. Indeed, Rawlinson had, as a result of his briefing by Haig, studied the scheme in conjunction with General Sir William Birdwood, then commanding the Australian Corps, and his chief of staff. They had concluded that to restrict the attack to south of the Somme would risk disruption from German artillery fire from the high ground around the Chipilly spur. They therefore recommended that this area be included in the attack. South of the river the divisions, supported by tanks, would leapfrog their way forward, but even though Haig had intimated that Rawlinson would be given the Canadian Corps, the Fourth Army commander considered that he would have insufficient troops to be able to penetrate more than 4 miles on the first day. In addition, Rawlinson was finding it difficult to arrange co-operation with the French, who viewed the high ground south of the River Luce as a problem. Haig stated, however, that he was prepared to lend Debeney some tanks to overcome this.[5] Before matters could be taken any further the Germans had struck once more, this time against the French, and the Amiens scheme was put to one side.

Going forward again to mid July, General Lawrence, reacting to his meeting with Foch on the 11th as any good chief of staff should in his master's absence, called in on Rawlinson on the way back to GHQ. Rawlinson urged him to consider the Amiens scheme, suggesting that its aim should be to regain the 1916 'battle line' on the Somme. Lawrence agreed to speak to Haig about it.[6] He also asked Rawlinson to draw up a plan on the lines of his post-Hamel proposal for an attack east of Amiens. Five days later, after his talk with Foch, Haig met Horne and Byng at the latter's HQ at Hesdin to review their plans for offensive action. Neither was happy with Haig's suggestion at the beginning of the month of a major attack in the Arras area at this time since the troops were not available. They agreed therefore on more limited operations, with the Canadian Corps especially to draw up plans for an attack on its own. Haig also sent Lawrence to see Plumer and ask him to consider the recapture of Mt Kemmel in the event of the expected German attack in that area being repulsed. Haig then travelled on to Rawlinson's HQ at Flixecourt. He stressed to the Fourth Army commander that his attack was to be the main operation on the British front and that the offensive preparations by his other armies would, he hoped, distract the Germans from what was happening in Rawlinson's sector. He wanted Rawlinson to advance to the River Luce and stated that he intended to ask Foch for Debeney to co-operate with an attack north-eastwards from south of Moreuil. He also intended to release the Canadian Corps to Rawlinson once the French had returned XXII Corps. Rawlinson was still keen to extend his line as far south as Moreuil, but Haig would only agree to him taking over from the

French down to the River Luce, pointing out that 'if our proposed attack is successful, the enemy in front of the French must retire because we have cut his communications.'[*7]

Rawlinson submitted his plan to Haig on 17 July, the day following their meeting. It was largely a matter of dusting down the original May concept and amending it in light of the fact that more troops were likely to be available to him. He justified an attack in the Amiens area on several grounds. The enemy's defences were weak, as Hamel had proved, and, thanks largely to the efforts of the Australians, his morale was low. Furthermore, there were few German reserves in this sector. The ground was suitable for tanks, there were good covered approaches to enable surprise, and there was excellent observation of the German line. The advantages of such an attack would be to drive the Germans out of artillery range of Amiens, shorten the Allied front and provide the possibility of 'inflicting a serious blow' on them in the aftermath of the failure of their Champagne offensive. As at Hamel, surprise was paramount especially in the deployment of the additional troops required. To give himself more room, Rawlinson wanted to take over the French line as far south as Moreuil, but this in itself would provide a cover story since it could be put about that it would free up French divisions to meet threats elsewhere. He was not keen on the French being involved in his attack for two reasons. It would make it very difficult to maintain secrecy and the problems of co-ordination would 'add greatly to the normal difficulties of such an operation.' These comments rather ignored what Haig had laid down at their meeting. If, however, the French were keen to take part he proposed that they should attack from the Montdidier area since this would lead to 'far greater strategical results' and would create fewer problems than a side-by-side assault. Rawlinson's dislike of French involvement was also in part on account of his frustration over

* In his diary entry for that day Rawlinson also noted that Haig 'seemed to think that the Bosche would not continue fighting through the winter and would probably do his utmost to come to terms in the autumn especially if he failed in Champagne as seems probable.'

trying to get Debeney to co-operate on further Hamel-like operations. On 11 July he had written in his diary: 'It is unsatisfactory to
have a man like Debeney to work with. He requires driving every
yard and is afraid of responsibility . . .'

The objective of the attack was principally a line 1 kilometre short
of the former outer defences of Amiens, which the Germans had
captured in March. This objective was represented by the so-called
Red Line. Rawlinson did, however, intend to exploit forward of this
to the outer defence line itself and if the Germans could be bounced
out of this, so much the better. If not, consolidation would continue
on the Red Line, which was some 6,000 yards from the existing front
line. There would, however, be an intermediate objective, the Green
Line, which was some 1,500 yards from the front line as it stood.
Attacks would also be made to secure the open right flank down to
Moreuil. If this was successful the Cavalry Corps could be used to
exploit and cut off the Germans facing the northern part of the
French First Army. The actual initial attack frontage was 16,000 yards
and, based on a requirement for 6 tanks for every 1,000 yards of
frontage and the fact that there were two objectives, Rawlinson
calculated that he would need 162 tanks, the Red Line objective being
11,000 yards only, and a further 36 tanks for the flank attack. This
equated to six battalions of Mark Vs. He also wanted two Whippet
battalions for exploitation beyond the Red Line. In terms of infantry
the Fourth Army bulwark at the time was the Australian Corps,
which was four divisions strong – 1st Australian Division being in
GHQ Reserve and under the administration of the Third Army. He
also had III Corps, which consisted of the 18th Division (also in GHQ
Reserve), the London Territorial 47th and 58th Divisions, and the US
33rd Division, but this was being acclimatized to trench warfare as
the culmination of its training with the BEF prior to probably rejoining the AEF out of which Pershing was intent on creating two
American armies. Finally he had the 8th Division, again in GHQ
Reserve and recovering from the battering it had received during the
German offensive on the Aisne at the end of May.

Clearly this force was not large enough to guarantee success and knowing that the Canadian Corps was reasonably fresh, with two divisions out the line, Rawlinson requested it to be sent to him. He asked for a further division, either 1st Australian or a British formation. He also wanted the 12th Division released to him, as well as the 8th, although this would have merely a line-holding role. Rawlinson intended the Australians and Canadians to make the main attack, but to give the Canadians room some adjustments to the Fourth Army's sector needed to be made. He therefore proposed that the Third Army extend its sector southwards to the Albert–Amiens road, an addition of 3,000 yards to its frontage, and III Corps would take over from the Australians as far south as the Somme. The Canadian Corps would be inserted south of the Australians, but would also take over the southern part of their sector up to the Amiens–Nesle railway.

Rawlinson stressed that this was merely the outline of the plan and that it would need to be considered in more detail by the corps commanders and the Tank Corps. It should be emphasized, however, that it was merely a limited attack and although there was talk of exploitation of success it was tentative. Certainly the Fourth Army commander did not envisage a decisive breakthrough.[8] But then neither did Haig at this juncture.

With a plan now in existence, on 17 July Haig replied to Foch's letter of the 12th. He dismissed the Robecq–Festubert option as pointless, but strongly recommended the Amiens attack. Foch replied, giving priority to the Kemmel operation on the grounds that if the Crown Prince did not attack the forces were already concentrated here for it. He also asked that preparations for the Robecq–Festubert attack continue because of the need to regain the mines. On the other hand, he was clearly enthused by the Amiens operation:

The combined operation of the British Fourth Army and the French First Army intended to free Amiens and the railway seems to me to be one of the most profitable to execute at the moment by reason of the prospects which it offers.

Foch added that Debeney was studying a similar concept, although his envisaged operation was even more limited.[9] He was, however, now in an ebullient mood. The German offensive had been stopped, with only small gains on the home bank of the Marne, and the time had come for the French to counter-attack, which they did on both flanks of the German salient. Their success enabled Foch to return the 12th and 18th Divisions to Haig, thus improving the prospects of Rawlinson's attack.

Although Foch had not as yet formally approved the attack, on 19 July 'Tavish' Davidson, Haig's chief of operations, telephoned Rawlinson to say that Haig had accepted his proposal and preparations for it could get underway. Rawlinson let Currie and Monash into the secret on the afternoon of 21 July and both apparently liked the concept.[10] Yet, there were still some doubts at GHQ over where and what sort of offensive action should be mounted, thanks to the threat of a further German attack in the Kemmel area, as a memorandum dated 22 July, which Haig asked his staff to draw up, makes plain. It noted that the bulk of the German reserves were still in the Courtrai–Lille–Douai–Valenciennes area and it was for this reason that the Second Army had been increased in strength to seventeen divisions, including two American. The memorandum then went on to consider a number of eventualities. Should the Germans attack at Kemmel and be repulsed the Second Army could counter-attack, assisted by the First and Fifth Armies. If, however, they did not attack and their reserves remained in place there would be a need to conserve the British reserves and therefore offensive operations on a smaller scale were the only option. Then again, if there was no German attack and their reserves were withdrawn from the British front or if they did attack but were repulsed without drawing in reserves from outside the Second Army then Rawlinson's proposal was the obvious answer. Its aim would be to remove the threat on Amiens and free up the railways running through the town to the west. The suggestion was that the British troops assemble behind the French lines, pass through them, and, if successful, establish the BEF's right flank on the River Luce. Yet, if the French were prepared to actively co-operate and push from the line Cantigny–

Grivesnes towards Hargicourt and Hangest 'a considerable advance of the French line might be achieved at very little cost and the front established on the old forward AMIENS defence line MERICOURT – CAIX – HANGEST.'[11] This, of course, again ran counter to Rawlinson's desire that the attack should be solely a British operation.

On the same day that this memorandum was written Douglas Haig and Ferdinand Foch met once more. While they were speaking in private, General John Du Cane, Haig's representative at Foch's headquarters, had a chat with Weygand. Du Cane reported to Haig in a letter sent that day that Weygand had told him that for the first time in 1918 the Allies actually had more divisions in reserve than the Germans, albeit by the narrow margin of 47 to 46. But he also warned that Debeney would probably have insufficient troops to be able to participate in the Amiens attack to the extent that had been envisaged for his First Army.[12] Then, on 24 July Foch convened a conference of the Allied commanders – Haig, Pershing, and Pétain. He got Weygand to read out a memorandum that he had drawn up. The main message was that the failure of the fifth German offensive marked the moment for the Allies to go over to the attack, especially since they now enjoyed numerical (thanks to the Americans) and material superiority. He listed the operations he had in mind – the freeing up of the Amiens–Paris railway and, in the Marne region, the Avricourt–Paris railway, together with attacks in the north to remove the German threat to Calais and Dunkirk and free up the mining area. He emphasized that these operations must take place in quick succession 'so as to embarrass the enemy in the utilisation of his reserves and not allow him sufficient time to fill up his units' and that surprise was paramount. But, according to Foch, the individual commanders did not appear to share his enthusiasm. Pétain described the French Army as 'worn out, bled white, anaemic'. Pershing expressed his frustration: 'The American Army asks nothing better than to fight, but it has not yet been formed.'* Haig rather echoed Pétain:

* Foch had finally agreed on 21 July that a separate US army be created.

'The British Army, entirely disorganised by the events of March and April, is still far from being re-established.' Foch then reassured them and sent each away with a copy of the memorandum.[13] Haig's comment on his fellow commanders at the conference was that they were in 'great spirits', which is somewhat contrary to Foch's recollection.[14] Be that as it may, all indicated to Foch on the following day that they were fully behind his memorandum. Indeed, on the same evening Davidson phoned Rawlinson to confirm that the Amiens attack was to go ahead.[15]

On 23 July Debeney mounted a Hamel-type operation. It took place some 3 miles south of Monreuil and was designed to improve the French position and test German morale. More specifically its aim was to enable the French artillery to engage the high ridges to the east of the River Avre in this sector. Selected to undertake the attack were the 3rd, 15th Colonial and 152nd Infantry Divisions of IX Corps, but they lacked tanks since the French armour was heavily engaged in counter-attacking the German salient across the Marne. They therefore asked the British for assistance and it was agreed that the 9th Tank Battalion should be sent south to help. The Battalion was first informed on 17 July and its commanders were briefed by General Bourgon, commanding the 3rd French Division with which the tanks would be operating, on the following day. That night the tanks began their move south. On 19 July the French sent infantry companies to train with the tanks at the 5th Tank Brigade Driving School and a further batch trained on 21 July. After some tanks had fallen victim to mechanical problems a total of 35 Mark Vs and four supply tanks actually deployed. Unlike at Hamel there was a one hour's preliminary bombardment, with the attack starting at 5.30 a.m. Being daylight Zero Hour was later than the tanks would have liked, but there was some cover from the fact that it was a cloudy day, with some rain, and that the French guns were using some smoke. Advancing behind a rolling barrage, the tanks and infantry soon achieved their first objectives and by 10 a.m. the assault had been successfully completed, the deepest advance being some 3,000 yards. Nearly 2,000 Germans were captured, together with 5 guns,

45 trench mortars and 375 machine guns. The total French casualties were just under 1,900, but it was noticeable that the 3rd Division, which was attacking in the centre, suffered no more heavily than the other two divisions and this was even though its frontage was over twice as wide and it faced by far the strongest defences. As for the 9th Tank Battalion, its casualties were surprisingly heavy. No less than fifteen tanks received direct hits and only one was repairable. Three of the knocked out tanks were in German hands, although at least one was blown up by its crew to prevent the enemy from learning too much about the Mark V. Even so, the French were delighted with their performance and conferred the Croix de Guerre on the 9th Tank Battalion. Moreuil, or Sauvillers, as the French called it, did much to boost morale of the French First Army.

Foch held another meeting on 26 July with Haig, Lawrence, Rawlinson, Montgomery (Rawlinson's chief of staff) and Debeney also being present. Perhaps satisfied by his rapid success at Sauvillers, the French First Army commander proposed merely a small operation south of Hangard on the River Luce as his contribution to the Amiens attack. It was an operation to which Foch had alluded in earlier correspondence with Haig and which Rawlinson and Debeney had discussed in the context of Hamel-type operations. Unsurprisingly, Foch now rejected this and demanded a plan that was more in keeping with that which Haig envisaged. Haig also noted in his diary that Rawlinson was still opposed to French involvement. The latter recorded in his diary that Foch turned down the Montdidier suggestion because there were not enough French troops to carry it out. Debeney would have to attack north of the River Avre, his objectives Moreuil Wood and Hill 110. Rawlinson again objected to the two armies attacking side by side because of problems of keeping the operation secret, but Foch overrode him. He also wrote:

The Austn and Canadn [Corps] will be on a narrow front with v. great depth but it will be difficult to get the reserves forward quickly and the Cavy [Cavalry] will not have much chance I fear. Debeney will have to attack 2 hours after we do. The crush of troops and guns will be excessive at first, but we must overcome these difficulties.

The reason for the French attacking at a later time was that they were lacking tanks and hence would need a preliminary bombardment. It is also worth noting that Haig supported Foch's view on the grounds of the lack of available British divisions to ensure success.

With the operation definitely confirmed, Lawrence wrote to all British army commanders, General John Salmond, commanding the RAF in France, and General Hugh Elles, the Tank Corps commander, on 27 July. He gave them an outline of Rawlinson's plan and then concentrated on the move south of the Canadian Corps. Critical to it was that the Germans should not be allowed to become aware of what was happening and not be tempted to redeploy their reserves. The Canadians themselves would be relieved in the line by XVII Corps (52nd, 56th, 57th Divisions) and then moved by 'strategic train' beginning on 1 August. To disguise the redeployment a number of deception measures were to be used. For a start, the Canadians were ordered to detach two battalions to Plumer's Second Army. They were to go into the trenches in the Kemmel sector, but not adjacent to one another, and then act as though they were preparing the sector for an attack prior to the arrival of the remainder of the Corps. They would be supported by the deployment of two Canadian Casualty Clearing Stations (CCS) and by Canadian and Tank Corps wireless sets, together with Plumer's own wirelesses from his reserve divisions and those from the First and Third Armies reserve divisions. To fox the Germans still further First Army was to deploy a wireless set from the Cavalry Corps, together with its own sets, behind the Arras sector. This was to be accompanied by increased air activity and the deployment of a tank battalion, which would train with the infantry during daylight hours and make little attempt to camouflage its tanks. Salmond was also ordered to occupy additional airfields in the Second Army sector and to increase air activity up until two days before the Amiens attack.

For Z Day, 10 August had been selected since this was the earliest date Rawlinson thought he would be ready. In the light of this Lawrence also attached an annex giving a timetable for the redeployment. Apart from the Canadian Corps move, the additional artillery which could be spared was to begin its move on 28 July. That of the Tank Corps would begin on 1 August and be completed five days later, while that of the Cavalry Corps would commence on 7 August. Finally the 1st Australian Division, which was detached to Third Army, would start to move on 8 August and complete by 5 p.m. on the following day.[16]

A meeting between Rawlinson and Debeney at which Davidson was also present took place on 27 July. They managed to agree boundaries and other details to their mutual satisfaction, but Rawlinson continued to worry over the secrecy aspect. The following day, 28 July, Weygand brought a personal handwritten letter from Foch to Haig. It stated that the French were rapidly pushing the Germans back towards the Rivers Ardre and Aisne, but were now being held on an unspecified river line. It was imperative that the Germans should not be allowed the time to regroup and so he asked Haig to bring the date of the Amiens attack forward from 10 August. Accompanying the letter was a 'special directive', also in Foch's hand, tasking the two armies to 'free Amiens and the Paris-Amiens railway, and also to engage and eject the enemy established between the Somme and Avre.' Debeney would be given four additional divisions and II Cavalry Corps. In a separate letter, and also handed over by Weygand, Foch gave Haig command of the French First Army for the operation. Haig was most grateful, as he was by Foch's agreement to return the remainder of the British XXII Corps earlier than he had previously stated.* Given the limited number of divisions that Rawlinson currently had available the attack could not be brought forward without the early return of this corps.[17] Rawlinson himself was told on the same day that the attack was to be advanced by 48

---

* The 12th and 18th Divisions were already on their way back and would join III Corps. Only their artillery had been used in the attack by the French First Army at Moreuil on 23 July.

hours – 'I do not know that this can be done.' He was also doubtful over an advance beyond the old Amiens defences. A visit to the Villers Bretonneux area did, however, reassure him that there was plenty of room to accommodate the Canadian Corps, additional artillery, and the tanks. During the course of this he came under German shell fire and his car was hit by a splinter.[18]

The same day, 28 July, also saw the first moves in the redeployment. All tank units were placed in GHQ Reserve, which meant that the armies could not employ them. The same applied to some Canadian artillery. Simultaneously GHQ ordered the moves of certain heavy artillery brigades to the Fourth Army.

GHQ BEF issued its formal operation order to Debeney and Rawlinson on 29 July. The aim of the attack was the same as stated in Foch's directive. The first phase was to secure the line Méricourt–Harbonnières–Caix–Quesnel–Hangest and put it into a state of defence. Once it had been secured Rawlinson was to push on towards Chaulnes, keeping his left flank on the Somme, while Debeney, with his right flank on the Avre, was to make for Roye. It also confirmed that the Fourth Army would be reinforced by the Canadian Corps, 1st Australian Division and the Cavalry Corps. Both Rawlinson and Debeney issued their orders two days later. Rawlinson's were brief, giving merely the area in which the attack was to take place, with the boundaries and objectives shown on a map. They also allocated the tanks to formations, with the Australian and Canadian Corps receiving the 5th and 4th Tank Brigades respectively, the Cavalry Corps 3rd Tank Brigade and III Corps 10th Tank Battalion. The 9th Tank Battalion was to be held in Army reserve. Debeney's orders were more detailed, but there was a flavour of caution in them. Since the British were unable to spare him any tanks, he would, unlike Rawlinson, require a preliminary bombardment. Hence, so as not to reduce the element of surprise, he would begin this at the moment Rawlinson launched his attack and his infantry would attack 45 minutes later. His XXXI Corps was to capture Moreuil and Mézières, as well as Génouville Wood and then advance towards Hangest, the implication being that it was not expected to reach this village on the first day. To its south IX Corps was to secure crossings over the Avre at Braches and northwards in preparation for X Corps crossing at Pierrepont on Day 2. This would also see XXXI Corps continuing its advance towards Hangest. Debeney also stressed the importance of secrecy. Corps HQs would nominate those officers working on the preparation of the attack by name and they were on no account to use the telephone to transmit their instructions.[19]

Rawlinson held another conference with his corps commanders on 29 July, the main purpose being to confirm that they were happy about the attack being brought forward to 8 August. Monash himself was not present since he had departed on leave to England, with Rawlinson's agreement, on 23 July. This was to include being present at the opening of Australia House in London by King George V and Queen Mary on 3 August. The proviso was that he was to stay in close touch with the War Office, a destroyer at Dover being placed on standby to rush him back to France if need be. Before departing, Monash had been through the outline plan with his chief of staff, Brigadier General Thomas Blamey, so that work on filling in the detail could begin. He also made it widely known that he intended to take three weeks' leave since 'no developments of any importance were to be expected' thus contributing to the overall deception plan.[20]

As Monash probably expected, his leave was curtailed and he returned to his headquarters at Bertangles on the evening of 29 July. Haig visited him two days later and Monash confidently told him that he 'had all the threads of the operation in his hands.' At this stage there had been no move to place cavalry formations under command of the Australians and Canadians and Haig suggested to Monash that a cavalry brigade be placed under his command to aid exploitation, a task for which his own corps cavalry regiment, the 13th Light Horse, was not trained.[21] Up until now, however, Rawlinson had not briefed the Cavalry Corps. On the same day that Haig visited Monash he and Rawlinson were present at a tank demonstration with the Australians at Vaux. During it they discussed the use of the Whippets of the 3rd Tank Brigade with the Cavalry and agreed that they should operate 'as a reserve in close touch with the contact squadns. To be called up as soon as any wood [or] village of MG nests holds up the Cavry advance.' He then had General Sir Charles Kavanagh, commanding the Cavalry Corps, to lunch, and briefed him on the operation, saying that he would describe it to his divisional and brigade commanders on 3 or 4 August.[22] The reaction of Brigadier General Archibald Home, the Chief of Staff of the Cavalry Corps was:

I fancy we are being pushed into it as another determined attack is being made by our friends at home on the Cavalry. The proposal is to abolish the Corps, turn one division into machine guns, one Division into Corps Cavalry and keep one Division mounted. This savours of Henry Wilson [Chief of the Imperial General Staff] as he hates the Cavalry ... If we make peace with the Boche on the Hindenburg line, then we don't want any Cavalry; but if we are going to beat him, we shall want every bus, car, horse, mule and donkey we can raise.[23]

The overwhelming need for secrecy permeated as far as London and Paris. At Foch's insistence neither the British nor French govern-ments, nor their respective war ministries, were told what was planned. Indeed, it was not until 1 August that British Prime Minister David Lloyd George obtained the first inkling of what was afoot. Canadian Prime Minister Sir Robert Borden told the Committee of Prime Ministers, which had been recently formed to give the Dominions a greater say in the conduct of the war, that he had heard the previous evening that the Canadian Corps was being moved to another part of the line to take part in an offensive. The spectre of Passchendaele immediately arose before the eyes of the politicians, but when they quizzed Sir Henry Wilson, the CIGS, he professed to know nothing about it. It is true that Haig had written to him on 24 July to tell him what had gone on at the conference with Foch on the same day, specifically stating the Generalissimo's intention during the next few weeks to 'regain the initiative' and to 'clear the main railway lines with a view to further operations.' Otherwise, on Foch's orders, no clarification came from France. That the British Government was worried is encapsulated in a letter written by Wilson to Du Cane a week earlier, probably immediately after Borden's revelation:

> The more we look into the question of our manpower the uglier it seems to be. Agriculture, Vital industries for ourselves and our Allies, Coal, Shipbuilding, Aeroplane & Tank Construction – & personnel – & so on & so forth show such formidable demands that little remains for the fighting services. The Cabinet therefore are anxious about the future. They do not want to end the war in an absolutely exhausted condition, if this can be avoided.

He went on to ask Du Cane to find out from Foch what his future intentions were with regard to major operations involving the BEF. As for the impending scheme the Cabinet were told that it was 'limited to a series of attacks intended to rectify the line.' The British Government remained apprehensive.[24]

CHAPTER THREE

PREPARATION

The complexity surrounding the preparations for the attack presented staffs at all levels with a major challenge, made even greater by the limited time available. The whole of the Canadian Corps had to be deployed from Flanders and moved into a sector between the Australians and the French. Likewise III Corps had to take over the existing Australian line north of the Somme. The Cavalry Corps and the 1st Australian Division had to be moved, albeit by not such a long distance. (See Maps 3 and 4.) Additional artillery, including several batteries of heavies, and nine tank battalions had to be taken into account, together with extra supporting services. A mass of extra ammunition had to be put in place. Once in position the new arrivals had to have the opportunity to familiarize themselves with the ground over which they were to attack. There were only ten days to do all this and the whole operation had to be carried out in such a way as not to arouse German suspicions.

Crucial to the deployment was the railway system. This had been severely disrupted by the German drives in spring 1918, but since then there had been a massive effort to improve the situation, especially in the construction of broad gauge lines. The German offensives had also had a benefit in that they had forced the railway operating system to adopt a more flexible approach. This was especially in the ability to speedily transport reinforcements from one part of the front to another, something which would now be urgently needed.

Security was paramount and to this end every officer and man in the Fourth Army was issued with a notice to paste into his 'small book'. Headed 'Keep your mouth shut' it exhorted the bearer not to talk to men from other units about the attack. Should he be taken prisoner he was to give the Germans no information other than his rank and name and was especially warned to be on the look out for 'stool pigeons' – Germans disguised in British uniforms intermingling with prisoners to pick up information.[1] This was not wholly successful. The Chief of Staff of the Canadian Corps was forced to issue an edict on 31 July:

> Officers have been talking about an offensive. Any officer who can be detected talking about an offensive in a Mess, or other public place, will be placed under arrest and court-martialled regardless of his rank.

It also drew officers' attention to the 'Keep your mouth shut' notice. In addition, the instruction gave some guidelines on reconnaissance. Officers were to conduct this singly or in pairs and not in 'large parties'. They were to avoid high ground and observation posts and not 'show maps or wave them about'.[2]

The Canadian Corps itself had begun to be relieved on 25 July, when the 59th Division took over from the 3rd Canadian Division in the line. The latter was placed in GHQ reserve, as was the 2nd Canadian Division, and at 24 hours notice to move. The 1st and 4th Canadian Divisions remained in the trenches and carried out a number of successful raids against the Germans during the next few days. Then, on 29 July, the Canadian Corps received a warning order from First Army stating that it was to be transferred to Fourth Army with a view to deploying 'at short notice' in event of a German attack to support the French in the Rheims–Soissons sector or the British Fourth and French First Armies. This was the cover story that was being put about. But on the same day, after receiving instructions from Rawlinson, Sir Arthur Currie wrote personally to his four divisional commanders to inform them of the real reason for the redeployment. He enclosed a map showing the boundaries and described the outline plan, which called for the initial assault to be made by three divisions, with the 4th Canadian

Division initially in reserve. This would then pass through the lead divisions to capture the Old Amiens Defence Line within boundaries, although it was not expected that this would take place before the second day of the operation. Currie stated that the attack would be a surprise one, using tanks and a creeping barrage, and that the Cavalry Corps would also be taking part, passing through the Canadian Corps on the first day and exploiting towards Quesnel and Fresnoy. He informed his commanders that he would hold a conference at HQ 3rd Canadian Division on the afternoon of 31 July and instructed them not to discuss the operation with their subordinate commanders. Any correspondence concerning the attack was to be addressed personally to Currie and was to be referred to by the codeword 'LC'.[*3]

The emphatic insistence on absolute secrecy did create enormous difficulties for the Canadian Corps Q Staff. Not until 29 July was Brigadier General G. J. Farmar, the senior Q staff officer, let into the secret. This meant that his subordinate staffs at divisional level had a mere 24 hours to plan the move south of the Corps. It was not just the troops themselves, but ammunition and other supplies which had to be deployed within the space of a mere nine days. The artillery ammunition requirement alone came to over 7,000 tons and Fourth Army's artillery dumps were so far back that a lorry could only make one trip per day from them to the forward artillery positions. There were only two roads leading to the Canadian Corps concentration area and so traffic congestion was a major problem, especially since the Australians were also using these routes. Because the Corps artillery did not begin to move until three days before the attack, its integral transport was not available to work within the Fourth Army area. Added to this was the fact that when the Canadian artillery transport did arrive the Fourth Army had insufficient fuel for its trucks. This shortage was only overcome by obtaining extra fuel

---

* LC stood for Llandovery Castle, the name of a Canadian hospital ship which had been torpedoed on 27 June 1918 while sailing back to Britain from Canada. Most of her crew, including a number of Canadian nurses, were lost.

from Abbeville, but the journey from here to Fourth Army's fuel dumps consumed a significant amount of fuel itself. Small arms ammunition (SAA) was another problem, not least because the Fourth Army's Q Staff were also kept in ignorance of the plan for some days and did not believe the Canadian demand for 10 million rounds of SAA. Consequently, it was issued in dribs and drabs. Yet, in spite of these difficulties the Canadians did have their requirements met, with the last rounds of ammunition for the guns arriving just a few hours before Zero Hour.[4]

On 30 July the Canadians were told that they were to be relieved by XVII Corps and that this was to be completed by 10 a.m. on 2 August. On that same day the Canadian Corps HQ moved from Duisans to Molliens Vidame, some 8 miles west of Amiens. In the words of J.F.B. Livesay, one of the official Canadian war correspondents:

There followed a week of strenuous preparation. 'Red tabs' are not popular in the army but no one who watched the staff officers of the Canadian Corps then and through the over charged weeks to follow could have anything but admiration and wonder. There is no Sunday in the army; and there are no specified hours, except that a man works until he can see no more, catches a few hours sleep, and goes at it again; in active operations officers of the General Staff and 'A' and 'Q' branches would work right through the 24 hours ... It was a breathless bustle at 'Molly-be-Damned', not least so for the staff of the Canadian Artillery, who had to work out in detail the ranges and the barrage of the great opening show. Then the Intelligence branch had the collection and collation of last-minute information, whether from our aircraft or by prisoners. Three clerks of the General Staff worked in a tent by themselves – all were under canvas and it rained a good deal – engaged day and night in copying out operation orders, which in great detail must be prepared and in the hands of the various commanders.[5]

The relief of the Canadian 1st Division began at 3 a.m. on the 31st. The Division was transported back to its billets by light railway and lorries. By noon on 2 August all units were in the Le Cauroy area and the process of moving south now began. The Division had been allotted no less than 101 trains, including thirteen for the artillery, and had three entraining stations, with a senior officer from each brigade in charge of each. The guns moved first, but an error in the movement orders did cause some problems. One of the destinations was given as Ligny-sur-Canche instead of Ligny-St Flochel. The villages were some 10 miles apart and this resulted in delays of four hours on this route, but otherwise the move went surprisingly smoothly. However, because of the short time available before the attack, the infantry had to be moved ahead of the divisional supply trains which did cause administrative problems the other end, although this was partly overcome by issuing each unit with an additional day's rations to take with it on its train. The Division eventually came to rest in the Hornoy area, 9 miles west of Amiens. This was regarded as 'a very fine area with comfortable billets, good roads, no traffic, where troops could get a good rest after detrainment and before the approach march.'[6]

The 2nd Canadian Division concentrated in the Cavillon area, closer to Amiens, by the end of 30 July. It then embarked on a period of training with the 9th Tank Battalion, fresh from its action with the French at Moreuil, with each brigade spending a day with the tanks. In the case of the 3rd Canadian Division its artillery and transport went by road and the Division occupied the Dury area, just to the south of Amiens, while the 4th Canadian Division area was centered on Hallencourt, 10 miles west-north-west of Amiens. Thus, by 4 August the complete Canadian Corps was concentrated behind the Australians.

The two decoy Canadian infantry units, the 27th Battalion and 4th Canadian Mounted Rifles, had a disconcerting time. The first intimation that the latter had of what was in store for them was a message from their brigade HQ on 29 July, which ordered them to move from their camp to Acq, where they would board a train at

4 p.m. on that day for an unspecified destination. Once they were on board they were told that they were travelling to the railhead at Arneke, 5 miles north of Cassel, and were in a 'strategic train', which differed from the normal troop train in that it travelled at a faster speed. They arrived at the railhead at midnight and were directed to a large field, where they passed the remainder of the night. Next day at noon they marched in 'oppressive heat' – luckily their packs were taken by lorry – to a tented camp at St Eloi. There they found themselves under the 41st Division. They entered the trenches in the La Clyte sector on 1 August, with one company in the front line and the others in support.

> The line consisted mainly of out-posts hurriedly made during the rear-guard action against the Germans on the Lys [in April 1918]. Very little work had been done in consolidating as all movement was observed from Kemmel Hill which was in the hands of the Germans.[7]

Patrolling by night was the main activity, but rain on the second day, combined with rumours of another move, did little for morale. Then, on 3 August, a shell struck the HQ of the front line company, killing Capt T. W. E. Dixon MC MM, a very popular officer, and wounding his second-in-command. Early the following morning the Battalion was relieved and once it was out of the trenches it picked up lorries, which transported it to Neurlet. Here they rested until midnight and then marched to St Omer, where they entrained. This time their journey took them via Boulogne, Abbeville and Amiens to Saleux, 6 miles to the south-west and where they detrained after a 10 hour journey. That night they marched to Boves, but had considerable difficulty in reaching their billets in the village because of the mass of traffic on the road. They were, however, reunited with their fellow Mounted Rifle battalions in the 8th Canadian Infantry Brigade.[8]

The experience of the 27th Battalion was roughly similar, although they left their billets in Grand Hullecourt early on 29 July and de-trained at Cassel. They went into a camp near Terdeghem and were placed under command of the 35th Division. On the following day, which was spent largely in resting and sport, as well as a large party from the Battalion attending the 35th Division theatre in the evening, they were visited by the GOCs of IX Corps (whose sector they were now in), 35th Division, and 104th Brigade. All these activities were designed to make the Canadian presence public as part of the deception plan. They relieved the 17th Lancashire Fusiliers in the Locre sector. They spent just 48 hours in the line and then, after a period in bivouacs, entrained at St Omer at 7 a.m., about the same time as the 4th Canadian Mounted Rifles, on 5 August, and also ended up at Saleux before rejoining the 4th Canadian Division.[9] As for whether the Germans were taken in by these ploys, their official post-war monogram on Amiens, *Die Katastrophe das 8t August 1918* states that they were aware of the Canadian presence in the Kemmel area, but had no idea that the Canadian Corps had moved south.[10]

For the Australians the main preoccupation at this time was the adjustment of their sector. In the north the 18th Division, which had for the past three months been holding the line opposite Albert, took over the sector immediately north of the Somme from the 5th Australian Division on the morning of 1 August.* Included in the ranks of the 18th Division was 1st Battalion 132nd US Infantry Regiment, which also took its place in the line. The 5th Australian Division then went into corps reserve in the Allonville area, just to the northeast of Amiens. In the south the 4th Australian Division relieved the 37th French Division in the sector immediately north of the Amiens–Roye road on 2 August. The cover story put about was that this relief had been necessitated by French losses during their Soissons offensive and that it would enable them to shorten their line. The plan was that this division would be in turn relieved by the 2nd and 3rd Canadian Divisions. This would leave the 2nd and 3rd Australian Divisions in the line. As for the 1st Australian Division, the beginning of the month found it in the line south-west of Ypres. It was relieved by the

---

* The 18 Div G Branch War Diary TNA WO 95/2017 mistakenly states that they relieved 3 Aus Div.

29th Division on 3 August and two days later left the Second Army and Flanders and was concentrated in the Allonville area by the end of 6 August, the 5th Australian Division having moved forward to the Villers Bretonneux area. As for the appearance of the Canadians this was explained away by stating that they were filling the gap created by XXII Corps being sent south to help the French.

While the Australians were disappointed that they were not being withdrawn for a rest, the various reliefs and arrival of the Canadians kept them occupied. Also, as with III Corps, they found themselves with Americans, in the shape of the 65th Brigade from the 33rd Division, under command. Two battalions had joined the 2nd Australian Division in the Villers Bretonneux sector and two others the 3rd Australian Division around Hamel during 26–27 July. What this did make clear was the declining strength of the Australian units. The 24th Battalion in the 2nd Australian Division had a trench strength at the time of 193 men, while the American company attached to them was 198 men strong. It meant that the battalion had more Americans in the line than Australians, but the additional strength was much welcomed and the Australians were most impressed by their guests' enthusiasm and willingness to learn.

The three divisions of the Cavalry Corps were positioned on 1 August as follows:

1st Cavalry Division – south of Doullens

2nd Cavalry Division – east of Etaples

3rd Cavalry Division – astride the Somme between Abbeville and Amiens.

The 3rd Cavalry Division, being already in the Fourth Army area, remained where it was for the time being, while the 1st Cavalry Division moved by two night marches to the western suburbs of Amiens during 5–7 August. The 2nd Cavalry Division also came by road, but required three night marches to reach an area just west of the 1st Cavalry Division and also just south of the Somme.

The move of the tanks was a more complicated business. At the end of July the 5th Tank Brigade (2nd, 8th, 13th Bns) was already with the Fourth Army, as was the 9th Tank Battalion, which was refitting after being in action with the French. The Third Army possessed both the 4th Tank Brigade (1st, 4th, 5th Bns) and the two Whippet battalions (3rd and 6th) which comprised the 3rd Tank Brigade. Further north with the First Army were the 2nd Tank Brigade (10th, 14th, 15th Bns), while the 1st Tank Brigade (7th, 11th, 12th Bns) were refitting and converting to the Mark V Star in the Tank Corps' dedicated training and base area at Bermicourt near St Pol. There was also the 17th Armoured Car Battalion, which had been serving with the French and was now on its way back to the British sector. Selected to take part in the Amiens attack were the 4th Tank Brigade, with the addition of the 14th Tank Battalion, to operate with the Canadians, and the 4th Tank Brigade plus 15th Tank Battalion with the Australians. Since III Corps had only limited objectives in the initial stages it was allocated just one tank battalion, the 10th, which continued to be administered by the 4th Tank Brigade. The 9th Tank Battalion made up the required total of nine heavy battalions and would initially be used to train infantry units as part of the Fourth Army reserve prior to being committed to the battle once it had completed its refit. The two Whippet battalions would operate with the Cavalry Corps, while the 17th Armoured Car Battalion would deploy to the Australian sector, since the terrain here was considered more suitable than that facing what would be the Canadian sector. Finally, five Tank Supply and two Gun Carrier companies were also allotted to the Fourth Army.

The movement plan for the tanks was approved as early as 30 July and entraining began the following night. This concerned the 4th Tank Brigade, together with the 14th and 15th Tank Battalions, as well as Tank Supply and Gun Carrier companies. Battalion and Brigade HQs went on ahead, but for security reasons were not allowed to tell their units their destination or to have any communication with them until they reached the detraining point, and the tanks and their crews travelled under sealed orders. Four detraining stations were used, each possessing ramps by which the tanks could be offloaded from the flat bed railway wagons. The whole operation was completed by the end of 4 August and went remarkably smoothly.[11] The 17th Armoured Car Battalion had disengaged from the fighting on the Marne on the afternoon of 27 July. On 1 August it began its journey to Fourth Army, coming to rest at Vaux-en-Amienois, just to the north of Amiens, two days later. There it spent its time giving its armoured cars a much needed overhaul.

The 9th Tank Battalion, meanwhile, was engaged in tank training with the Australians. While Hamel had served to remove much of the Australian mistrust of tanks, a considerable number of them still had little or no experience of operating with them. On 31 July there was a demonstration at Vaux-en-Amienois in the presence of both Rawlinson and Haig. The 25th Australian Battalion provided the infantry. One of its members recorded:

> The ground was prepared, as much as possible, to resemble a battle ground, having large holes in it (like a battlefield), barbed wire, trenches, etc. We had about 1200 yards to 'capture'. The barrage was represented by a smoke bomb thrown about 100 yards from where we started, immediately after which 3 tanks set out in the direction of the enemy, represented by a few men holding flags. About 10 yards or more behind the tanks we advanced. The second 'wave' of men was about 20 yards behind the first. The tanks manoeuvred in a really marvellous manner, crawling in and out of trenches, over them and around them, blazing (or rather pretending to blaze) away with their guns at the unfortunate (also imagined) occupants of these trenches. Only especially strong outposts were indicated by the attacking party (ourselves) by means of a smoke bomb thrown by one of us, which landed in or near the supposed strong point. The tank nearest immediately lumbered on in the indicated direction and 'gambolled' over the supposed occupants of the trenches. Our advance was made in short rushes. The stunt was very realistic except, of course, there was no Fritz enemy to oppose us, and no shells, etc.[12]

Another battalion then took the 25th's place. Both Haig and

Rawlinson expressed their appreciation of the success of this training demonstration, with Haig commenting: 'Remarkable progress has been made since Cambrai, not only in the pattern of Tank, but also in the methods of using them.'[13] The training also further increased the Australian confidence in tanks.

Besides preparations for the offensive, in the Fourth Army sector the main interest at the beginning of August was what was happening in the Albert sector. During the night of 1–2 August III Corps noticed that the German artillery was more active than usual. This was especially so in front of Albert itself and included gas shelling. In daylight it became clear that the Germans were withdrawing. Patrols were sent out by the 47th and 58th Divisions and discovered that the German front line trenches had been abandoned. The 58th Division established that the Germans had withdrawn from west of the River Ancre in its sector, while 47th Division on its right reported them in strength to the south and west of Morlancourt, which itself lies south-west of Albert. The following night further patrols were sent out and confirmed that the Germans had pulled back east of the Ancre, but could not identify their new front line. During 3 and 4 August further patrolling took place. This confirmed that the Germans continued to hold Meaulte and west of Morlancourt in strength and, although they had destroyed the bridges over the Ancre elsewhere, they still retained those in Albert itself. III Corps accordingly adjusted its line to the Amiens–Albert railway, apart from Albert itself, where its front line now took in the outskirts of the town.

In the Australian sector the Germans largely contented themselves with intermittent shelling, including some gas. This was not out of the ordinary and there was no indication that the Germans had any inkling of what lay in store for them. They had, however, identified the fact that the Australians had relieved the French north of the Amiens–Roye road and on the night of the 3rd they raided the outposts of the 51st Battalion around the ruined village of Hourges. The raiders came from the 1/373rd Infantry Regiment in the 225th Division and succeeded in surrounding one post and capturing a sergeant and four men, although they left ten dead in front of the post and had a further man captured. But, as the Divisional War Diary put it, those captured 'could have no knowledge of [the] coming operation and would innocently mislead the enemy.'[14] This was indeed so and was later confirmed by a captured German report, which spoke of the sergeant's refusal 'to make any military statement' and that he 'could not be shaken in his resolve by any means employed'. As for the other prisoners, 'whether their statements are pretence or truth there is no means of proving; all were reticent and only after a lot of talking to did their tongues become loose.' They did admit to having relieved the French on 31 July, but stated that there were no preparations being made for an attack, although they did give details of the Australian dispositions.[15] Yet, with the Canadians poised to relieve that 4th Australian Division on the following night, there was concern. It was highly likely that the Germans would make further raids and if they discovered Canadians in the line they would certainly be alerted that something was afoot. Consequently Rawlinson decided to delay the relief until the night before the attack. In the meantime, the Australian 13th Brigade, which was part of the 4th Australian Division, took over the complete divisional front on the night of 4 August and came under the command of the 2nd Canadian Division the following morning.

On that same day, 3 August, there was another high level conference between Foch and Haig. The French counter-attack on the Marne was continuing to drive back the Germans, who had now withdrawn to the east bank of the Vesle. Foch was certain that they were disintegrating and wanted to take advantage of this. He was concerned that the plan as it stood laid too much emphasis on consolidating the old Amiens outer defence line at the expense of exploiting initial success. He also said that he was considering involving the French Third Army to the south of Debeney as well. Haig assured him that the advance would continue to the Roye–Chaulnes line as soon as the reserves had been brought up. Two days later Haig saw Rawlinson, Debeney and Kavanagh and impressed on them Foch's wish that exploitation should be more positive.

By this time the attacking troops were beginning to deploy. The same technique was to be employed as at Cambrai in that all moves forward would be done by night, with the noise of the tanks being masked by overflying aircraft. As for the artillery, Bombardier R. T. Gemmell of the 11th Australian Field Artillery Brigade recalled: 'As we were going up quite close to Fritz's line all the chains had to be muffled and the wheels enwrapped in straw so as to make no noise.'[16] It had been decided not to dig fire positions for the guns, of which there would be some 1,300 field and 160 heavies, since there was too great a risk of detection from the air. Instead they were deployed in the open and concealed with camouflage netting. In addition, ammunition was dumped by the guns – 600 rounds per 18-pdr gun, 500 for each 4.5-inch howitzer, 200 for each 12-inch howitzer, and 400 each for the 60-pdrs, 6-inch guns and howitzers, 8-inch and 9.2-inch howitzers. This again all had to be done by night, and in what would become the Canadian sector it was not possible to begin this in earnest until 3 August, when the Canadians had been largely deployed. To begin with there was a shortage of lorries until those belonging to the heavy artillery ammunition columns had arrived and the nearest Fourth Army ammunition dump was some distance away, meaning that the lorries could make only one trip per day. Thereafter, it was lack of fuel which provided the limiting factor. Yet, the ammunition was delivered in time, although it was at the expense of a certain amount of small arms ammunition and grenades.

The overall artillery fire plan called for a creeping barrage, with the 18-pdrs opening fire at Zero Hour 200 yards ahead of the start line. They would increase their range by 100 yards after three minutes and then again after a further two minutes. Thereafter they would continue to lift their fire by 100 yards at three minute intervals. Then, on the eleventh lift 100 yard range increases would be made every four minutes. In all there would be no less than forty lifts. Each corps would superimpose the fire of its 4.5-inch howitzers on that of the 18-pdrs and some of the heavies would also fire a deep barrage to interdict the deployment of German reserves in the area of the old Amiens outer defence line. The majority of heavies would, however, be employed on counter-battery fire. Much work had gone into locating the German batteries, through air reconnaissance, flash spotting and sound ranging, and a reasonably accurate picture had been built up. As for the types of ammunition to be fired, there were some variations among the corps. The Australians opted for HE with instantaneous fuzes, while the Canadians preferred shrapnel. When the first objective had been reached the artillery would lay down a smokescreen while it was consolidated and the next wave deployed. Field batteries would also be moved up to support the next phase.

Effective communications were essential if the attack was to maintain its momentum. Fourth Army orders recommended extensive use of mounted messengers and this was to be one of the major roles of the corps cavalry regiments. This was especially since there would be no time to lay line if the advance was rapid. Pigeons were another key means of communication and each corps, together with the three tank brigades, was allotted a number of birds, with the Cavalry and III Corps having two lofts, the Canadians and Australians three each, and the tank brigades one each. The RAF would also be used extensively to report on progress. Each corps was to have a dedicated squadron to fly contact patrols, as would the Tank Corps which had had No. 8 Squadron dedicated to it for the past few months. These aircraft, which were RE8s, would have special markings, either in the form of streamers or painted on panels on the tailplane or underneath the lower wing, to indicate with which formation they were working. Troops on the ground would use panels and flares both to mark their positions and to call down SOS fire.* In terms of the 5th Tank Brigade, it set up an advanced HQ at Pouilloy and had telephone lines laid to the HQ Australian Corps and its divisions. When the attack had begun a Brigade Report Centre was to be established on the western slope of the Cerisy valley and this would be reinforced by two wireless tanks. A tank would then be used to lay a cable between the report centre and advanced Brigade HQ. Battalion advanced HQs were initially attached to one of the infantry brigades

---

* When the guns were not firing they were laid on targets which would best help disrupt possible enemy counter-attacks.

they were supporting. Once the Green line had been reached, battalion HQs would deploy to the Cerisy Valley, where the tanks would rally, and would be in contact with Brigade HQ by runner. Likewise, the companies communicated with their battalion HQs by runner. Some pigeons were allocated, twenty-six pairs, and these were given to the armoured cars of the 17th Battalion and those tanks going to the furthest objectives.

Apart from the squadrons dedicated to support the various corps through contact patrols, the RAF had a range of other tasks. Its key role during the preparatory phase was to prevent the German air arm from detecting what was about to take place. The Germans did, in fact, note a significant amount of traffic in the Fourth Army area on 1 August, but did not consider it out of the ordinary. Thereafter the weather closed in, preventing meaningful air reconnaissance, until the 7th. The deployment of the additional squadrons required was left to the very last moment and when the weather did improve on 7 August German aircraft reported heavy air activity around the airfields of Bertangles and Bovelles, but that was all they were able to discover. In all two RAF brigades, V and IX, would be involved. There was, however, some confusion over the command chain. Brigadier General L. E. O. Charlton, the commander of V Brigade, was directly responsible to Rawlinson, but Salmond controlled the operation of all squadrons which were not part of V Brigade and also had the ear of the Fourth Army commander. There was therefore a danger of co-ordination problems. Apart from six army co-operation or corps squadrons (RE8s and Armstrong Whitworths), there were three fighter reconnaissance squadrons (Bristol Fighters, DH4s), fifteen fighter squadrons (SE5s, Camels, and one squadron of Dolphins), one night fighter squadron (Camels), five day bomber squadrons (DH9s, DH4s) and five of night bombers (FE2bs, Handley Pages). The day bombers would be launched at first light on 8 August to attack German airfields and then in the evening switch to railway stations through which German reserves might pass. The night bombers would then take over this task, as well as attacking billets, railways and roads. The roll of the fighting scout squadrons was two-fold. The fighter squadrons were to provide cover for the day bombers, which would attack at low level, and some of the Camels would also be used in the ground attack role. Two of the corps squadrons in V Brigade, No. 9 supporting the Australians and No. 5 the Canadians, would also be charged with laying smokescreens. No. 9 Squadron was also to have the unique task of dropping machine gun ammunition to III Corps and the Australians during the advance.

The Tank Corps was also involved with ammunition resupply in the shape of its Supply and Gun Carrier companies. The former used converted Mk IV tanks, with twenty-four making up a company. Each supply tank would carry ammunition and engineer stores and a typical load was 10 boxes of small arms ammunition, 2 Stokes mortars, 1 box Very lights, 7 boxes of grenades, 50 boxes of trench mortar bombs, 50 cans of water, 20 Lewis Gun drums, 1 box of SOS flares, 100 shovels, 50 picks, 50 coils of barbed wire, 30 short and 30 long pickets, 250 sandbags, 50 sets of rations and a power buzzer.[17] It will be seen that these were items which would be particularly needed for consolidating the objective. Other supply tanks were dedicated to replenishing the fighting tanks. The Gun Carriers had, as their name suggests, originally been designed to carry an artillery gun – 60-pdr or 6-inch howitzer – which could be fired from the chassis without dismounting it. By summer 1918, however, the two Gun Carrier companies in existence had been converted to the supply role and would carry similar loads to the Supply tanks. The great advantage of these two vehicles was that they were less vulnerable than horse-drawn transport or infantry carrying parties.

As for the move up of the troops, the 102nd Canadian Battalion (4th Canadian Division) had arrived in the Fourth Army area early on 4 August, having travelled overnight by bus from Berneville, south of Arras. It spent the day resting up in the village of Fresnes-Tilloloy, 25 miles west-north-west of Amiens. After dumping their packs and the officers' bedding rolls, 'little dreaming that it would be three weeks before we saw them again', they set off eastwards at 9.30 p.m. that night. This first march took them to Metigny, just over 9 miles as the crow flies, and they arrived at 2 a.m. That evening the Battalion faced more of a challenge:

At 9pm we fell in again ready to move off, but for some reason unknown were kept standing around for an hour before we actually set out on what was officially stated to be a 21-mile march; 25 miles was more probably the distance covered, and covered as it was in battle order and yawning stomachs it seemed like 30. It is not easy to understand why some provision was not made for a bite to eat on these long night marches. When battalions marched by day a stop was always made for lunch, and sandwiches or their equivalent were invariably carried in the haversack; why the darkness should have been presumed to counteract hunger is a mystery.

There was consolation once dawn came in the countryside they were passing through, 'open and billowy' and, compared to Flanders and the very north of France, the villages were more 'widely scattered' and 'larger and more prosperous in their appearance.' The 102nd arrived at their destination, Creuse to the south-west of Amiens, at 9 a.m. on the 6th. The following night took them to Boves Wood just south-east of Amiens. There some 50,000 men and 25,000 horses were concentrated, but 'the undergrowth was so dense and the over-head cover so luxuriant' that it was easy to hide these numbers from prying eyes.[18] The 42nd (Royal Highlanders of Canada) Battalion observed in its war diary of its march to Gentelles Wood (the forward assembly area for much of the Canadian assault force) on the night 6–7 August: 'One of the remarkable features of this march was the tremendous amount of troops, transport, tanks, guns and other machinery of war which was placed on the road up, making our progress very slow.'[19]

For the Australians in the line, the 2nd Division had to relinquish the US 129th Infantry Regiment on 5 August. This returned to its parent US 65th Infantry Brigade, but left the 6th Australian Brigade very stretched. As LCpl D. T. R. Wilson of the 24th Battalion recorded in his diary:

> We did miss them as our Battalion front was 2000 yards and extraordinarily long for a unit. Our company this time was 60 strong including all ranks ... There were very few men in the line. Our Commanding Officer remarked that the line was being held by Christian Science. It was, I know. I had to patrol the line at intervals to see how the lads were; two here & two there at intervals of 30 or 40 yards ... [20]

In the meantime, there had been further developments at the higher command level. On the afternoon of 4 August Rawlinson duly briefed the Cavalry divisional and brigade commanders – 'I have not given them an unlimited objective but told them to put the infry [infantry] onto the Amiens Def[ence] line.'[21] However, the day before Haig and Lawrence had had Foch and Weygand at Mouchy le Châtel. With the Germans now falling back from the Marne, Foch was keen to exploit the French success as much as possible and hence his emphasis on the need to advance beyond the Amiens defence line. Thus Haig had agreed to Ham, rather than Chaulnes, as Rawlinson's ultimate objective. That Debeney had also given an additional four infantry and three cavalry divisions further reflected Foch's determination to launch a full blown offensive.

In the light of what Foch had laid down Haig held a conference at Rawlinson's headquarters at Flixecourt on the morning of 5 August. Present were Rawlinson, Debeney and Kavanagh. Haig stated that he felt that Rawlinson was placing too much emphasis on consolidating the Amiens defence line and not enough in exploiting surprise. He told Rawlinson that, while he was to put the defence line in a state of defence he was not to delay – 'at once reserves must be pushed on to capture the line Chaulnes–Roye.' Rawlinson's view was that the Canadians would play the lead part and he had already arranged for the 3rd Cavalry Division, together with a Whippet battalion, to be attached to them, but Haig wanted the cavalry to be prepared to exploit anywhere across the whole front and ordered a cavalry brigade plus Whippets to be attached to the Australians, as he had already suggested to Monash. Haig's reasoning behind this was:

> If the Cavalry are placed under the orders of the Corps Commanders in the first place, then the Corps Commanders will have an interest in seeing that it is given every opportunity of pushing through.[22]

Haig was clearly thinking of Cambrai for which the cavalry had remained under the command of its own corps at the outset and this had failed to move it forward in sufficient numbers in time to exploit the breakthrough achieved by the tanks and infantry. Consequently, Rawlinson attached a brigade from the 1st Cavalry Division. He was also to be given further divisions to support the Australians and Canadians.*[23]

Debeney also explained his plan. He said that he would carry out a rolling attack, beginning with his XXXI Corps immediately adjacent to the British Fourth Army attacking at 45 minutes after Zero Hour, with the aim of reaching Hangest by the end of the first day. To its south IX Corps would advance four hours after Zero with the object of protecting XXXI Corps's southern flank. The other two corps, X and XXXV, would attack north and south of Montdidier when the situation permitted, with the latter probably not attacking until the second day with the aim of linking up with the Fourth Army in the Roye area. He intended II Cavalry Corps to follow up behind XXXV Corps. In further orders issued to his corps on 6 August Debeney emphasized the need to press on with all speed, with strong-

---

* These were the 17th, 32nd and 63rd Divisions, although only the 32nd was about to be immediately deployed and would be virtually promised to the Canadians.. The other two divisions were out of the line, but would not receive orders to move until 11 a.m. on 8 August.

points being overcome through envelopment and divisions not waiting for neighbouring formations to catch up.[24]

Fourth Army issued further orders on 6 August. Once the Cavalry Corps had secured the outer Amiens defences it was to 'push forward in the direction of the line Roye–Chaulnes with the least possible delay.' This was reiterated in amended orders issued by the Cavalry Corps on the following day. They stressed that ' . . . on reaching the line of the Amiens outer defences, the Divisions will hold the line with the minimum number of men whilst the bulk of the Divisions pass as far east of that line as possible, pushing strong reconnaissance to the line Roye–Chaulnes'.[25] Simultaneously the Canadian Corps, reinforced as necessary, would follow on behind the cavalry, keeping close touch with the French, while the Australians, 'pivoting on the Somme between Méricourt and Etinehem, will swing forward their right so as to keep touch with the Canadian Corps.' The III Corps task would be to establish a defensive flank between Etinehem and Dernancourt.[26] While additional reserves were being made available there was concern at GHQ over them being deployed in time. A memorandum written by Tavish Davidson to Lawrence on 7 August encapsulates this:

> If the battle goes well, the troops succeed in reaching the red line early, and it appears probable that they will be given further objectives during the day, – And, if it is the intention in these circumstances to push on the next day and [sic] the following day and continue fighting —
>
> Then it is essential that the GHQ reserves should be pushed up on the 8th and the Fourth Army be informed by 11am [sic] that these reserves or a portion of them are released for that purpose.
>
> If the reserves are not released in sufficient time as suggested above, we shall have a repetition of the Loos incident.*

---

* This refers to the attack at Loos on 25 September 1915, when Sir John French held the reserves – Guards Division and unblooded 21st and 24th Divisions – too far back. He did not release them to Haig, then commanding First Army, until midday. Haig wanted to use

If we are to push on and exploit success, some fresh troops must pass through the Canadians on the second day in order to let the latter reform and fill up with ammunition and food and be in a condition to follow up and continue the battle on the third and fourth days.[27]

As we shall see, problems over the deployment of the reserves did arise.

The biggest scare during the preparatory period came in the III Corps sector. The origins of it go back to 21 July, when Monash had approved another 'peaceful penetration' action, namely to secure the Brick Beacon ridge south of Morlancourt. This would deny the Germans valuable observation posts, but, in spite of this, Rawlinson was unwilling to give his approval. However, on 25 July, while Monash was on leave, Rawlinson had a change of heart and agreed that the 5th Australian Division could make this attack prior to its relief by III Corps. It was duly mounted on the night of 28/29 July and by dawn the objective had been achieved. An encouraging sign was that many of the 128 prisoners captured appeared happy that the war was over for them. III Corps duly took over this sector. On the night 5/6 August the 58th Division began to relieve the southern half of the 18th Division's sector immediately north of the Somme. It was a complicated operation, which involved the 18th Division's 54th Brigade sidestepping northwards to allow the 174th Brigade to enter the trenches. It was made more difficult by the conditions. The trenches themselves were those recently captured by the Australians and were very shallow since they had prevented the Germans digging them deeper. The recent rain had not helped and had turned the trenches into a boggy morass. The night was also dark, with no moon. The 8th Londons (Post Office Rifles) were to relieve the 2nd

---

the 21st and 24th Divisions to exploit his initial successes, and threw them into the attack on the following morning. They had been on the march throughout the intervening time, had no chance to look at the ground over which they would attack and were up against a now consolidated German defence. The result was a bloody repulse.

Bedfords, who in turn would relieve the 8th East Surreys on their left. Because of the conditions the relief took considerably longer than expected and by 3.30 a.m., with some of the Post Office Rifles still making their way up, the commanding officer of the 2nd Bedfords decided that he would delay relieving the East Surreys until daylight. Fifty minutes later all hell was let loose.

Determined to reclaim the Brick Beacon ridge and preceded by a heavy artillery and trench mortar barrage four battalions of the crack German 27th Division assaulted. The Post Office Rifles had by this time got their two right hand companies in place, but the two on the left had not yet completed the relief and it was on them and the Bedfords and East Surreys that the attack fell. The Post Office Rifles managed to hold where they were and formed a defensive flank, but the Germans succeeded in penetrating to a depth of 800 yards, overrunning a forward command post which was being prepared by the Royal Engineers for the commander of the 54th Brigade, Brigadier General L. W. De V. Sadleir-Jackson. They captured the RE working party, including its officer, but shortly afterwards were driven out by the 2nd Bedfords. Further counter-attacks by the 8th East Surreys and 6th Northamptonshires enabled half the ground to be recaptured by 10 a.m., but fighting continued for the remainder of the day. This attack threw up a number of problems. To begin with, the Germans captured no less than 5 officers and 231 other ranks. Besides infantry-men and engineers they also included a number of artillerymen engaged in dumping ammunition in preparation for the 8 August attack. While none were likely to have been briefed on the details of the assault at this time, they would almost certainly have deduced from the preparations that something major was in the offing. Yet, according to the Germans, none of them gave any indication of the impending attack and none of those involved in the assault appear to have recognized the significance of the dumped artillery shells or Sadleir-Jackson's future battle headquarters.[28] The commanders and staffs within III Corps and at HQ Fourth Army were not to know this, however, and all they could do was to watch for any intelligence indicators that the Germans opposite were being reinforced.

Another problem was that the German attack had thrown III Corps' planning into disarray. The wedge which the Germans had driven in the line left no proper forming-up point for the initial assault on 8 August. Sadleir-Jackson was therefore ordered to recapture the lost ground. He carried this out on 7 August and succeeded to a degree, although the Germans still held a wedge in the left centre sector of his line. The 48 hours of virtually continuous fighting also left the 54th Brigade in no state to carry out its part in the main attack and so the 36th Brigade from the 12th Division was at the last minute deputed to take its place.

By now the final deployments were being made. The tanks had been steadily moving up. They lay up, largely in villages, during the day and were carefully camouflaged. The bulk of the 5th Tank Brigade, which would be supporting the Australians, had been gradually moving forward from the night of 30/31 July. During these marches the tank commander walked ahead so as to guide his tank. This could be hazardous, as the 13th Tank Battalion found during its move from Vaux to Querrieu Wood on the night 4/5 August. One officer was crushed to death and another badly injured by their tanks, mainly because they had tripped on loose barbed wire. Earlier, on the night 30/31 July, the 2nd Tank Battalion suffered an officer and NCO killed and two other ranks wounded from a chance bomb that fell near the tanks while they were moving to Querrieu Wood. By 6 August the Brigade was concentrated in villages lying to the west of Hamel, but disaster struck No 1 Gun Carrier Company, which was in an orchard close to Villers Bretonneux and with its tanks loaded with small arms ammunition, 3-inch mortar bombs and grenades. A shell happened to hit one and the subsequent explosion of the munitions on board caused sympathetic detonations of those aboard other tanks. Only five out of nineteen could be saved by driving them out of harm's way.

Once in their forward assembly areas there was much work to be done in terms of tank maintenance. Air photographs were closely studied, especially oblique shots, which tank commanders found to be very helpful, particularly since the 1:20,000 maps issued to each tank commander arrived late and they were unable to study them as closely as they might have done. Most commanders also had the opportunity to study the ground from artillery OPs around Villers Bretonneux. They noted that the ground varied considerably on either side of the Villers Bretonneux–St Quentin road. To its north it was characterized by steep valleys and banks, while to the south it was flat and colourless, with little cover for the tanks. The forward assembly areas themselves were some 3,000 yards behind the infantry start line and the routes to it were marked with white tape. The 5th Tank Brigade noted that the rate of taping achieved was 1,500 yards per hour going forward to the start line, but when carried out the reverse way it was 4,000 yards per hour.[29]

The preparations of the 4th Tank Brigade were very similar. One of the essential but tedious tasks during the deployment phase was ensuring that the tracks made by the tanks had been covered up by daylight. Capt Wilfrid Bion* of the 5th Tank Battalion overcame this in an ingenious way. He arranged for the last tank in his section to tow a makeshift harrow weighted down with personal kit. His battalion was to be the extreme right hand one, operating in support of the 3rd Canadian Division. This meant having to cross the River Luce in order to get into position. Of the two tank companies operating with the Division a crossing place for one was identified at Domart in the extreme north of the sector, but because this lay a mere 1,000 yards from the Germans it was decided that the tanks would not cross until Zero Hour. For the other company, of which Bion's section was part, the only possible crossing place was a ruined bridge and in the early evening of 7 August Bion had to take a party of his men to fill the river at this point with rubble from the bridge and fascines so that the tanks could cross. Before this and since the ruined bridge lay across the boundary with the French, he was

---

* Bion had previously distinguished himself at Cambrai, being recommended for the VC but awarded the DSO instead for continuing to fight his tank after it had been disabled and keeping the Germans at bay. He would later receive the Legion d'Honneur for his part in the Amiens attack.

ordered to report to the headquarters of the First French Army to meet some staff officers of the French 42nd Division to explain to them precisely what his tanks would be doing. In particular they would help the French capture the village of Villers-aux-Erables. His own French was shaky, but he eventually found an officer who spoke some English:

My impossible, ever-so-funny 'parlez-vous' sixth form French meeting his, presumably, 'baccalaureat' English, was not a suitably reassuring back-cloth for a serious dialogue. I did not feel frivolous. I felt in every possible way incompetent. We declared ourselves satisfied with the result of our laborious stammering match, saluted each other and parted.

Then, having completed his task at the ruined bridge, Bion settled down to await the arrival of the tanks.[30] Captain Cyril Falls was acting as a liaison officer to the 42nd Division and apprehensive about the attack. Writing in his diary on 6 August:

So all the old tricks are coming out of the conjurer's box. I have seen it too often before – the Somme, Messines, Ypres, Cambrai – to be fully confident of a great success on this occasion. But one thing is sure: if we take the knock this time after Ludendorff has shown us how it is done, we may as well give up.

That night:

I lay awake in my bunk for some time thinking of the assembly of the troops and tanks on the tiny spit of land between the Avre and the Luce, and its dangers. If the Boche were to find it out and launch quite a small attack, or even to deluge that position with high explosive and mustard gas, what hellish confusion and loss there would be![31]

Many of the Canadian infantry spent 7 August in Boves and the wood of the same name:

Boves, a small village, lying astride the river Avre seemed dead in the daytime, but at night it was the centre of seething activity. Soon after twilight, from hidden crannies came creeping tractors, lumbering tanks, huge guns, thousands of wagons and innumerable limbers, all preparing to move forward, towards the front. Out of the houses poured troops who formed up wherever they could find a space. Drivers who had been cleaning and oiling their harness during the day in their billets, were limbering-up their teams. Lorry drivers were tinkering at their engines. No one would recognise the innocent little place of the day time.[32]

Inevitably there was increasing congestion during the last nightly moves. The Canadian 116th Battalion (3rd Division) took seven hours during the night 6/7 August to cover the 4 miles from Boves to Gentelles Wood, with the one road available aggravating the congestion. Then:

With but little sleep, reconnoitring commenced almost at once, and in order to observe secrecy, small parties were sent forward to Domart Wood. The Commanding Officer, Intelligence Officer and Company Commanders only were able to reach the forward system and make a quick reconnaissance at close range. Owing to the broken nature of the ground the assembly area was limited and positions for one company had to be found forward of the front line, held by the troops then holding that sector. All these areas had to be thoroughly reconnoitred and positions taped off, which was an extremely difficult and hazardous task due to the night activity of enemy machine guns, but thanks to the assistance of the Australian Outpost Company then holding the line, who personally pointed out the most favourable positions, everything was completed satisfactorily.[33]

The tape laying was hazardous and the greatest fear was that one or more of those involved might be wounded and then captured by the Germans, especially if they were identified as Canadians.

For those spending their last day before the attack, Thomas Dinesen* of the 42nd Canadian Battalion (Royal Highlanders of Canada) was in Gentelles Wood:

All day long we rested in this pleasant spot – we even had permission to make a little fire here and there under a thickly branched tree and do a bit of cooking. The regular meals are good and plentiful, of course, but we never miss a chance of eating unlimited quantities of extra food. The last tin of baked beans was opened – there's no reason to go into battle with a haversack heavier than was absolutely necessary! We washed and shaved carefully in order to look our best before Fritz ... Our equipment was inspected for the last time: Gas-masks, rifles, ammunition, shaving kit, iron rations – everything was OK. Some of us were presented with an extra gift – mine was a big and heavy bag containing a dozen or so Mills bombs! Just before sunset we had to fall in for a final parade. Then supper – and at 10pm we were again fighting our way through the throng on the Amiens – Roye road.[34]

In the Australian sector Monash issued a special order of the day to be read out to all troops. He made the point that for the first time in the war the complete Australian Corps would be engaged and that the operations of the past four months had been in preparation for 'this greatest and culminating effort'. He assured his men that 'this battle will be one of the most memorable of the whole war' and that

* Dinesen was a Dane and the sister of Karen Blixen of 'Out of Africa' fame. He joined the Canadian Army after failing to be accepted by the British and US Armies. He was to win the Victoria Cross at Parvillers on 12 August during ten hours of desperate close quarter fighting when he five times went forward to subdue German machine guns. He was also awarded the French Croix de Guerre and commissioned.

he had every confidence in them. He concluded: 'I earnestly wish every soldier of the Corps the best of good fortune, and a glorious and decisive victory, the story of which will re-echo throughout the world, and will live for ever in the history of our home land.'

In the III Corps area the 36th Brigade (12th Division) had been placed under command of the 18th Division, and one of its battalions which would make the initial assault was the 7th Royal Sussex. They only gathered what was in store for them that day when the CO and his company commanders went up to carry out a reconnaissance, having understood that their brigade was to relieve the now battered 54th Brigade. Sadleir-Jackson, who was still fighting the battle to regain the ground lost on the night 5/6 August, told them what was to happen next day and put them in a trench from where they could see something of the terrain. They then attempted to get forward to the front line, but could obtain no clear idea of where the assembly area for the attack would be or what the precise objectives were. Lt Col A. L. Thomson decided that nothing more was to be gained and returned to his battalion. By now it was 5 p.m. and the 7th Royal Sussex had finally received their orders for the next day:

There was a great deal to be done before marching off at 8.30pm. It was difficult for the company commanders to explain much to their subordinates, for the battalion's assembly positions could not be given and its objectives were obscure even to those who had seen something of the ground. Zero hour was not to be disclosed until after the march had begun.

During the march up the 7th Royal Sussex suffered badly from German shell fire. One shell struck a company HQ and its lead platoon. Another hit a platoon from another company, also causing heavy casualties. In spite of this, the pitch black of the night, and the very uneven ground, the battalion managed to pick up its guides and was in position by 2.45 a.m. Their difficulties were not yet over:

There were no troops in the line taken over, but some wounded men in a dug-out were of assistance in giving roughly the lie of the land. They did not, however, know of the position of any other troops, although they said that they thought there were some isolated posts still remaining in front. Our patrols could not find any of these posts, so that orders had to be given to all ranks to look out for them as they advanced. Not much more time remained and patrols were not able to gain touch with the 58th Division, which was supposed to be on our right. C Company was in touch with the 9th Royal Fusiliers [the other 36th Brigade assault battalion] on the left.

Matters were not helped by the thick mist that developed an hour before Zero Hour.[35] The 12th Division also suffered gas shelling in its assembly areas between 9.30 p.m. and 12.30 a.m. This also affected the 18th Division's deployment, especially its field batteries.

As for the 58th Division, they appear to have had an easier time, not least because they were already in the line. A Post Office rifleman:

> Around 2.00am on 8 August our Coy officer, Capt Thomas, told us we were going over the top and we should meet him in the front line at a specified time. The rum ration was shared out and somehow the surplus fell into the care of Bill Murray, L/Cpl stretcher-bearer. The rest of us were so heavily laden with extra bandoliers of ammo, Mills Bombs in our pockets, as well as a box of them carried between two. All was quiet, except for an occasional spray of German machine-gun bullets aimed at nothing in particular, so we elected to stay on top while we made our way to Capt Thomas. A shout from Bill Murray and we joined him in the communication trench. A bullet had gone through the petrol can containing the rum. We emptied our own water bottles and replaced the water with rum![36]

Indeed, the Division's casualties were only slight during the forming up phase.

Immediately south of the Somme the 3rd Australian Division managed to avoid congestion by laying out four tracks, two for each of its initial assault brigades. These avoided roads and villages as much as possible. Consequently, the deployment went 'without a hitch' and the troops were ready in their jump-off positions an hour before Zero and this having had a 15 minutes rest halt during the march. Cpl J. S. Finney of the 44th Battalion (3rd Australian Division) had been involved in laying out the tapes from the lying up positions to the start line:

This had to be done in as silent a manner as possible, and everything had to be done by signs. Occasionally up would go a Fritz Very Light and everything we were doing would have to remain in abeyance and it was absolutely necessary for us to remain in whatever position we were in at the time the light went up if not for our own safety for the safety of those who were out either cutting the wire or assisting us in laying the tape. At times we could hear the muffled snip of the wire cutters. The snip that seemed like the crack of a whip. We knew then that another stumbling block in the form of a wire was cut. It was now that Fritz got it into his head to give us a Good-night salvo and over came his iron rations. We got down full length in the nearest shell hole and patiently waited (as there was nothing else we could do) until he considered he had done enough. On ceasing this he traversed a machine gun two or three times and then settled down for the night.[37]

Likewise, 5th Australian Division, which would pass through the 3rd after the first phase, also had an uninterrupted deployment. For the past two days they had been lying up immediately west of Villers Bretonneux and did not leave their assembly areas until 2 a.m. on the 8th.

Below these two divisions were the 2nd and 4th Australian Divisions. They also had few problems over their final deployment, although the 4th Australian Division, which would be committed to the second phase, did report some problems with the fog. The 2nd Tank Battalion was employing two companies to support the 2nd Australian Division and all bar one tank, which had mechanical problems, were in position by midnight.

In the Canadian sector and just south of the Amiens–St Quentin road the 2nd Canadian Division's 4th Infantry Brigade relieved the Australian 50th Battalion at 1.15 a.m. and the remainder of the Division was fully deployed just over two hours later. On its right the 1st Canadian Division's experience was similar, with its reserve brigade concentrated in front of Gentelles. No more than the usual German harassing fire was encountered. The 3rd Canadian Division would operate south of the Amiens–Roye road and had the problem of the River Luce to contend with. They managed to overcome this and the forward brigades were in position by 2 a.m. As for Wilfrid Bion's tank company:

At 9.50 [p.m.] Handley Page bombers were due to start flying along the front; the noise of their engines was supposed to cloak the roar of tank engines so the enemy would not become suspicious. Soon we heard the characteristic pulsating tone* . . . Just then from two miles away we heard the roar of the first tank engine starting up . . . The tanks, after the first one, helped to screen each other. As each engine started, the driver throttled down to slow speed so that the roar soon became a diffuse murmur, and the murmur became an undifferentiated noise like traffic on the roads; it was just possible to believe that the enemy might be deceived.

---

* The Handley-Page bombers of No. 207 Squadron carried out this task. In spite of the improvement to the weather on 7 August very low cloud developed during the evening and only two of the aircraft were able to take off after several abortive attempts. They then flew for three hours up and down the line. The pilots, both Canadian, were later awarded DFCs for this work.

After what seemed an interminable wait:

> The first of the huge shapes came out of the blackness, in low
> gear, so that the idling engines could easily propel the tanks
> forward without strain. They were exactly on time. The intense
> relief . . . Something made us look back to the bridge over the
> Luce. It had gone; utterly and absolutely vanished behind a
> dense wall of fog.

Using his compass and map to obtain the right bearings, Brion now
had to hastily get tape laid to enable the tanks to get to their start off
positions. This they did.[38]

Zero Hour had been fixed for 4.20 a.m. It would appear that in the
Canadian Corps at least the views of the divisions on when it should
be were taken into account. Thus 1st Canadian Division had recommended 4.15 a.m., but 'higher authority, making necessary cor-
rections to allow for a waning moon' had decided that it should be
five minutes later.[39] This was an hour before dawn. Zero Hour was
disseminated to the troops during the night. In the case of the 40th
Australian Battalion, which was one of the line holding battalions,
the commanding officer, concerned that the Germans might pick up
the message if it was passed by telephone *en clair* to his companies,
organised a simple code:

> The agreement was that a number of rations of jam should
> mean that zero hour was at so many minutes after 4am, and
> a number of rations of butter so many minutes before 4am.
> However, zero hour was fixed at 4.20am, and accordingly a
> telephone message went to companies: 'Send 20 rations of jam
> to Battalion Headquarters at once. Acknowledge.' Now the
> OC B Company happened to be away from his headquarters
> when the message arrived and another officer was present
> who naturally thought that there were 20 men at Battalion
> Headquarters in urgent need of jam. So he set the Company
> Quartermaster-Sergeant to work, and the Company

Quartermaster-Sergeant went round posts and dugouts and begged or borrowed small portions of jam from protesting men. A few minutes before zero hour a breathless runner dashed into Battalion Headquarters with a large tin containing a small quantity of hopeless-looking mixture of several kinds of jam which he put in front of the Adjutant. 'With Capt Bisdee's compliments, sir, he can't get 20 rations, but here's enough for 12.'[40]

At 3.30 a.m., however, a German 5.9cm and 77mm bombardment broke out astride the Australian–Canadian boundary in the area of the Villers Bretonneux–Marcelcave railway. It hit the right half of the 7th Australian Brigade (2nd Division) and on 4th Canadian Brigade (2nd Canadian Division). The 26th and 27th Australian Battalions, together with the 19th Canadian Battalion did have some casualties. The belief was that it was the noise of tank engines which had alerted the Germans. Indeed, earlier the 2nd Canadian Division had asked Corps HQ if artillery fire could be increased to drown it out, but had been refused. Those under this fire therefore just had to use the cover they could find and hope that the Germans were not adopting their tactic of disrupting the attack before it had been launched. In fact, the Germans had heard the engine noises and had decided to mount a raid. The barrage was put down to cover it, but the raiders, from 148th Infantry Regiment (41st Division), found the front line trenches immediately south of the railway empty, since they had just been vacated by the 50th Australian Battalion, and withdrew. The barrage itself continued almost until Zero Hour.

There was a similar incident in the III Corps sector, when the 18th Division's field batteries were shelled at 3.40 a.m. for five minutes as they got into position. Again there were fears that the Germans had realized what was going on. What had actually happened was that one of the battalion commanders of the 265th Infantry Regiment had called down the fire after receiving reports that British troops in fighting kit were lying out in front of his battalion's positions. The German artillery had, however, been ordered to conserve ammunition and hence the briefness of the bombardment. Further fire would only be brought down if the infantry requested it, which they clearly did not.

The truth of the matter was that the German High Command was complacent. In an order of the day dated 4 August Ludendorff stated:

At the present moment, we occupy everywhere positions which have been strongly fortified, and which we have, I am convinced, effected a judicious organisation in depth of the infantry and artillery. Henceforth, we can await every hostile attack with greater confidence. As I have already explained, we should wish for nothing better than to see the enemy launch an offensive, which can but hasten the disintegration of his forces.[41]

The reason for his satisfaction was that in the immediate aftermath of the Hamel attack he had laid down a scheme of defence applicable to the whole front. In essence this was to consist of a forward zone and a main line of resistance. The former would be a belt some 500–1000 yards in depth, but lightly held with just patrols and machine-gun nests and was designed to degrade any attack before it came up against the main line of defence, behind which reserves would be positioned. Staff officers had been sent to von der Marwitz's Second Army to check that it was conforming to the concept and had expressed themselves satisfied. In fact, the situation on the ground was very different.

Apart from the two areas where German fire was out of the ordinary the remainder of the front was relatively quiet. Gunner James Armitage of 30 Battery Australian Field Artillery wrote in his diary:

We got out on the flat marshy ground where our guns were to be sited. It was utterly still. Vehicles made no sound on the marshy ground. There was no talking and only an occasional random burst of German machine-gun fire and an odd gun going off in the distance. Only the constant display of enemy Very lights going up from their trenches worried us. The silence played on our nerves a bit. As we got our guns into position you could hear drivers whispering to their horses and men muttering curses under the breath, and still the silence persisted, broken only by the whine of a stray bullet or a long range shell passing high overhead.

We started putting out our lines of fire, calculating our charging fuse settings so that our shells would keep bursting ahead of our advancing infantry . . . Each crew's world centred around his gun, but we could feel that hundreds of groups of men were doing the same thing – preparing for the heaviest barrage ever launched.[42]

Padre Frederick Scott with the 1st Canadian Division:

The Colonel [CO 16th Battalion] ordered me to stay in the trench, but I had made up my mind to go forward and see the companies which were going over in the first wave. They lay along the side of a road some distance down the slope in front of us. In making my way there I passed a trench where the 5th Battalion was waiting to follow up the advance. A German machine-gun was playing freely upon the spot, but no one got hit. When I came to the advanced companies of the 16th Battalion, I passed along their line and gave them my blessing. It was splendid to meet and shake hands with those gallant lads, so soon to make the attack. They were in high spirits in spite of the seriousness of their enterprise.[43]

2Lt Percy Smythe, who was in the 24th Australian Battalion's Battle Surplus:

The atmosphere seems tensely charged with excitement tonight. Everybody is keenly interested about tomorrow's great battle, and wondering how the tide will go. Optimism is running at a high pitch. This is the first time the Australians will have been given a fair open go with unlimited objectives. Usually they have been limited to an advance of a mile or two at the most, and the prisoners and booty captured were not worth the sacrifice of life entailed. Thank Heaven the days of close warfare have gone, and such slaughter-house battles as Pozières are a thing of the past.[44]

Finally, Rawlinson wrote in his diary that night:

There is nothing to show that the Bosche knows what is coming S of the Somme. We shall have 8 excellent Divns and 350 tanks against him and three Divns of Cavy ready to pass through any hole that is made. I have great hopes that we may win a big success.

CHAPTER FOUR

THE GREEN LINE

With the fog growing thicker the attackers began to count down the minutes to Zero Hour. The 17th Australian Battalion:

> At 10 minutes past 4, company commanders quietly passed the order: 'Stand-to,' and presently an equally quiet-voiced runner, looming-up silently out of the mist, would report his platoon 'all present and correct'. Meanwhile, the tanks had crept forward to their allotted positions in front of the waiting infantry. 4.19 – Wristlet watches, previously synchronised, were raised to eye level, while the second hands ticked out that last fateful minute. Twenty seconds to go – 10, 5 – Zero! And simultaneously the gigantic orchestra of 680 guns crashed into the opening bar of the overture of the 'Battles of the Hundred Days'.[1]

Bertie Cox, a Canadian gunner, in a letter to his three brothers:

> Every gun shot together and the thing was off. I never heard anything like it in my life, neither has anyone else, as it was about the biggest show that has ever been staged on the Western Front. Several times I could not hear my own gun fire, and for half the series I laid and fired the gun myself. After 3 hours I was practically deaf.[2]

Major Donald Coutts, the 24th Australian Battalion's medical officer:

> The noise was terrific – away in the distance you could hear

our heavy 12" guns pounding away, and all around us, the 18 pounders and 4.5 [inch howitzers] were cracking away as hard as they could go. You could hear our shells whistling overhead. Everyone had to keep down in the trenches for the first ten minutes, because the trajectory of the 18 pounders was low on account of the short distance they were firing.[3]

Three minutes into the barrage and the assaulting troops began to move forward.

North of the Somme III Corps would be employing three divisions from Morlancourt south to the River Somme. (See Map 5.) The attack would be opened by 18th and 58th Divisions, with the 12th Division in the extreme north joining in two hours later. The key objective was the Chipilly Spur, whose guns threatened the Australian advance south of the river. Thereafter the Corps would form a defensive flank, which would be the primary responsibility of the 58th Division.

It was the 58th Division that was faced with the bare upland of the Chipilly Spur. The Somme in this sector was characterized by steep banks, cliffs in some places, and steep ridges. The Division identified Sailly Laurette as another key objective. To this end the 174th Brigade would carry out the initial assault on the Green Line, but would take the 2nd/10th Londons from the 175th Brigade under command. This battalion would be responsible for seizing Sailly Laurette. The attack would be supported by ninety 18-pdrs and thirty 4.5-inch howitzers, with the field guns providing the creeping barrage and the howitzers shelling the deep valleys running down to the Somme. In addition, heavy artillery would bombard German gun positions, machine-gun nests and villages known to be strongly held. Ten tanks from the 2nd Tank Battalion were also allotted, two of them specifically to support the 2nd/10th Londons. Once the Green Line had been reached there would be an hour's pause to allow the 173rd Brigade to pass through, together with the 53rd Brigade (18th Division) on its left. They would carry on to the Red Line, with the 173rd Brigade being responsible for the Chipilly Spur and 53rd Brigade Gressaire Wood.

The attack began well, with the German front line being quickly overrun, in spite of resistance from the 27th Division. The 2nd/10th Londons under Lt Col E. P. Cawson did especially well to secure Sailly Laurette by 6.30 a.m., as well as the quarry and sunken road to the north-east of the village. They captured some 500 Germans. This was in spite of the thick fog, which did not disperse until 8.30 a.m. The remainder of the 174th Brigade, with the 7th Londons on the left, 6th Londons on the right, and the 8th Londons in support, were to clear Malard Wood, the eastern edge of which represented the Green Line. The 6th Londons were to actually clear the wood, which they intended to do by sending two companies round the north face and the other two round the south face. A platoon commander with one of the companies advancing to the north end of the wood:

Except for the front line itself, the Hun seemed to have made very little in the way of organised defensive positions, beyond machine-gun posts, relying more on the ground itself . . . Ridges were strongly held, but on our approach were surrendered, the enemy either running away, or themselves surrendering. I found one tank, with which was one of our officers and a number of men of both 6th and 7th Battalions, and we helped them clear out one or two enemy posts . . . It was broad daylight by now, but the mist was, if anything, thicker than ever, and it was impossible to make a straight line for my place, but from a knowledge of the ground obtained from maps, I knew that if I worked round the wood, keeping it to my right, I should eventually get where I wanted. So with five men I started off. We met and passed several other parties going in different directions and . . . at last we worked round to the east of the wood and there found a small party of the 7th and 8th Battalions . . . digging in. Passing them we pushed on to the quarry, which was the main landmark given to our company, and to our surprise we found no one there at all – friend or foe. Pushing on again, we came to a track junction which had been given to me as my platoon's objective, but no sign of our men could be seen anywhere.[4]

The fog and the shape of the terrain, which tended to slope down towards the river, caused the attacking units to both become scattered and drift to the right. Even so, the Green Line was secured.

The lead battalions of the 173rd Brigade (3rd and 2nd/4th Londons) followed up closely behind the attackers and the intention had been for them to move round the northern edge of Malard Wood in order to reach their jump-off positions on the Green Line. But, largely thanks to the fog, they became mixed up with the 174th Brigade and went through the wood instead. As they exited on the far side they came under very heavy machine-gun fire and were unable to reach their forming-up positions. In addition, the 2nd/4th Londons became mixed up with the 18th Division while trying to overcome the opposition on the Green Line. The Brigade's follow-up battalion, 2nd/2nd Londons, was sent forward in an effort to restore the situation, but when the time came to initiate the second phase there were only a few troops available to take part in the attack and not many of these reached the stiff cliff overlooking the Somme. The Chipilly Spur thus remained in German hands and machine-gun fire from there not only drove the attackers back into Malard Wood, but also interfered with the Australian advance south of the river. This necessitated another attempt on it, which was carried out by the 2nd/10th Londons at 7.30 p.m. Supported by a heavy barrage they managed to reach the outskirts of Chipilly village but were driven out by machine-gun and small arms fire. That ended the 58th Division's day.

On the left of the 58th Division, the 18th Division's main task was to secure the Bray–Corbie ridge. The attack would be initiated by the 53rd Brigade and the 36th Brigade from the 12th Division which had been brought in to replace the battered 54th Brigade. Apart from not knowing the ground and the fact that the fog prevented the tanks from arriving on time, the 36th Brigade, led by the 7th Royal Sussex and 9th Royal Fusiliers, and 7th Queens, which had been loaned from the 53rd Brigade, moved forward ahead of time – at 4.10 a.m. so as to keep as close as possible to the creeping barrage. It was the same with the 53rd Brigade to their south.

The 36th Brigade attacked with the 7th Queens on the left, 9th

Royal Fusiliers in the centre and 7th Royal Sussex on the right. According to the last named:

> From the moment of starting it was obvious that the attack would have to be taken slowly. The heavy mist, the uncertainty as to the presence of any troops in front, the exposed flank to the right, and the lack of knowledge of the ground or of the enemy's defences all made caution necessary. In spite of the dense barrage by our artillery, the enemy rifle and machine-gun fire was at first heavy, though mostly over our heads; enemy shell-fire, once the advance started, was negligible. As soon as we covered the wide No Man's Land we found the enemy was manning short lengths of deep trenches, mutually supporting each other, and that there was little or no wire. The trenches were very difficult to locate in the echoing mist, and the attack became a mixture of hide-and-seek with blind-man's-bluff. Any attempts at orderly progress were made more difficult by the appearance of units from other formations which had lost their way in the fog, and casualties became heavy during this period.[5]

On the other flank 7th Queens were held up by machine guns. Their commanding officer Lt Col Christopher Bushell VC DSO* came forward and personally led a successful attack on these, although he himself was mortally wounded. This enabled the 36th Brigade to reach and recapture the remaining ground lost to the Germans on 6 August, but they failed to reach the Morlancourt–Malard Wood road. At 7 a.m., and to plan, the 53rd Brigade now passed through, advancing astride the Bray–Corbie road. In the south the 10th Essex stormed forward in the fog and, after fierce tussles with men of the German 27th Division which cost them some 200 casualties, secured the road. Leaving the 36th Brigade to consolidate this they pressed

---

* He had won his VC for inspirational leadership of his battalion, although severely wounded in the head, on 23 March 1918 during the German offensive and had only recently returned to 7th Queens.

on, their numbers down to some eighty men. But they were out of touch of the battalions on their flanks, the 8th Royal Berkshires and 7th Royal West Kents, and there appeared to be no Germans to their front. To keep direction they hugged the Bray–Corbie road. Then the fog lifted and they found that they were just a few hundred yards from the north part of Gressaire Wood. More remarkable was that immediately in front of them were two well-camouflaged German artillery batteries, with their crews taking a stand easy. It was too good a chance to miss and the Essex immediately charged in and captured the lot. Lt Col E. M. Banks, who was commanding, knew that he had too few men to provide a proper escort for the prisoners and so ordered them to go back under guard of one of his wounded men. Matters for him were made easier by the fact that the Germans gained the impression from Colonel Banks' orders that they were about to be shot and to placate him some took their boots off. He therefore ordered the remainder to do the same and they departed. He now took stock and concluded that he had reached his objective on the Red Line, but there were still no other friendly troops around. He therefore sent a runner back. Half an hour later, at about 8 a.m., elements of the 7th Royal West Kents, which had also managed to make their way up along the Bray–Corbie road, linked up with the Essex and a protective flank had now been formed, albeit a very weak one.

It was now that the Germans began to counter-attack. The first assault came from the Morlancourt direction and was against the Royal West Kents. The Essex then came under fire from Gressaire Wood. Meanwhile the 8th Royal Berkshires on the right had managed to reach the western edge of the wood, although their commanding officer was hit no less than five times by machine gun bullets when they stumbled across a number of machine-gun nests. When the fog lifted they found themselves very exposed and under heavy fire and after hanging about for three quarters of an hour and suffering increasing casualties they were forced to withdraw to the Green Line. This left the 10th Essex on their own and at 9 a.m. they were counter-attacked from Gressaire Wood. With their rear threatened by the attack on the Royal West Kents and beginning to be outflanked Colonel Banks had no option but to withdraw. He damaged the breechblocks of the guns he had captured so as to render them unusable and, under machine gun fire from both flanks, withdrew the 2,000 yards back to the Green Line. Only fifteen men, including the commanding officer, made it back.

Back on the Green Line the 36th Brigade was also experiencing some problems. When the fog lifted the 7th Royal Sussex on the right flank realized that they were short and to the right of their objective on the Green Line. They had also been unable to make contact with the 58th Division on their right. Now aware of counter-attacks to their north, they were ordered to stay put while the Brigade's reserve battalion, the 5th Royal Berkshires, passed through and did reach the Green Line.

In the far north the 12th Division was to attack between the River Ancre and Morlancourt. The main object was to get onto the spur immediately north of Morlancourt. The 35th Brigade was to carry out the attack with all three of its battalions – 9th Essex on the left, 7th Norfolks in the centre, and the 1st/1st Cambridgeshires on the right. The reason that Zero Hour was at 6.20 a.m., two hours later than the remainder of the Fourth Army, was that the German defences in this sector were strong and it was decided that a preparatory bombardment was needed. The Essex and Norfolks were successful in their attack and were soon consolidating on their objective. The Cambridgeshires ran into problems, however. While the left attacking company reached its objective that on the right suffered heavy machine-gun and rifle fire, especially from its flank. The result was that both companies were forced to withdraw to the start line. Their commanding officer, Lt Col E. T. Saint DSO, pleaded to be allowed to make another attempt and this was agreed. Another barrage was laid on and co-ordination carried out with the 18th Division on the right to ensure that this time the Cambridgeshires' flank was not exposed. The new attack was mounted at 12.15 p.m. and was totally successful, with the two companies involved capturing over 300 prisoners, as well as a number of machine guns and trench mortars.

Thus, by the end of the day the 18th Division was firm on its objectives, but the 18th and 58th Divisions had been able only to achieve the Green Line. Gressaire Wood and, more significantly, the Chipilly Spur remained in German hands. The latter would cause the Australians south of the Somme some problems.

The essence of the Australian Corps plan was that the initial assault would be made by the 3rd Australian Division in the north and the 2nd Australian Division in the south. Once they reached the Green Line, which was scheduled for 6.20 a.m., two hours after Zero Hour, they would consolidate and then the 4th and 5th Australian Divisions would pass through and take on the Red and Blue Lines, the latter representing the old Amiens outer defences. It was estimated that the advance on the Red Line would begin four hours after Zero Hour. The Australians would be supported by the 5th Tank Brigade, whose tanks were allocated as follows:

2nd Tank Battalion plus one company of 13th Tank Battalion to the
    2nd and 5th Australian Divisions
13th Tank Battalion less one company to the 3rd Australian Division
8th Tank Battalion to the 4th Australian Division.

In addition, one and a half companies of the 15th Tank Battalion would each be allotted to the 4th and 5th Australian Divisions for the attack on the Blue Line. The tanks of No 1 Gun Carrier Company were to be used for carrying infantry supplies, with two each to the 2nd and 3rd Australian Divisions and nine each to the 4th and 5th Australian Divisions. No 4 Tank Supply company would support the fighting tanks, with a section of six tanks being allocated to each tank battalion. Finally, twelve of the 17th Armoured Car Battalions' cars were allocated to the 5th Australian Division, with the remaining four being under the direct control of the Australian Corps for a special mission, of which more later.

An hour before Zero aircraft began to overfly the front to drown the noise of the tanks moving up to the start line. The tanks themselves started their engines half an hour before Zero and then covered the final stage in column. Each battalion used the same formation for the attack (see Diagram 1.). First would come a line of scouts to point out machine gun posts and strongpoints to the tanks, which followed line abreast behind them. Then came the two lead companies, each with two platoons up and two in support, with the sections in each advancing line abreast in single file. The two supporting companies followed on behind using the same formation. The follow-up battalions also advanced with two companies, but with their platoons in artillery formation and their men in single file. The tanks needed to get ahead of the infantry, apart from the scouts, and deploy in line by the time the barrage made its first lift at Zero plus three minutes. In spite of the fog they achieved this – those tank commanders with compasses found them invaluable.

The 3rd Australian Division attacked with its 11th Brigade on the left, immediately south of the River Somme, and the 9th Brigade on the right. The 10th Brigade was to hold the original front line until the 4th Australian Division had passed through. Each assault brigade was supported by a company of the 13th Tank Battalion and eight Vickers from the divisional machine-gun battalion. The remainder of the machine guns would lay down a barrage at Zero Hour. No less than nine field artillery brigades would be used to lay down the main barrage. They were organized in three 'sub-groups' – A, B, and C. Once the Green line had been secured, one sub-group would move forward to act as 'mobile artillery' for the 4th Australian Division. A second would be deployed to cover the Blue Line, while the third was then placed in corps reserve.

The barrage opened on time and four minutes later, after the first lift, the attack began. Fog, smoke and dust made it difficult to keep direction, but some comfort was gained from the fact the inevitable German counter barrage, which came down ten minutes after Zero Hour, was weak and after a time ceased altogether. The single file formation also helped to maintain control and direction. Even though, in the words of Captain C. Longmore, commanding A Company of the 44th Battalion, which, with the 42nd Battalion, kicked off the 11th Brigade attack:

The whole line became hopelessly mixed, all ranks simply doing the best they could and keeping going somewhere in the direction of their own moving barrage. Company and platoon commanders never even saw their tanks; sometimes they heard them, but that was all. No company or platoon commander that morning had any influence over his men. He simply became an individual, blind to everything except what he tumbled over, and not knowing anything about the unit he was supposed to be in command of. However, as it happened, there was no need to worry. Every Digger or small party of Diggers when they found themselves apparently isolated pressed on – always in the direction of the barrage. There was no sitting down waiting for orders.[6]

The obscuration inevitably slowed the advance and it fell behind the creeping barrage, but this is where the tanks came into their own. Looming out of the fog as they did they struck terror into the Germans, with machine-gun crews surrendering after hardly firing a shot. However, some tanks did experience problems with communication trenches which they were unable to see in time and became ditched after falling sideways into them. Seven out of the twelve tanks of B Company, which was operating with the 11th Australian Brigade, fell victim to this and another was put out of action by a mine before reaching the Green Line.* This, however, did not deter the Australians. The 9th Australian Brigade had, for instance, feared that Accroche Wood, which lay just beyond the start line, would prove a problem since it was known to be strongly held. In fact, the opening barrage had driven the Germans into their dugouts and when the tanks and infantry arrived most of the defenders emerged merely to surrender.

* According to the 28th Australian Battalion, one of whose cookers later ran over a mine without detonating it, they were contained in kerosene tins, with the tops protruding a few inches above the ground, and were buried in groups of six. (Browning, Neville *The Blue & White Diamond: The History of the 28th Battalion 1915–1918* p.418 the Author, Perth, 2002). It is hardly surprising therefore that the tanks failed to spot them in the fog.

The upshot of all this was that the 9th Australian Brigade had secured its portion of the Green Line by 6.50 a.m., its 33rd and 35th Battalions holding the line and the 34th Battalion in support. They also had 8 trench mortars and 24 Vickers machine guns. The 11th Australian Brigade was somewhat later in consolidating, mainly because some platoons of the 41st Battalion lost their way in the fog. Even so, by 7.30 a.m., they were also firm, with the 41st Battalion, having passed through the 44th Battalion, on the right and the 42nd Battalion on the left, but echeloned back along the south bank of the Somme so as to provide a protected flank. Such was the initial success that the 42nd Battalion was able to deploy its cookers and give the men a hot breakfast by 9 a.m. As the Battalion History commented: 'This was considered a remarkable achievement, as never before had the cookers been so close to the front line in an attack.'[7] There was, however, concern from the outset over liaison with III Corps, especially that machine-gun nests on the north bank of the Somme might threaten the left flank of the 3rd Australian Division. Consequently, two platoons from the 39th Battalion had been detached to the 42nd Battalion on 6 August. Their task was to advance along the north bank of the Somme, although no effort appears to have been made to physically liaise with III Corps. One platoon advanced along the tow path, while the other covered the swampy ground abutting the river. Both came across barbed wire entanglements, against which their wirecutters proved ineffective. The latter platoon therefore used rifle butts to beat down the wire and as they were doing so they spotted a German machine-gun team withdrawing through the fog. The Australians opened fire, but missed. The platoon then continued into Sailly Laurette, where a number of German machine-gun posts were located. Yet, such was the shock of seeing the Australians that the crews immediately bolted into a cellar and then surrendered. The other platoon also captured a machine gun. The total bag of 8 machine guns and 40 prisoners was then escorted to the rear while the remainder of the two platoons continued on to their objective.

The experience of the 2nd Australian Division was much the same, although there were instances of German troops being bypassed. The 5th Brigade was able to use the Roman road running from Amiens to Brie as a guide, keeping it on its right to start with. It also used the old inner Amiens defence line as an initial objective, with 19th and 20th Battalions securing this and the 17th and 18th Battalions then passing through to the Green Line. All twelve tanks of B Company 2nd Battalion, which was supporting the Brigade, crossed the start line, but soon afterwards two were immobilized by land mines and another two received direct hits. The four battalions did become intermixed in the fog, but the inner Amiens defence line was quickly overrun. The first serious opposition came just short of Warfusée-Abancourt. Lt N. F. Wilkinson, whose machine guns were supporting the 19th Battalion:

... on our right a battery of machine-guns began to spit around us. Following us was a tank and we quickly got it to charge this nest of guns. Right at them the tank went, firing through the now clearing mist at the battery. Their fire ceased, and we rushed forward and came upon all the guns intact, but their crews had gone under the shelter of the mist and in fear of the tank which surely would have mowed them down if they had remained a little longer at their post. We went on again, and there lay the mound which was the limit of our attack, and where we quickly got our guns into position for a counter-attack, should it develop.[8]

Under a prearranged plan, the 17th and 18th Battalions now passed to the south and north of the village respectively. The right forward company (B) of the 17th Battalion, worked its way round to the south of the village and with the help of a tank captured three 4.2-inch howitzers. C Company on the left of B had problems when its HQ became separated from the platoons in the fog. The company commander located a tank, which was dragging a mass of barbed wire. Every time it changed direction the wire behind it swung backwards and forwards causing the infantrymen to give it a wide berth. None-

THE DAY WE WON THE WAR

theless, it helped them capture four machine guns. As Captain
Harnett and his HQ approached the southern outskirts of the village,

> ... they observed, in a sunken road ahead, a battery of 4.2-inch
> howitzers which the enemy was attempting to withdraw. They
> shot the horses and captured the four guns intact, but the crews
> escaped. Nearing the south-eastern edge of Warfusée a battery
> of 5.9-inch howitzers was seen to be firing point blank on the
> 7th Brigade, which was advancing on the right. The enemy
> gunners had not observed the party, which, led by Harnett,
> dashed forward on the flank and captured the four guns,
> together with one officer and 45 gunners.[9]

The 17th Battalion's A Company was supporting B Company and got
round the southern side of the village, thus enveloping it. Five tanks
then moved in, crushing the houses that lay in front of them. The
infantry then entered the village throwing grenades into dug-outs
and cellars, which persuaded the elements of the German 152nd
Regiment (41st Division) which were holding it to surrender. Lt Col
E. D. Bryce DSO, commanding the 2nd Tank Battalion, personally
took one of these surrenders. He had followed the advance on foot,
with his reconnaissance officer, RSM, and three orderlies. When
they reached the outskirts of the village the shell fire became quite
heavy and wounded his reconnaissance officer in both legs:

> While his wounds were being attended to by my Medical
> Orderly 6 German officers came out of a dug-out and sur-
> rendered – among them a Battalion Second-in-command. I
> asked him whether they had been expecting an attack, and he
> replied that they had been told from behind that British Tanks
> were in front ready to attack, but had heard nothing more
> definite than that. I then made him get some other prisoners
> and carry Captain DILLON back.[10]

What had actually happened was that the headquarters of the two forward battalions of 152nd Regiment had their joint HQ in a house on the western outskirts of the village and the senior commander had organized a number of machine gun posts to cover the approaches from this direction. Some of these were overrun by the 17th Battalion supported by a tank. The two German battalion staffs were also driven out of their house and into dug-outs and it was clearly some of these whom Bryce had captured. Other prisoners also confirmed that the noise of vehicle engines over the past few days gave indications that there might be an attack, but that there had been no further information.

To the south of Warfusée a company of the same German regiment, seeing nothing because of the fog, fired blind into it. They then became aware of tanks approaching from behind them, followed by Australian infantrymen advancing at the double. There was therefore no option but to surrender.

The 7th Australian Brigade attacked south of the Roman road. Initially the German defences appeared to be little more than lines of scattered posts which were easily overcome in the fog. Just short of Card Copse and close to the inter-corps boundary with the Canadians, however, the 28th Battalion came across a belt of wire entanglements. As the men made for a gap in it they came under heavy fire from a strongpoint just beyond and were forced to go to ground since no tanks had arrived to support them. This was part of the main defences of the German 18th Infantry Regiment, the centre regiment of the 41st Division. One of the 28th Battalion's company commanders, Lt Alfred Gaby, then found a further gap in the wire, passed through, got onto the German parapet and, after firing his revolver into the trench, took the surrender of a German company and four machine guns. Lt Shorrock achieved a similar feat a short distance away.* By this time the tanks had come up and resistance ceased, leaving the way open to the Green Line, which the Battalion reached at 6.55 a.m.

---

* Gaby was awarded the VC for this feat, but was sadly killed on 11 August by a German sniper. Shorrock received the DSO.

On the extreme right the 21st Battalion's primary task was to provide a flank guard and to liaise with the Canadians. Two companies were allocated to this task and followed the line of the railway, quickly meeting up with a liaison platoon provided by the 19th Canadian Battalion. The Battalion was able to give help to the Canadians in the capture of Marcelcave, (about which more later). By 6 a.m. the fog was beginning to thin and tanks were able to spot targets visually rather than just rely on driving towards the noise of machine gun fire.* This enabled the advance to speed up, passing north of Marcelcave, which was still resisting the Canadians, and by 8 a.m. the 2nd Australian Division was firm on the Green Line.

The Canadian Corps made its initial attack with three out of its four divisions – 2nd in the north, 1st in the centre, and 3rd in the south. The Canadians suffered a number of disadvantages when compared to the Australians. First, they did not know the ground so well, having had little opportunity to study it visually. They also had further to advance to the Green Line, in some cases almost twice as far. In addition they had the problem of the River Luce, which cut across the southern half of their sector. Furthermore, because the French attack was taking place later they would have to initially secure their southern flank. The 4th Tank Brigade supported the attack. The 1st and 2nd Canadian Divisions each attacked initially with just one brigade, the others successively leapfrogging through until the Blue Line had been reached. Because of the River Luce the 3rd Canadian Division attacked with one brigade north and the other south of the river.

In the north the 4th Canadian Infantry Brigade attacked with two battalions up. Significantly at 4.10 a.m., just ten minutes before Zero Hour, the Brigade Major sent a written message to all four battalions:

---

* Each tank had an Australian infantryman, who knew the ground, on board and they helped to identify targets, as well as liaising with the following infantry. In some cases they also helped the tanks to find their way through the fog.

In the event of the operations on the 8th of August being carried out according to plan the Canadian Corps will be continuing the advance in conjunction with the troops on either flank on 9th August.[II]

This indicated that Currie had had a late change of heart over his previous belief that the attack was merely a limited one to regain the Amiens outer defence line. Be that as it may, the 19th Canadian Battalion on the extreme left was subjected to a bombardment in its forward assembly area from 3.20 a.m. until just before Zero Hour. This caused casualties, but the battalion, together with the 21st Battalion on its right, set off on time. The tanks, from the 14th Tank Battalion, did not materialize, having been held up by the fog. One platoon from the 19th was deployed just north of the railway line to maintain contact with the Australians, which was to prove very beneficial. Initially, with the Germans totally taken by surprise, the opposition was slight, but at about 5.30 a.m. the 19th Battalion came up against a well wired strongpoint called Jaffa Trench. This had been known about and it had been planned that the tanks would devote particular attention to this. They were not present and so Captain R. H. Bliss, who was commanding the attacking companies, organized an attack. Assisted by the Lewis gunners of the 21st Australian Battalion, Bliss's men overran the strongpoint and continued towards their main objective, the village of Marcelcave. This had been the subject of special orders by the 19th Battalion. The village was to be bombarded for just over two hours by 6-inch howitzers and as soon as the fire lifted the assault was to go in, with one section of tanks crossing the railway so as to attack from the north. Bliss arrived on time, but again no tanks were present. Even so, and further assisted by the 21st Australian Battalion and men of the neighbouring 21st Canadian Battalion, as well as a tank from C Company 2nd Tank Battalion, the attack went ahead. The tank, followed by the Australians, entered the village from the north and the Canadians from the west. The HQ of the German 148th Infantry Regiment was captured, including its commander, as well as numerous other Germans. A number of artillery batteries were also seized.* The capture of Marcelcave was a good example of the excellent co-operation that existed between the Australians and the Canadians and was also the last resistance met before the Green Line, which ran just to the east. Indeed, by 7 a.m. the 4th Canadian Infantry Brigade was firm on it.

The 3rd Infantry Brigade opened the 1st Canadian Division's attack. It was supported by twenty-two tanks of the 4th Tank Battalion. Unlike those supporting the 4th Canadian Brigade these arrived on time, apart from one which had ditched during the approach march but did catch the others up after the attack had started. Plans to give the crews a two hours' rest in the forward assembly area came to naught, however, because travelling in low gear increased the fume problems inside the tanks and many crewmen suffered, which slowed progress. The Brigade attacked with three battalions and two others in support, one borrowed from the 2nd Canadian Infantry Brigade. On the left the 14th Battalion (Royal Montreal Regiment) moved quickly through the German outpost line and did not meet any significant opposition until reaching Morgemont Wood, 2,000 yards from the start line. They came under fire from eight machine guns. Passing round the flanks of these they left them to be dealt with by follow-up troops. When they came up against the main line of resistance the 14th Battalion came under heavy fire. Bringing down their own fire from the flank caused white flags to be raised and so the Canadians got up and moved forward. This, however, was met by renewed firing. Further heavy fighting followed and then 'the enemy raised two White Flags but in view of the results of the former ruse, no notice was taken of these flags by our men, and the enemy garrison was exterminated.'[12] Thereafter resistance was slight and the Green Line quickly reached.

In the centre the 13th Battalion (Royal Highlanders of Canada) met their first serious resistance in Hangard Wood West as soon as they

---

* Bliss received the DSO for his day's work and the tank commander, Lt C. R. Percy-Eade, who had insisted on obtaining a receipt for his capture of the village from the Australians, the MC.

crossed the start line. There was much wire here and German snipers were very active. The leading companies used the same tactic as the 14th Battalion, bypassing it on both flanks and leaving the supporting companies, aided by two tanks, to do the mopping up. Further resistance was met on the other side of Hangard Wood and was overcome with the help of two Stokes mortars. Their final significant fight came in Pelican Ravine where the German gun lines were situated. The gunners fought hard to prevent the capture of their pieces, but in vain. Finally, on the right the 16th Battalion (Canadian Scottish) initially met little resistance as it advanced along the north bank of the Luce with its pipers playing. Indeed, in the words of Lt Col C. W. Peck CMG DSO, the commanding officer, 'I found the pipes of the greatest usefulness, not only to encourage and inspire the men, but the keen ear of one piper could detect the tones of the others through the dense fog and enabled us to identify companies in the advance.'[13] It was not until they arrived north of the village of Demuin that they came under heavy fire. At one point the commanding officer and his HQ group came under the direct fire of a machine gun as they came round the corner of a high bank. His piper was killed, but the Battalion Scout Officer, Lt Alexander MacLennan MC, then crept forward along a sunken road and killed all five of the crew with his revolver, earning a bar to his MC. A similar incident occurred when they reached Aubercourt, where a single machine gun held up the advance until one of the runners, Pte Sumner, managed to get round behind the gun and despatch the crew. Like the other two battalions, the Canadian Scottish reached the Green Line on time. By then 12 out of the 22 supporting tanks were still running. Among the weapons captured were 18 guns ranging from 203mm to 77mm, 15 heavy trench mortars, 2 grenade launchers, and 30 machine guns. More than 900 prisoners fell into their hands, including a complete regimental headquarters, and at a cost of 144 Canadian Scottish killed and wounded.

The 3rd Canadian Division had a more complicated task in that it had to attack both north and south of the Luce. There was also the problem of the southern flank in the fact that the French attack

THE DAY WE WON THE WAR

would begin later. North of the Luce the 8th Brigade had the relatively simple task of quickly seizing the village of Hangard and the ground north of Demuin, as well as securing the bridge over the Luce to the latter. They would then halt so as not to cramp the advance of the 1st Canadian Division to their north. It was known that the Germans had prepared the Demuin bridge for demolition and two tanks from C Company 5th Tank Battalion, each carrying a crib and manned by picked crews, were to take the most direct route to the bridge and only engage the enemy if their way was barred. One of the tanks would also carry a Canadian engineer officer to remove the charges from the bridge. The crib-carrying tanks would be followed by the other fourteen tanks in the company. If the bridge proved impassable six tanks, which were to halt well short of the bridge until the situation was clear, were to make best speed for the Domart bridge and then try to catch up the infantry. When the two crib tanks arrived at the bridge they found that it was blown, but one dropped its crib in the gap and this enabled all the tanks to get across the river.* Eight tanks reached the Green Line and by 6.20 a.m. all the 8th Canadian Brigade's objectives had been achieved.

The 9th Brigade was to attack south of the River Luce. Its initial frontage was comparatively narrow – just 1,500 yards, although this would increase to 2,500 yards on the Green Line, which lay 2,000 yards from the start line. Three battalions would assault to the Green Line – 58th on the left, 116th in the centre, and the 43rd on the right. The 52nd Battalion would be in support and twenty-eight tanks from the 5th Tank Battalion would also take part. While its B Company would cross at Thennes in the French sector, A Company had to use the bridge at Domart, which was only 1,000 yards from the German front line. Swampy ground also extended 500 yards from the river's banks. The upshot was that its tanks would not begin to move until

---

* This is taken from the 5th Tank Battalion's report on the operation in its war diary (TNA WO 95/111). The 8th Canadian Brigade war diary entry for 8 August states, however, that the bridge was initially found to be intact and that four tanks crossed before it collapsed. It does not mention what happened to the other tanks.

twelve minutes before Zero and would have to proceed in single file. The last tank actually crossed the river three minutes before Zero Hour and was only some 150 yards clear of the bridge when the German counter-barrage came down and it received a direct hit from a shell. Since the fire was heavy the company commander decided to deploy his tanks at once for fear that another would be immobilized and block the passage of the rest. Three tanks, however, immediately became bogged in the swampy ground. Nevertheless, the remainder pressed on.

As for the Canadian infantry, the 58th Battalion initially attacked with one company, which, after some difficulty with the marshy ground close to the River Luce, as well as wire entanglements and some heavy machine-gun fire, overcame the German outpost line and pushed out patrols towards Demuin. C Company then passed through and, supported by tanks, attacked the village, securing it by 6.20 a.m. B Company, which had made the initial attack, now joined C, with both occupying a line east of the village. It was now D Company's turn. Its objective was the hamlet of Courcelles. Attacking frontally and from the north and east, it overwhelmed the defenders, and secured the high ground beyond, on which ran the Green Line. Finally, A Company moved up and joined D and the Green Line. The Battalion had captured some 400 prisoners.

The main obstacle barring the way of the 116th and 43rd Battalions was Dodo Wood, otherwise known as Rifle Wood, which Rawlinson considered the key initial Canadian objective.[14] To the north-west of this, and on the road running south from Hangard, there was a strong German defensive position known as the Bade trench system, which lay in the right half of the Battalion's sector. The 116th's first task was to eliminate this and then advance to Hammon Wood, which actually lay beyond the Green Line. Apart from the wood itself, its particular target was German batteries believed to be just north of the wood. A Company was given the task of dealing with the Bade trench system. C Company would then pass through and get round to the northern edge of Hammon Wood. D Company would follow C and move behind the wood, while B Company did the actual mopping up within the wood. As the Battalion History expressed it:

> From a study of the map and intelligence provided it seemed that even with little opposition the turning movement to be made would be extremely difficult, and that the leaders of all units would be called upon to exercise their best judgement and skill in order to ensure success, especially in view of the fact that very little opportunity was to be given them for making a personal reconnaissance.[15]

A Company began to move at 4.28 a.m. and in just over half an hour the complete battalion was advancing. The tanks, however, with no opportunity for reconnaissance and in the fog, experienced early difficulties in finding their way and tended to operate on the flanks, apart from two which went through the Battalion assembly area and nearly ran down a number of men as they crossed the start line. The German counter-barrage, which came down five minutes after Zero Hour, also caused some casualties in the assembly area. A Company met fierce resistance from the Bade system and all its officers quickly became casualties. CSM Fenwick, although wounded, rallied the company and the opposition was overcome, a feat which later earned him the Military Cross. The Company, now reinforced by details from Battalion HQ, got into position to give covering fire to C and D Companies moving round to the north of Hammon Wood. They encountered a number of machine-gun posts, which were quickly overrun. They decided to use Demuin village as their launch pad for the attack on the wood, liaising closely with the 58th Battalion. Germans, however, were firing on A Company from high ground on the right, preventing it from giving the necessary fire support to the other companies. C and D returned the fire and forced the Germans to surrender. This enabled B Company to advance. The guns to the north of Hammon Wood were overrun, their crews firing over open sights in a desperate effort to prevent capture. The wood was cleared and the 116th Battalion was firm on its final objective by 7.30 a.m.

This left the 43rd Battalion on the extreme right. The key initial objective was Dodo or Rifle Wood, which lay 800 yards and uphill from the start line. B Company was to make a frontal assault on this, while A Company swung round the left flank so as to attack it from the north. The other two companies would then successively secure Hollon Wood and Vignette Wood, which was known to house a German battery. The 43rd had one further task. The French were concerned about a ravine which ran along a re-entrant just to the south of Dodo Wood. It had therefore been decided to form a small inter-Allied unit, with one platoon from the 43rd and one from the French 94th Infantry Regiment. The whole was under a French officer acting under the orders of the 43rd Battalion and its task was to advance along the inter-army boundary with the French, which ran just south of Dodo Wood and then passed through Hollon Wood. This was a highly successful innovation. In the words of the Battalion report on the operation: 'The whole of their attack was a splendid exhibition of GAELIC [sic] dash and HIGHLAND fury in assault. The kilts and the horizon blue swept all before them.'[16]

As for the main attack, the German counter-barrage fell on the forward assembly area as the companies were moving out, as it did with the 116th Battalion, and there were casualties. One of the shells also hit the RE dump containing smoke projectiles to be used to cover the ravine south of Dodo Wood and this served to increase the obscuration. Furthermore, of the eight tanks allotted to help in the capture of Dodo Wood, only two got into action. Four others were to operate on the Roye road. B Company had a hard fight to clear Dodo Wood and it took two hours to rid it of the numerous machine-gun nests. Indeed, some 40 machine guns were captured, together with 20 trench mortars. The other companies had problems in keeping direction in the fog and became very intermingled as they pushed up the hill to outflank Dodo Wood:

Touch could not be maintained and men in small groups were pushing forward with all sense of direction lost in many cases, but the determination to press on was there, and officers and NCOs were ready to assume control and lead the men forward.

In this way the Companies, mixed up it is true, but controlled fighting units none the less, arrived at the top of the hill, and as they reached the high ground, found the mist thinning and visibility improving rapidly.[17]

This also had a disadvantage. A German 5.9-inch battery and another of 77mm guns positioned south of Vignette Wood engaged the tanks supporting the Canadian Highlanders on top of the hill and knocked out three of them. Even so the 43rd achieved all its objectives on schedule at a cost of 21 killed and 173 wounded.

The French First Army's main problem was the rivers Avre and Luce. This was especially so for the XXXI Corps, which would attack next door to the Canadians. In particular, the 42nd Division on the left first needed to cross the Luce and then attack south-east, with the 37th Division on its right. The overall objectives were the heights of Moreuil Wood (scene of an epic action by the Canadian Cavalry Brigade in March 1918), then Mézières and Génouville Wood, and subsequently to continue the advance towards Hangest-en-Santerre. Moreuil itself would be encircled. Meanwhile IX Corps to the south would attack Saint-Ribert and Braches before pushing on towards Hangest. During the night 7/8 August the 42nd Division deployed over the Luce using a number of crossing places, as did the field artillery. The Division would attack with the 94th Infantry Regiment on the left and the 8th Battalion Chasseurs on the right. Behind them were the 332nd Regiment and the 16th Battalion Chasseurs respectively. Two hundred guns were in support:

At 4.20 one officer per battery raised his arm. At the command – a simple 'Go!' and then along the Boves – Domart road up to the Avre an immense flash of lightning, made up of 200 flashes, at the same second, illuminated the horizon. 200 thunderclaps, bursting at once, made the ground tremble, 200 formidable explosions gave the retort … After that there was a dis-continuous rumble. The ground shook as in an earthquake; the vibrating atmosphere, howling and whistling with the passage of all this steel.[18]

While the field artillery concentrated on the forward German trench system, the heavy pieces engaged known battery positions and suspected locations of reserves.

At 4.20 a.m. the 94th Regiment and the 8th Chasseurs began their advance. This was behind a rolling barrage, which lifted 100 metres every three minutes to beyond Magdeburg Trench. Here, in order to reduce the effects of the German counter-bombardment, they would pause to allow the 37th Division to come up on the right and then all would go on together. Each half section had a light machine gunner at its head and the officers led the way, using a compass bearing to keep direction. In just over 15 minutes the leading elements had covered the 600 metres to Magdeburg Trench. Other German defences, little more than foxholes, were empty apart from a few bodies, although one of the companies of the 94th Regiment did find a German officer and 15 men behind them. All were shocked and surrendered immediately. While the barrage continued, with the field artillery firing two rounds per minute, the infantry waited in the German trenches for the French Zero Hour proper.

Suddenly, a powerful throbbing . . . it is a British tank! Our allies had come before the appointed hour. At all events, liaison is already assured. But no! The passage of this machine in the midst of the companies of the 94th caused an extraordinary stir. This blind machine was lost in the fog; suddenly it passed over a sleeping soldier and now it wandered about. Eventually its hatch opened and a young man, with long blond hair, got out and came up to the colonel and asked him where he was. He had little understanding of French. With a gesture, the colonel pointed him towards the Andrea ravine where, in a better situation, it could render service in strengthening liaison and securing the flank. But one could not shoot at nothing; he knew nothing, had nothing more to explain. He left the colonel disquieted about the support of the tanks, so well organised yesterday.[19]

This was one of Captain Wilfrid Bion's four tanks from B Company the 5th Tank Battalion. Their task was to help the 94th Regiment capture the village of Villers-aux-Erables. In fact, it was the only tank to play any significant part in the attack, since one received a direct hit when moving from the deployment area and the other two were misdirected by a French liaison officer.

The French attack proper got underway at precisely 5.23 a.m. The first phase was to clear Moreuil Wood. The German 18th Reserve Regiment had two companies covering the northern edge of the wood and another company in Dodo Wood. These had been virtually obliterated by the bombardment. Behind them the 4th Bavarian Regiment had two companies inside Moreuil Wood and another holding Villers-aux-Erables. Apart from being discomforted by some machine-gun fire from Dodo Wood, which the Canadians were still trying to clear, the advance proceeded rapidly against the now dazed defenders. At one point a company from the 94th fighting to clear Longuet Wood, between Moreuil and Dodo Woods, came across a German captain. He asked whether the French were in strength and was told that there were two divisions behind the attackers. 'Now we are f——d!' was the reply.[20] It took little over an hour for the 42nd and 37th Divisions to reach the first objective, which lay astride the Demuin–Moreuil Road. There was then a pause for an hour while the French artillery prepared the ground for the next phase. The situation in Dodo Wood was still obscure, however. General Deville, commanding the 42nd Division, was at one point in favour of delaying the next phase until it could be confirmed that the wood was clear, but the commander of the 94th Regiment assured him that he was holding several German prisoners from the wood and that there was no problem. Later, Captain Cyril Falls, the British liaison officer with the 42nd Division, went across to HQ 3rd Canadian Division in Domart to obtain news of the Canadian advance. They could tell him little, apart from the fact that their advance was going well.[21]

Back in London news of the attack was given to Sir Henry Wilson that morning. It had been agreed on 6 August that Foch's British liaison officer, Brigadier General Charles Grant, should travel to London on the 7th to inform the authorities, but not before the assault had actually begun. Grant briefed Wilson just before he went off to attend a meeting of the War Cabinet. Present at it were both the Australian and Canadian prime ministers. According to General Grant the former expressed concern over the Australians being involved in view of their recent heavy casualties. Wilson apparently replied that at that very moment they were racing the Canadians to be the first to reach the Somme. When asked about the scope of the operation Wilson responded with the flippant comment that it was 'to enable the officers of the Royal Naval Air Service to take their little "tartines" to tea at Amiens.' He was then accused of knowing about the attack beforehand on the basis that he had mentioned freeing up the Amiens railway as an option for the BEF, together with liberating the Bruay mines and recapturing Kemmel, in an earlier paper to the War Cabinet. Wilson assured those present that he had not known which of these courses Foch had decided to put into effect. His case was supported by Du Cane, who wrote Wilson a letter on the afternoon of the 8th stating: 'At the earnest request of Marshal Foch and the CinC I refrained from giving you particulars of the offensive which began this morning up to the last moment.'[22]

CHAPTER FIVE

TO THE BLUE LINE AND BEYOND

During the first phase of the attack the forces earmarked for the advance beyond the Green Line had followed up closely. By now the fog had begun to clear. Gunner James Armitage, with the 8th Australian Field Artillery Brigade:

> On either side of us as far as we could see was a great wall of field guns – what the papers were to describe later as 'a wall of guns, wheel to wheel, along the entire front'. Actually the guns were at 20 yard intervals but that was close enough. All guns were still in action and the sight of all this massed artillery right out in the open, without a spot of cover, was a sight to see.[1]

In the case of the 3rd Canadian Division, its reserve formation, the 7th Brigade was tasked with securing the Red Line within the divisional sector. It had crossed the River Luce on specially prepared bridges, beginning at Zero Hour. It reached the Green Line and passed through the 8th and 9th Brigades. It was clear that the Germans were still reeling from the initial assault. On the left the 49th Battalion had the most difficult approach march, but still attacked on time and the only significant opposition it met was from a machine gun in Cerfs Wood, which was quickly overcome and they reached the Red Line at 10 a.m. In the centre the 42nd Battalion overran two German batteries before reaching its objective at 10 a.m. and then pushing patrols forward of the Red Line. On the extreme right the Royal Canadian Regiment also formed an international company of one Canadian and one French platoon. Lt J. W. Miller's platoon also helped the

French to secure Mézières by moving into the east end of the village and holding on until the French arrived. Their main attack, supported by tanks, quickly took them through Valley and Wheelbarrow Woods. Lt W. G. Wurtele was commanding C Company:

We had a few casualties, mainly from snipers in the trees, which we disposed of as quickly as we could locate them. Here I have a confession to make. About one third of the way to our objective we came across a section of a German 4.2 Artillery Battery with two guns still hot, situated on the high ground overlooking the ground we still had to take including a walled 'maison blanc' farm which looked like an ideal German stronghold. In spite of the Hague Convention I intimidated a young German who spoke English to reveal that it was manned by German machine guns, in spite of his efforts to reveal only his rank, name and serial number. We still had one of the fifteen tanks that were to support us . . . and we got this one to put 40 or 50 of his two [sic – six] pound shells into the 'maison blanc' and some 40 Germans immediately went beetling down the road, abandoning their position. This wiped out any remorse I may have had, as these Germans, with the 10 or 12 machine guns they left behind, could have wiped out a lot of our men and held up the advance. [2]

They were firm on the Red Line by 9.45 a.m.

The story was much the same with the 1st Canadian Division. Almost as soon as its 3rd Brigade had reached the Green Line the 1st Brigade passed through. However, the 2nd Battalion (Toronto Regiment) on the left did experience a problem while moving up to the Green Line. It was advancing by platoons in single file when it ran into heavy machine-gun fire just to the east of Morgemont Wood. It was a pocket of resistance which had been bypassed by the 14th Canadian Battalion and cost the Toronto Regiment some thirty casualties before the Germans were forced to withdraw at the double. Nevertheless the Battalion crossed the Green Line at 8.20 a.m. It then came up against determined opposition from the high ground between Lemaire Wood and Stove Wood. Reinforcements and tanks were called for, while the Lewis guns and snipers sought to suppress the fire. After 35 minutes reinforcements arrived and the advance resumed, with covering fire being given by twelve Lewis guns from the edge of Lemaire Wood. Two tanks were then spotted and these helped to force the Germans to withdraw. After encountering one or two more machine gun nests the Battalion reached the Red Line at 11.30 a.m.

The 4th Canadian Battalion had less trouble in the centre. Its main objective was the village of Cayeux-en-Santerre which necessitated crossing the River Luce. This was carried out by the right hand company, which advanced up the river valley in the face of machine-gun fire and then used a high bank just south of the Luce from which to rush the village. The Red Line at this point ran through the centre of Cayeux and so the company took up position here. The left hand assault company kept north of the river and after dealing with machine-gun fire from Lemaire Wood and Ruisseau Wood, the latter with the help of a tank, it also reached the Red Line. The right hand battalion, the Eastern Ontario Regiment, which advanced along the south bank of the Luce, quickly captured Ignacourt and then encountered a number of machine-gun nests which it dealt with using its own resources since the tanks had not caught up. The Battalion then advanced into the valley south of Cayeux, but suffered casualties from German artillery fire. It pressed on and secured the high ground east of the village by 11 a.m.

The 2nd Canadian Division passed the 5th Brigade through the 4th Brigade on the Green Line. It advanced with two battalions leading, each on a two-company front, at 8.20 a.m. Initially the infantry led, but after a quarter of an hour the tanks passed through. Artillery support was reliant on the heavies which laid down a creeping barrage some 600 yards ahead. The main resistance came from Pierret Wood, 900 yards from the start line, and Snipe Copse to its south. The 24th and 26th Battalions had a hard fight for these, but they yielded a good number of prisoners and a number of guns, including a 150mm battery. Thereafter the advance quickened. Wiencourt-l'Equipée was secured at 9.20 a.m. and Guillaucourt, 1,700 yards further east half an hour later. About 100 prisoners were taken in each. Indeed, it was noticeable that the Germans did not make much effort to defend the villages, preferring copses, sunken roads, and clumps of bushes. The tanks were of especial help in overcoming these and enabling the Brigade to reach the Red Line in good time.

In the Australian Corps sector the second phase of the attack began at 8.28 a.m., when the 4th and 5th Australian Divisions passed through the 3rd and 2nd Divisions respectively. In the south the 5th Australian division advanced with its 15th Brigade right and the 8th Brigade on the left, the 14th Brigade being in support. Each of the two leading brigades had an 'exploiting detachment' consisting of Vickers and Lewis guns and their crews carried on board Mark V Star tanks. Nine of these tanks, with a total of 16 Vickers and 16 Lewis guns, were allocated to each brigade, the idea being that they would advance straight to the Blue Line and hold it with the tanks until the infantry came up. The two brigades also had a company of Mark V tanks each drawn from the 2nd and 10th Tank Battalions to lead the attack, while the two 2nd Tank Battalion companies which had taken part in the advance to the Green Line would also be used, primarily to help capture Bayonvillers. A field artillery brigade, light trench mortar battery, engineer detachments, cyclists from the Australian Corps cyclist battalion, a machine-gun company, and sections from the corps cavalry regiment, the 13th Australian Light Horse were also under the command of each brigade. And, as they were very much 'all arms' formations, they were designated 'brigade groups'. In addition, the Division had the 1st Cavalry Brigade, twelve cars from the 17th Armoured Car Battalion, and two companies of Whippets attached.

The outline plan was for the 8th and 15th Brigades to leave their start line, which lay some 1,000 yards behind the original front line, at Zero plus one hour so as to reach the Green Line at Zero plus four hours, i.e. 8.20 a.m. Once they reached the Red Line the exploiting detachments, which up until then would travel 600 yards behind the leading brigades, would pass through and make for the Blue Line.

They would be followed up by the leading brigades, with the 14th Brigade remaining in reserve throughout. The cavalry would pass through the infantry 'as soon as circumstances permitted' in order to exploit the success achieved and the armoured cars would be let loose once the Roman road was open.

The 15th Australian Infantry Brigade crossed its start line on time and used compass bearings to maintain direction in the fog. They crossed the Green Line on schedule, with Mark V tanks taking the lead. Very soon they came across abandoned German 77mm guns. However, the 57th Battalion also encountered a 5.9-inch battery, which engaged over open sights. As the company involved prepared to attack a tank drove directly at the guns, but was knocked out 40 yards from them. Another tank got round to the flank and the gun crews then surrendered. According to Jimmy Downing, who took part in this attack with the 57th:

Thereafter it was fairly plain sailing. Whenever we found ourselves in trouble, we signalled to the tanks,* and they turned towards the obstacle. Then *punk-crash, punk-crash!* As their little toy guns spoke and their little, pointed shells flew, another German post was blown to pieces. *Punk-crash!* A brick wall tottered and crumbled amid a cloud of red dust. We passed the place. The machine-gun and its crew were crushed and dead.[3]

The experiences of the 59th Battalion on the left were much the same. They had been ordered to skirt round to the south of Bayonvillers, the one village between the Green and Red Lines within the Division's

---

* A system of signals between the tanks and infantry had been worked out prior to the attack. The tank would fly a Green and White flag to indicate a strongpoint overrun so that the infantry could move up to it and a Red and Yellow flag if it had been knocked out or was broken down. The infantryman would place a steel helmet on his bayonet (they went into the attack with bayonets fixed) if he wanted the tank to come to him so that he could point out a target to it. Obviously during the first phase, when the fog was still thick, this system did not work and the tanks were guided merely by the noise of German firing.

sector in order to maintain the momentum of the advance. As it was, both battalions reached the Red Line at 9 a.m.

Enemy guns of all calibres were passed during the advance but the fighting was too brisk and the advance too rapid to allow the affixing of labels or the marking of captures accurately.[4]

The only significant problem came just before the Red Line was reached when some of the supporting guns began to fire short. This was reported, but two guns continued to fire short which did cause some disruption.

Of the two supporting battalions in the 15th Brigade, the 58th Battalion on the left was tasked with reducing Bayonvillers. They were given six tanks to help them and these moved into the village covered by machine guns placed on the high ground to the north and south. In fact, the bombardment had created such damage that there was little resistance and the village was secured by 11 a.m. with two 9.2-inch howitzers captured, although three of the tanks were knocked out in the process. By this time the cavalry, Whippets and armoured cars had passed through. Meanwhile, on the right flank the 59th Battalion and two platoons of the 60th Battalion had assisted the Canadian advance by engaging Germans withdrawing from Pleuret Wood and Wiencourt.

The 8th Australian Brigade passed through the Green Line at 6.20 a.m. with the 30th Battalion on the left and 31st on the right. The 32nd Battalion was in support 450 yards behind and the 29th Battalion in reserve and a further 450 yards to the rear. Progress was initially rapid, but then, on the right, German field batteries engaged the tanks from concealed positions and knocked out five before being outflanked and captured by the 31st Battalion. Machine nests were encountered, but the supporting artillery proved very effective in helping to deal with these. According to LCpl Len Clarkson of the 32nd Battalion snipers were also a problem:

We were advancing in artillery formation when crack! crack!

rang out from the copse ahead of us, and bullets started to whistle past our ears. We had certainly found him, and undoubtedly he found us. We lay down for a while for it was getting a bit too hot with bullets whispering around us in the grass . . . Then came the order to advance, and we hopped up again. The snipers got to work again and two or three bullets whistled within an inch of my head, and I thought to myself 'it won't be long now', but we kept on wondering whether the next one would hit us or not.[5]

Just short of the Red Line there was further resistance in the Morcourt Valley. At the southern end of this a gap appeared between the two leading battalions and a company of the 32nd Battalion had to be deployed. The Germans here were quickly overcome in a 'short sharp action' with the help of the tanks which resulted in the capture of 200 prisoners and a good deal of weaponry. It turned out to be a rest camp and P. F. Lewis of the 32nd Battalion recorded:

. . . all the prisoners seemed quite happy in their situation, their only worry being to exchange their heavy helmets for the light round cloth cap they wore out of the line. This they were allowed to do. I felt rather sorry for one chap who had his leave pass for home in his pocket.[6]

By 10.30 a.m. this brigade was also firm on the Red Line.

Meanwhile the 1st Cavalry Brigade had been on the move. It had an advanced guard consisting of the Queen's Bays, a section of guns from I Battery RHA, a mounted machine gun section, and an RE troop. By 8.30 a.m. the brigade was in touch with the infantry around Bayonvillers and was ordered to 'push through infantry whenever opportunity offered'. By 9.15 a.m. the Bays' right hand squadron was in action south of Harbonnières

With regard to the 4th Australian Division its two leading brigades, the 4th and 12th, were organized in similar fashion to those of the 5th Australian Division, except that the latter and the other brigade

(13th) in the Division had three battalions only. Each brigade was supported by twelve Mark V and nine Mark V Star tanks. The former were supplied by the 8th and the 13th Tank Battalions and the latter by the 15th Tank Battalion. The 12th Brigade on the right crossed the Green Line on schedule and initially met some resistance from Lena Wood, but this was quickly dealt with and four guns captured. Thereafter the lead companies bypassed woods, leaving the supports to mop them up. Machine-gun nests were either dealt with by the tanks or outflanked and rushed.

The 4th Brigade had a more complicated task in that the ground it had to cover was broken by re-entrants enclosing streams running into the Somme, as well as the marshes along the south bank of the river. It also had to deal with the fact that the 58th Division had failed to reach the dominant Chipilly Spur on the north bank. It was also short of four Mark V tanks, which had broken down en route. On the left, and advancing with its left flank on the Somme, the 15th Battalion's principal objective was the village of Cerisy. The tactic adopted by the tanks of the 13th Tank Battalion to cope with the undulating ground was to leave the infantry on a crest and then advance into the next valley, suppressing any fire that they met and then halting on the next crest to allow the infantry to move up.[7] This enabled the 15th Battalion to quickly capture Cerisy. The only significant opposition came from a machine gun in one of the houses on the outskirts, which caused some casualties before a tank fired into the building and brought down its walls. The main problem came from across the river, where German infantry could be seen making for the Chipilly Spur. An Australian 18-pounder battery, which was following up, immediately came into action and engaged them. However, hidden 77mm guns on the Spur now opened fire and began to knock out tanks. It was the 8th Tank Battalion which suffered mainly, losing a total of thirteen tanks to shell fire and a further one to a mine during the day. Using their own Lewis guns and recently captured German machine guns, the 15th Battalion managed to suppress this fire by forcing the gun crews to take cover.

The 14th Battalion, which was in the centre, had been cheered on its way to the Green Line by

> ... the trotting through the advancing infantry of a battery of field artillery, which went into action alongside of them. Such incidents had been seen in army manoeuvres in Egypt, but it was an absolute novelty as far as practical warfare in France was concerned.[8]

Apart from being discomforted by a supporting howitzer, which was firing short and killed some of the Battalion's stretcher bearers and wounded its doctor, it had suffered little loss by the time it passed through the Green Line. It was now faced by a valley, on the other side of which ran the Cerisy Ridge. There was heavy machine-gun fire from the moment that the Battalion began to descend into the valley, its supporting tanks in the lead. The advance quickly assumed the form of short rushes from one shell hole to another. Casualties began to mount, but when the tanks reached the ridge the fire began to slacken and finally ceased. By 8.50 a.m. its part of the ridge was secured. A Company on the left could see swarms of Germans fleeing on the low ground close to the Somme and was overlooking the village of Morcourt. They decided to take advantage of the German confusion and seize it. While part of the company carried out a flanking move the remainder, with one of the six Mark V tanks supporting the Battalion leading the way, moved towards the village. It had been the headquarters of the German 202nd Regiment and its commander, Major von Rathenow, managed to escape by car. Two of his officers, one with the regimental canteen funds, were not so lucky when they tried to do the same on horseback. Both were shot. The company had to pause, however, because the heavies were still firing on the western corner of the village. It therefore contented itself with getting Germans out of their dug-outs and what the Australians called 'souveniring'. Indeed, the loot they unearthed both in quantity and value 'exceeded anything of which the 14th had had experience'.[9] Once the supporting artillery fire had lifted from Morcourt, the

Battalion entered it and then pushed two companies on to the next ridge, which represented the Red Line. Once they were on this they, too, were discomforted by the German artillery fire from the Chipilly Spur and were forced to temporarily withdraw to a nearby sunken road. The arrival of the 16th Battalion, which was passing through to tackle the Blue Line, drew this fire away from the 14th, enabling them to continue digging in on the Red Line.

In terms of 'souveniring' it was the 13th Battalion, the right hand assault unit of the 4th Brigade, which enjoyed the most fruits. It advanced south of Morcourt and was also subjected to fire from the Chipilly Spur, but was secure on the Red Line at 10 a.m. Morcourt Valley, however, proved to be a veritable treasure trove. To quote the Australian Official History:

> ... when the British 'heavies' lifted their fire from the wooded Morcourt valley, the 13th found among canteens, stores, transport lines, and shelters, teeming with unresisting Germans, more souvenirs than it had time to collect. Among three tiers of huts were an officers' mess (with fresh grapes and eggs), two canteens with good pre-war cigars, a store of photographs and boxes of maps, and a pay office where one man blew open a case with 25,000 marks in notes. Wagons piled with stores, apparently just arrived, one vehicle containing six machine-guns, were near the track on which the 13th hurriedly reformed, and 60 horses were picketed there.[10]

The 16th Battalion now passed through the Red Line, but did suffer from fire across the river. Furthermore:

> In this final movement the 16th had to swing around on the left from an imaginary line stretching from the south bank of the Somme to the south side of Morgan Wood and then advance 2,500 yards on a front of 2,500 yards. This move was to conform with the course of the River Somme, which at this point formed the letter U. It was up the right hand side of this letter U that

the battalion had to advance and finally dig in on a line which linked up with the old Amiens Defence Line.[11]

It succeeded in doing this, but its now depleted strength was not sufficient to hold such a wide frontage. Hence, the 13th Battalion had to stop its looting and move up to take over the right half of the sector.

The 12th Australian Brigade's progress was much more straight-forward. The terrain, although covered with small woods, was less broken than that facing the 4th Brigade. Co-operation with the tanks worked very well, especially when it came to dealing with machine-gun posts. In the case of the woods the tactic employed was for the lead companies to outflank them, while the rear companies mopped up. The Brigade was firm on the Red Line by 10.30 a.m. The 45th Battalion, which was the left hand assault unit, recorded that its casualties were a mere 4 killed and 44 wounded and that it captured 400 prisoners and 'an immense amount of war material'. This included 25 guns, ranging from 8-inch howitzers to 77mm field guns, 8 trench mortars and 18 machine guns.[12]

From 10.20 a.m. the creeping barrage came to an end, although the heavies would continue to engage targets. Soon after this General Currie and his chief of staff, Brigadier General N. W. Webber, arrived at their advanced HQ at Gentelles. Currie instructed Webber to visit HQ 4th Canadian Division to ensure that its troops were moving forward quickly for the next phase. Webber set off on his horse and in his words:

I made straight across country which was deserted entirely but, on rounding the corner of a small wood, suddenly saw a bunch of Germans in column of fours marching towards me. My batman & I whipped behind the trees prepared to make a fight of it & had another look. We saw that the Germans were unarmed & were carrying, in the middle of the column, three Canadian stretcher cases: their sole escort to the cage near Boves![13]

Now it was the turn of the Cavalry to take the lead.

The forces available to exploit the initial success of the attack were the Cavalry Corps, with two Whippet battalions attached, the Canadian Independent Force, and the 17th Armoured Car Battalion of the Tank Corps. The Cavalry Corps was given the mission of seizing and holding the outer line of the Outer Amiens Defences from the Fourth Army's southern boundary on the Amiens–Roye road north to the Villers Bretonneux–Chaulnes railway, which, in effect covered the Canadian Corps sector. The 1st and 3rd Cavalry Divisions would initially be employed, with 2nd Cavalry Division in reserve. The former would operate in the north and the latter in the south. Each would have a Whippet battalion attached. The timing of actual advance would be decided by each divisional commander on the basis of the reports from their patrols. It was to be essentially when the infantry began their advance from the Green Line. Although the Cavalry were to be prepared to patrol as far even as Nesle, the Whippets would not operate more than one kilometre east of the Cavalry Corps' main objective. As for the Canadian Independent Force, this had the task of securing the 3rd Cavalry Division's open southern flank on the Amiens–Roye road, as well as acting as the link between the leading cavalry elements and the infantry. The role of the 17th Armoured Car Battalion was totally separate to that of the Cavalry Corps and Independent Force and will be covered later in the chapter. In addition to the use of the Cavalry, Mark V Star tanks, carrying Vickers and Lewis gun teams would race to the Blue Line and Blue Dotted Line (in the case of the Canadians) and help the horsemen hold it until the infantry arrived.

On the night of 7/8 August the Cavalry Corps had moved from their concentration area and passed through Amiens to a waiting area just east of the fork of the Amiens–St Quentin and Amiens–Roye roads. The spectre of their failure to react in time to the breakthrough at Cambrai had impressed on Sir Charles Kavanagh, their commander, the need for them to deploy as far forward as possible. Hence the heads of their columns were in the Cachy area, just one kilometre behind the Canadian front line. The 1st Cavalry Division was to advance astride the Amiens–Chaulnes railway, which would mean that one of its brigades, the 1st, would actually pass through the 5th Australian Division rather than the Canadians. The 3rd Cavalry Division's main initial problem was crossing the River Luce, but prior reconnaissance had established a crossing point at Ignacourt. At 7 a.m., with the 5th Australian Division having reached the Green Line, the 1st Cavalry Division began to move forward. An hour later the 3rd Cavalry Division also commenced its advance.

As far as the 1st Cavalry Division was concerned its 1st Brigade passed either side of Bayonvillers and caught up with the advancing Australians at about 8.30 a.m. By 9.45 a.m. they had looped round both sides of Harbonnières and the lead regiment, the 5th Dragoon Guards, was ordered to exploit towards Framerville. As they approached Vauvillers A and C Squadrons came under machine-gun fire. B Squadron, which was in the rear, swung north-east and then came across three trains – one broad and two narrow gauge. The latter two steamed off towards Vauvillers, but at that moment the broad gauge train was hit by a 25lb bomb dropped by a marauding Camel from No. 201 squadron.* The squadron, assisted by a patrol from the Queen's Bays (2nd Dragoon Guards), then took all the passengers prisoner. They turned out to be troops who had just returned from leave. It then overran a field hospital and, swinging south to the east of Vauvillers, caught four artillery batteries on the move. These surrendered, but as Capt Mitchell, the squadron commander, was organizing them to be sent back, his men came under machine-gun fire. Since his strength was now reduced to twenty men, Mitchell got five of the captured guns put out of action and then withdrew to the hospital. Here they joined A Squadron, which had, together with C Squadron, dismounted to contain the

---

* This Camel was almost certainly flown by South African Capt T. M. Williams of 65 Sqn. He reported attacking the rearward train of three, dropping two 25lb bombs on it and seeing it break in half. He had joined the RFC in 1917 and had already shot down nine enemy aircraft with 65 Sqn. He was subsequently awarded the MC and DFC, remained in the RAF after the war and rose to be its Inspector General 1948-51.

opposition in Vauvillers. A patrol was sent out towards Framerville, but was fired on by an armoured car bearing a tricolour and one man was hit. This car belonged to the 17th Battalion, which clearly had not expected their own cavalry to be operating in this vicinity. In parallel with this action a squadron of the Bays charged into the valley south of Harbonnières and captured a number of Germans, but was then discomforted by German machine guns which could not be dislodged, even with the help of Whippets. Another Bays squadron moved round to the north of the village and managed to reach the Old Amiens Defence Line.

Behind the 1st Cavalry Brigade nine Mark V Star tanks of the 15th Tank Battalion were supposed to take machine-gunners of the 5th Australian Division forward and lead the advance to the Blue Line. But by 10.20 a.m., when the Division was due to begin its advance to the Blue Line, its Mark V Stars had not arrived on the Red Line. The cavalry and Whippets had already passed through and the divisional commander decided to press on regardless, especially since he still had support from the 2nd Tank Battalion. The right hand battalion, the 57th, also moved quickly to the objective and put out posts up to 400 yards beyond it. Advancing on the left, the 59th Battalion's first task was to clear Harbonnières. At about this time Lt Col Bryce, commanding 2nd Tank Battalion, was continuing to follow up his tanks on foot:

The shelling having decreased, we went towards HAR-BONNIERES and found Lt. ROTTERILL'S Tank stationary in a sunken road about a quarter of a mile from the village. This was about 10.15am, and he was presumably waiting according to the Time Table for our fire to lift from the Village, though for some time previous there had been very little shelling of HARBONNIERES itself. After telling Lt. ROTTERILL to push on to the Village we went forward and again waited a few minutes at a point about 200 yards north of the Village, near the railway line.

At that time there appeared to be no one in HAR-

BONNIERES, though we had seen infantry making for the lower end and they might have been in that part of the village. The troops near us were engaged in locating positions to dig in and apparently it was not intended that they should enter the village.

After a few minutes, seeing two Australians approach, we went across, and I instructed an Orderly, Pte DEASON, to place the flags in the top window of what seemed to be the most prominent house. He entered the house (approximately 10.30am) as the two Australians, who had bombs ready; but that house proved to be empty.

After the Australian flag* and our Battalion flag had been fixed outside the window, we sat down outside to have some food, but were immediately fired on by a machine gun from a house higher up. My Sergeant-Major and Orderlies started to stalk the machine gun post with their revolvers, but before they could do anything two tanks belonging to 'A' Company, 13th Battalion entered the village higher up, and no more firing was heard.[14]

With the village cleared, the 57th Battalion pushed on to the Blue Line and secured it, apart from on the right where a small wood containing numerous machine guns denied them access and there were no longer any tanks available. It also relieved the 5th Dragoon Guards, whose casualties in men had been surprisingly light – seven killed and 57 wounded – although they lost 122 horses and many of their men had become detached through providing prisoner escorts for the 750 Germans it had captured and in searching German HQs.

Having cleared the Morcourt Valley, the 8th Australian Brigade sent strong patrols out towards the Blue Line without waiting for its Mark V Stars. These did, however, appear and exploited beyond the

* According to Bean Vol 6 p.581 fn85 this flag had been given to him personally by General Monash.

Blue Line. Capt Henry Smeddle, one of the 8th Tank Battalion section commanders, wrote:

> The enemy were evidently unaware of the rapidity of our advance, for just as we were about opposite Harbonnières we saw an ammunition train steaming into the station as if nothing was the matter. It was immediately shelled by all the 6-pdr guns of the approaching tanks. One shell must have struck a powder van for suddenly the whole train burst into one great sheet of flame ... It was followed by another one, a passenger train rushing up fresh troops; this was running on another track and ran right into our lines where it was captured, complete with personnel.[15]

In terms of the trains this appears to tally to a large extent with the incident involving the Sopwith Camel train attack. However, the 15th Tank Battalion report on the attack states that the train which was hit was at Framerville.[16] This makes more sense in that this village faced the Blue Line in the 8th Brigade's sector. There is a further complication. The 31st Battalion captured a railway gun which had been used to bombard Amiens. It was, in fact, a 280mm 1904 model naval gun, which fired a 620lb shell to a distance of over 19 miles. It came complete with its engine and eight wagons, although one of the wagons had been destroyed, apparently by air attack. There were, however, two other pilots who reported a successful attack on a train. These were Lts Gates and Misener of No. 201 Squadron. They reported that they were flying in company in their Camels when they spotted three trains just to the north-east of Harbonnières. They attacked them with 25lb bombs and stated that they scored several hits. The British Air Ministry monograph states that two of the trains made off towards Vauvillers, but that the third had been badly damaged. The account then goes on to state that this was the troop train captured by the 5th Dragoon Guards.[17] Interestingly, the Australian Official Historian concludes that the train struck in the Harbonnières area was that with the railway gun and implies that it was the 5th Dragoon Guards who captured it. He also cited the official German monograph, which stated that two aircraft attacked the train and that the commander of the gun crew loosed off some four shots 'into space' before it was attacked.[18] Whatever the case, the 8th Australian Brigade listed the railway gun amongst its booty and the task of dealing with it was given to the 8th Australian Field Company RE. Cpl John Palmer:

We had been sent up with a quantity of Amanol to blow up the large gun ... However Les Strachan one of our sappers in the party had been a driver in the Western Australian railways, and he found there was still a head of steam, he asked for a fair go, instead of blowing the gun up he got the engine going, we were told then to try to get it back if possible into a cutting so it could be camouflaged.[19]

They were successful in this and the gun was eventually exhibited in Paris.*

The Whippets of the 6th (Light) Tank Battalion had a generally successful day, with thirty-four eventually rallying at the end of the day.[†] They found it difficult to co-operate closely with the cavalry, since the latter moved much faster, but they were also very vulnerable to machine-gun fire. Communications were also a problem and individual tank commanders often had to use their own initiative. A case in point concerned one of B Company's tanks. This had a series of unique adventures, which only surfaced after the war was over, when the tank commander was repatriated after being a prisoner of war. Musical Box, as the tank was called, was crewed by Lt C.B. Arnold, Pte C. Ribbans, the gunner, and the driver, Pte W. J. Carnie. During

---

* After the war the gun was sent to Britain for onward transmission to Australia as a war trophy. While the carriage was destroyed the gun itself can be seen in the grounds of the Australian War Memorial, Canberra to this day.

† Of those that failed to rally two had mechanical problems, two were ditched, two received direct hits and two were burnt out.

the initial advance Musical Box found itself the leading tank. At this stage it had not passed through the leading Australian infantry and their supporting Mark Vs, whom Arnold noticed were being engaged by a German battery, which succeeded in knocking out two Mark Vs. Arnold then took on the battery by driving diagonally across its front so that he could fire on it with both his machine guns. Then, using a conveniently placed belt of trees as cover, he got round to the rear of the battery, causing the crews to abandon their guns. After conferring with the Australian infantry and another Whippet section, which had now arrived, Arnold continued east, running alongside a railway embankment. He then passed through two cavalry patrols. The first was being troubled by German fire from a cornfield, which Arnold successfully suppressed.

Proceeding further east, I saw the second patrol pursuing six enemy. The leading horse was so tired that he was not gaining appreciably on the rearmost Hun. Some of the leading fugitives turned about and fired at the cavalryman when his sword was stretched out and practically touching the back of the last Hun. Horse and rider were brought down on the left of the road. The remainder of the cavalrymen deployed to right, coming in close under the railway embankment, where they dismounted and came under fire from the enemy, who had now taken up a position on the railway bridge, and were firing over the parapet, inflicting one or two casualties. I ran the machine up until we had a clear view of the bridge, and killed four of the enemy with one long burst, the other two running across the bridge and on down the opposite slope out of sight.

Arnold then continued on his way and entered a small valley between Bayonvillers and Harbonnières, which his map told him contained German hutments. He could see some German troops hastily packing their kits, while others were making off eastwards. He opened fire on the hutments and the troops around them, his gunner at one point even dismounting and entering one of them. Arnold then turned his attention to waves of withdrawing infantry, which he engaged as he 'cruised up and down' for the next hour or so. He did not see any other friendly troops and realised that he was on his own. At the same time, he and his crew were beginning to suffer. They were carrying spare tins of fuel on the outside of the tank and these had inevitably been punctured, allowing the fuel to run into the cab. The resultant fumes, combined with the effects of bullet splash and the growing heat inside the crew compartment, was making breathing very difficult and they were forced to breathe through the tubes of their box respirators.

Undeterred, Musical Box continued its progress. Arnold could see an airfield in the distance with an observation balloon hoisted above it. There were also masses of mechanical and horse transport about. The crew engaged all this, as well as further lines of withdrawing infantry. By now Musical Box was forward of the Outer Amiens Defence line and south of Vauvillers. Her crew came across some wagon lines, which they proceeded to beat up. They then turned to engage further men and horses in a small copse. At this point they came under the most intense machine-gun and rifle fire:

When at all possible, we returned the fire, until the L.H. [left hand] revolver port cover was shot away. I withdrew the forward gun, locked the mounting and held the body of the gun against the hole. Petrol was still running down the inside of the back door. Fumes and heat combined were very bad. We were still moving forward and I was shouting at Driver Carney [sic] to turn about, as it was impossible to continue the action, when two heavy concussions followed one another and the cab burst into flames. Carney and Ribbans got to the door and collapsed. I was almost overcome, but managed to get the door open and fell out on to the ground, and was able to drag out the other two men. Burning petrol was running on to the ground where we were lying. The fresh air revived us, and we all got up and made a short rush to get away from the burning petrol. We were all on fire. In this rush Carney was shot in the stomach

The village of Hamel on 5 July 1918, the day after its capture by the Australians.

The Allied high command for Amiens with King George V. Front row left to right – Rawlinson, Debeney, Foch, the King, Haig, Pétain, and General Fayolle (commander of the French Reserve Army Group). The bareheaded figure in the rear and on the right is Rawlinson's chief of staff, Maj. Gen. A. A. Montgomery.

A Handley Page 0/400 bomber of 207 Squadron RAF. These were used to drown the noise of the
tanks moving up on the night of 7/8 August. It had a crew of 4 or 5 and a top speed of 80 mph

FE2b night bombers were very active during the battle. They were 'pushers', with the engine mounted in the rear of the fuselage.

The wrecked tanks of No. 1 Gun Carrier Company in an orchard near Villers Bretonneux after a German shell had caused the ammunition that many were carrying to explode on 6 August.

Canadian 60-pounder guns in action.

Lt Rupert Downes MC of the 29th Australian Battalion briefs his platoon. Its meagre strength – less than 50 per cent of war establishment – is typical for the Australians by this stage of the war.

The headquarters of the 8th Canadian Brigade during the attack. The Brigade successfully seized Hangard and the bridge at Demuin over the River Luce during the first phase.

Recently captured Germans near Morcourt just south of the Somme. At the time the area was under fire by German guns on the Chipilly spur, their fire being adjusted by a German observation balloon.

Elements of the 15th Australian Brigade consolidate on the Green Line, while a Mark V Star tank of the 15th Tank Battalion advances towards the Blue Line, which it successfully reached

A section of Austin armoured cars from the 17th Battalion Tank Corps advancing along the old Roman road east of Warfusée-Abancourt. Each is armed with two ball mounted Hotchkiss machine guns and the lead car flies the French *tricolore* for identification purposes.

Canadian cavalry bringing in prisoners. During the four days of the battle the Fourth Army captured some 19,000 Germans and the French a further 11,000.

The German 280mm railway gun which was captured by the 31st Australian Battalion. It had been used to shell Amiens.

French Renault tanks await the order to advance. The lead tank is armed with a 37mm Puteaux gun and that behind it has a Hotchkiss machine gun. The Renault was the first tank to have a fully revolving turret.

This overrun German transport park in the Australian sector is indicative of the German Army's 'Black Day'. The notice reads 'Group Collecting Station: Entry Forbidden'.

The attack resumes. A Mark V tank from the 10th Battalion Tank Corps moves forward on 9 August to take part in the attack on Morlancourt, north of the Somme. It survived the day, but its 6-pounder gun and three machine guns were put out of action.

An armoured car of Brutinel's Independent Force covering the open right flank of the Canadian Corps on the Amiens–Roye road, 9 August. The cars were built by the US Autocar Company and were armed with two Vickers machine guns.

Lancers of the 2nd Cavalry Division pass through the village of Beacourt-en-Santerre en rout
to Le Quesnel, 9 August. The opportunity for the cavalry to break through had by now passed

The final resting place south of Vauvillers of Lt Arnold's Whippet tank 'Musical Box', which had wrought such damage on the Germans on 8 August. Photographed the following day and now a collecting point for wounded.

Field artillery signallers of the 58th Division on Chipilly Spur after its capture. They are using a heliograph, one of the many methods of communication which were employed during the battle.

Members of the 8th Londons (Post Office Rifles) with a haul of captured machine guns.

A 13th Battalion Tank Corps tank dealing with German machine-gun nests near Lihons while supporting the 85th Canadian Battalion, 10 August.

French artillery passing a disabled tank, with members of a Canadian Scottish battalion talking to crew members.

Exhausted Australians in a captured trench by Crépey Wood, just to the north-west of Lihons, 10 August. Note the abandoned German 77mm field gun.

French troops dug in on the south side of the Amiens–Roye road at Bouchoir, 11 August. The road marked the inter-army boundary and Canadian troops can also be seen.

Sir Douglas Haig congratulating the Canadian 78th Battalion (Nova Scotia Highlanders) at Domart on 11 August.

King George V, with General Pershing, inspecting men of the US 33rd Division on 12 August. The 131st Regiment could not be present as it was still in the line.

General Currie, the Canadian Corps commander (and the tall figure on the right), inspecting captured artillery. Some 450 German guns fell into Allied hands during the four days of the Amiens attack.

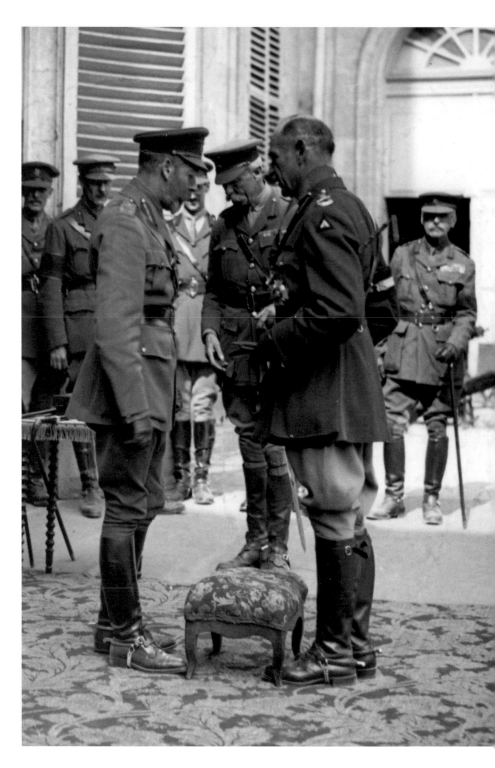

King George V knights Monash at the Australian Corps HQ at Bertangles.

and killed. We rolled over and over to try to extinguish the fumes [sic – flames?]. I saw numbers of the enemy approaching from all round. The first arrival came for me with a rifle and bayonet. I got hold of this, and the point of the bayonet entered my right forearm. The second man struck at my head with the butt end of his rifle, hit my shoulder and neck, and knocked me down. When I came to, there were dozens all round me, and anyone who could reach me did so and I was well kicked. They were furious.

Arnold and Ribbans were eventually rescued and rigorously inter-rogated before being evacuated to Germany.* [20]

At 1.30 p.m., patrols and an aircraft reported that the Germans were massing against the 57th Battalion for a possible counter-attack. By this time the Exploiting Detachment in its Mark V Stars had finally arrived and was placed under command of the Battalion's CO, as were the dismounted cavalry from the Bays. The attack did not materialize and the CO returned to the problem of securing the Blue Line on his right. At this stage the Canadians, who were his next door neighbour, had not reached the Blue Dotted Line and hence an effort on his own would leave his right flank exposed. He therefore sent runners to the 6th Canadian Brigade requesting that they join him in a further advance. The Canadians apparently declined, however, stating that they intended to remain where they were. It then transpired, unknown to the Australians, that the dismounted cavalry on the right did push forward to the Amiens Defence Line and were relieved by the 6th Canadian Brigade. The result of this was that the 57th Battalion was left with an indentation in its line.

The 3rd Cavalry Division, with the 3rd (Light) Battalion Tank

---

* Lt Arnold eventually ended up in a POW camp at Freiburg, where he was reunited with his brother, Capt A. E. Arnold MC, also of the Tank Corps. The story of Musical Box began to emerge on 9 August 1918, when advancing troops came across it, with 20-40 German dead lying around the tank. Arnold himself was later awarded the DSO (London Gazette 4 Oct 19) and Pte Ribbans the DCM (LG 2 Dec 19). Pte Carnie has no known grave, but is commemorated on the Vis-en-Artois Memorial.

Corps attached, was also on the move well before 9.30 a.m., with the Canadian Cavalry Brigade crossing of the Luce at Ignacourt completed at 10.25 a.m. It was followed by the 7th Cavalry Brigade, which was complete on the far bank by 11 a.m. The Canadians headed south, with Lord Strathcona's Horse in the lead, and made contact with the Independent Force on the Roye road before 11 a.m. Two sections of Whippets accompanied this regiment and initially advanced ahead of the horsemen, who overran the village of Fresnoy-en-Chaussée, taking 125 prisoners. As a result they became separated from the Lord Strathcona's. Two crews had also been wounded and the others were faint from the heat and fumes inside their tanks. After a pause they rejoined the Strathconas.

By this time the Royal Canadian Dragoons had passed through. They also had two Whippet sections attached. An anonymous troop leader describes the advance:

We had 8 tanks with us and they were having a bit of a time at this juncture. The tank commander, mounted on a horse, was riding at full gallop to and fro among his command and his flow of language was a delight to the ear. Really, if he was a cavalryman, whose carefully groomed horse had fallen and rolled in the mud, the minute before inspection, he could not have done better. The chief tenor of his remarks seemed to be that the tanks could travel a blanket-blank faster in the back areas where training had been carried on, than they were doing at that time. One tank was in trouble and its commander was on top like a brakesman on a freight train. At a critical moment he allowed his hand to stay for a second on the top of the exhaust pipe but only for a second. His remarks were not in any way appointed to be read in the churches. All this was going on while moving along at a trot and canter with the odd shell bursting and the hollow wooden tattoo of the machine guns over Beaucourt.[21]

This illustrated the fact that the Whippets found it difficult to keep up with the cavalry. Even so, they moved to deal with the machine-gun fire, which was from the north of Beaucourt, and eventually silenced it. They also drove the crews away from a German battery. This left the Dragoons without tank support, but they now attacked the village of Beaucourt. Captain Roy Nordheimer:

The squadron was riding hell bent for election for Beaucourt, with swords drawn and yelling like mad. Lieutenant Steve 'Bramwell' Booth, who was the brigade galloper, was riding alongside of me and right at the start gave a grunt and fell dead off his horse. We were losing heavily on that ride. A horse is a good target and the gunners had a field day, for 130 odd men and horses are a great temptation. The squadron commander had his horse shot under him and I can see him yet, caught by one leg and waving his sword and cursing like a blue streak. We reformed just outside Beaucourt and the squadron, by then only about fifty ranks, rode through and reached our objective in front of the village, taking up position on the left of the LSH.[22]

The Royal Canadian Dragoons had 9 killed, 47 wounded, and 6 men posted as missing, but also lost 125 horses. The Fort Garry Horse also joined in the attack on Beaucourt, but its casualties were much lighter. The Canadian Cavalry thought of pushing further forward but the intense machine-gun fire coming from Beaucourt Wood, some 2 kilometres to the east of the village, dissuaded them and they remained where they were until relieved by the 11th Canadian Brigade at 5 p.m.

The 7th Cavalry Brigade operating north of the Canadians faced similar problems with woods south of Cayeux. The 6th Cavalry Brigade was deployed in support and the 7th then successfully charged the wood, bagging over 200 prisoners. The Whippets helped considerably in this, getting round the eastern side of the wood and engaging a large number of Germans. The Canadians were, however, still held up by Beaucourt Wood and so at 1.40 p.m. the GOC issued orders for the 6th Cavalry Brigade to turn the wood from the north and north-east and then continue south-east to secure the Canadian Cavalry Brigade's ultimate objective of the Outer Amiens Defences east of Le Quesnel. The 6th Cavalry Brigade was to head for the Amiens defences east of Caix, while the Canadians were to reorganize and then take over the support role. This was largely achieved by 2.30 p.m., with only a small portion of the Outer Defences to the east and south-east of Le Quesnel remaining in German hands. The Whippets themselves managed to reach the outskirts of Le Quesnel but found it too strongly held and lost one tank, which was hit and set on fire, killing its crew. A Company of the 3rd (Light) Battalion was supposed to be attached to the 6th Cavalry Brigade but found itself instead assisting the 4th Canadian Division.

By this time the 2nd Cavalry Division had been deployed. Its 4th Cavalry Brigade advanced through the Outer Defence Line towards Rosières-en-Santerre and Vrély to its south, but, as the 1st Cavalry Division experienced at Vauvillers, the Germans were holding this line too strongly for the cavalry to penetrate.

Of the exploiting forces it was undoubtedly the Austin armoured cars of the 17th Battalion Tank Corps which enjoyed the most success. The Battalion was attached to the 5th Australian Division and spent the night of the 7/8 bivouacked on the side of the Villers Bretonneux–Vermand road, some 4 kilometres west of Villers Bretonneux itself. Attached to it were three tanks from the 5th Tank Brigade, the idea being that they could tow the armoured cars across any shell torn ground. Each also carried an Artillery bridge for placing across trenches. Of the sixteen cars available, twelve would exploit any breakthrough by the Division, while the other four were to carry out a long distance reconnaissance east along the Villers Bretonneux–St Quentin road under the direction of the Australian Corps. This road was to act as the centre line for the Battalion, with six cars operating to the north of it and six to the south. Each car had axes and gun cotton to remove obstacles. They also carried pigeons, which would be their main means of communication.

At Zero Hour the cars began to advance as far as they were able and then waited for the 5th Australian Division's pioneers to clear the road ahead. Three and a half hours after the attack was launched the road was reported clear and the cars passed through the village of Warfusée-Abancourt accompanied by two towing tanks (the third had to be left behind with fuel feed problems). The going was initially very slow because of the numerous trees and branches which had been blown across the road by artillery fire, but with help from the towing tanks these were cleared and the cars passed through the Australian infantry, which was now on the Green Line just east of the village. They then passed through the barrage being fired on the withdrawing German troops and began to engage the latter with their machine guns. Seven kilometres east of Warfusée they reached a railway dump at La Flaque and caught a loaded train just leaving. They holed the engine's boiler, captured the crew and the complete train. The four cars operating under Corps HQ then pushed on towards Foucaucourt, while the main body split, with half turning north to Proyart and the remainder south to Framerville.

The Foucaucourt contingent continued east, engaging Germans as they did so. They were then engaged by a field battery. Lt Blencowe's car fought a duel with it, but he was eventually blown into a ditch, while his other car was also damaged and withdrew to be repaired. Blencowe himself noticed a line of telegraph poles on the side of the road and destroyed these with gun cotton to disrupt German communications. He then managed to obtain a tow for his car and withdrew. The other section also had both cars hit. Lt Kenyon's had its engine set on fire and he and his crew had to abandon it. His other car suffered damaged turrets, but he carried on, turning south to Framerville, where he found the road blocked with dead horses and limbers and so returned to the main road. He managed to salvage the guns from his knocked out car, but then was again engaged by the same battery as before and so retired.

The main body continued on to 2 kilometres west of Foucaucourt, creating further confusion, but was eventually frustrated by German transport wagons, a number of which had collided with one another and blocked the road. The northern group then turned north-west to Proyart. Here they found German troops eating a meal in their billets and dispersed them. They also pursued a truck full of troops and inflicted several casualties. Turning east towards Chuignolles they came across a German staff car. They killed the occupants, apart from the driver, whom they sent with the car back to the Australian lines. On their way back they encountered several other Germans withdrawing and who did not think that the cars were hostile.

Most spectacular was the effort of the southern group. Its target was Framerville, which was known to hold a German corps HQ. Indeed, prior to the attack Monash had given the 17th Battalion the pennant from his staff car to fix to the HQ should they capture it. The plan was for No. 7 Section (2Lt James) to block the roads to Framerville from the Amiens–St Quentin road and for No. 6 (2Lt Berd) and No. 8 (Lt Rollings) to actually enter the village, with Rollings himself going directly to the headquarters. The cars of No. 7 Section duly took up position, accounting for many stragglers as they streamed back eastwards. They also found a German staff car, whose occupants were taking cover in a ditch. These surrendered and one of the Austins then took the staff car in tow and back to the Australian lines. Lt James noted in his report that 'the enemy appeared to be completely taken by surprise and did not seem to realise that the cars were British.' No. 6 Section entered Framerville down its main street, which was very narrow. Again, total surprise was achieved and a large amount of horse transport was destroyed, as were three artillery limbers without guns. These, however, blocked the narrow street and Lt Berd's cars had to retrace their steps.

This left Lt Ernest Rollings, a former Welsh policeman who had been commissioned into the Tank Corps and won an MC at Third Ypres after service as an infantryman, and No. 8 Section. He duly entered Framerville and went straight to the corps HQ, which he entered, seizing as many documents and maps that he could, although he made no mention of this in his after-action report, and duly fixed Monash's pennant to the entrance. The plan was for the Framerville sections to continue south to Vauvillers. In Rollings' own words:

After mopping up all we could find I searched every road, track and field to try and [sic] get to VAUVILLERS but could not do so, so I returned to the centre of the village again, and was just in time to greet 4 Staff Officers who rode up to the HQ. These were killed, one being dragged away by the stirrups till the horse fell. By this time a good crowd of the enemy had also come up from their dugouts, etc and we again cleared the village.

Rollings then set off back towards Villers Bretonneux, but ran into No. 6 Section who told him that they had orders to patrol the roads as far as Foucaucourt. They began to do this, but came under short range fire from German guns. The car therefore reversed back out of trouble. While Rollings was halted and taking a look round, 'a German came out of a dugout close by carrying some pigeons. My Driver killed this man and we brought back the pigeons in the car.' He then tried once again to get Vauvillers by track, but eventually decided to re-enter Framerville. As he was doing so he came across the staff car encountered by No. 7 Section. Rollings returned to his company HQ and was ordered to try to reach Lihons, some 3 kilometres south-east of Framerville. However, on the east side of Harbonnières, which lay between the Red and Blue Lines, he found his way blocked by a German steam wagon. He tried to get round this obstacle by means of using tracks, but without success and hence returned to Battalion HQ west of Villers Bretonneux.

Rollings summed up his experiences:

Nearly every German we saw waited till we were close up till they discovered who we were, they were absolutely dazed. Men running from the [Australian] Infantry came right up, in some cases as near as 50 yards before they realised what was happening. It was real murder. Absolutely no artillery fire on either side, it is by far the finest fighting day I have ever had.

Indeed, the sixteen Austins, operating on their own and sometimes as much as 5–6 kilometres ahead of the advancing infantry, had created an atmosphere of alarm and confusion in the German ranks out of all proportion to their numbers. Remarkably, too, their casualties were very light. Four officers and four men were very slightly wounded and of the cars only one was lost, although seven suffered mechanical problems.[23]

For the Canadians, whose 4th Division was to pass through to the Blue Dotted Line, it was the 1st Tank Battalion's Mark V Stars, totalling thirty-four, which would lead the advance. Each carried one Vickers and two Lewis gun teams, the former being drawn from No. 3 Company 4th Canadian Machine Gun Corps and the latter from the 11th and 12th Infantry Brigades. Each tank would also carry an infantry or machine gun officer, a runner and an infantry scout who would work with the tank commander. This meant that in addition to its eight-man crew it would be carrying an additional fourteen men.* But, as the Company's after-action report pointed out:

> To my mind the scheme in General [sic] had not been given sufficient thought. The tank people themselves thought we should have all been together for at least a week to get everything perfect ... Owing to the shortness of time the men did not know until zero hour who the Officer was to lead them. This did not add to their confidence. The men did not also know their tank Officer or their tank crew.[24]

The Division itself would advance with its 12th Brigade on the left, 11th Brigade on the right and the 10th Brigade in reserve. At 12.40 p.m. the lead brigades passed through the 3rd Canadian Division on the Red Line. On the right the 11th Brigade advanced to Beaucourt with little difficulty, with the 54th Battalion and cavalry combining to capture the village. Both were then held up by machine-gun fire

---

* Each Vickers team consisted of an NCO and four men, while the Lewis guns had a crew of three men each.

from the west face of Beaucourt Wood. A Company of the 1st Tank Battalion moved to attack the wood, but lost no less than nine of its tanks to a German battery situated in the open. The Commanding Officer of the 54th Battalion realized that the wood would have to be captured if the advance of the Division was not to be jeopardized. Even though it was not in his sector and he lacked supporting artillery and trench mortar fire he led his men into the attack across the open ground to the wood. Although he and his men did have some cover provided by the smoke of a burning tank casualties were heavy, but the survivors managed to gain a lodgement. The 102nd Battalion on the right then also attacked and eventually at 4.30 p.m. the wood was cleared. The two battalions then took a position on the east side of the wood although this was still some 3,000 yards short of the Dotted Blue Line. The Brigade's right hand battalion, the 75th, was similarly frustrated. Advancing across open ground it came under fire from the villages of Le Quesnel and Fresnoy, the latter being in the French sector but not yet reached by them. The surviving Mark V Star did manage to get to the outskirts of Le Quesnel with its machine gun teams, but was forced to withdraw. The CO therefore decided that a frontal attack on Le Quesnel was out of the question. There were signs, too, of German reinforcements moving up. Hence the 75th Battalion dug in where it was, linking up with the 54th Battalion to the north. The reserve battalion, the 87th, was deployed to the west of Beaucourt.

The 12th Canadian Brigade fared better on the left. They initially faced opposition from machine guns in the woods north-west of Beaucourt and from the northern edge of Beacourt Wood but overcame this with the help of tanks, a field battery and a 6-inch trench mortar. Six Mark V Stars from the centre company managed to reach the Blue Dotted Line, although because of the 11th Brigade being restricted in its advance by the stiff resistance, they were forced to withdraw some 1,500 yards with their machine-gun teams. On the left, though, four tanks got to the Blue Dotted Line south of Caux and held there. Lt F. M. Macdonald, a machine-gun officer, was in the first tank to arrive on the objective:

... we pushed forward to the Dotted Blue Line with the cavalry and ahead of the infantry on the frontage of the 12th Brigade. Continued machine gun fire and bursts of shell fire were encountered during the remainder of the advance. For this reason we had to travel inside the tanks all the way. Several of the men became weak and sickened by the fumes inside the tank. By using anti-gas tablets and also a solution we had for the purpose, most of them recovered.* Two, however, had to be left behind to be evacuated. The cavalry moving with us, or ahead of us, but on many occasions they met with hostile machine-gun fire and sustained heavy losses.

We also met fire from anti-tank rifles and a few bullets from these penetrated our tank. Slight casualties were also caused from splinters inside the tank. By continued concentrated fire on the revolver loop holes in the tank, the enemy succeeded in breaking the loop-hole frames and causing casualties. My tank officer was fatally wounded in the head. His NCO was killed and two of the tank men were later mortally wounded. One of the Lewis Gun men and the scout were killed. After a direct hit on our tank it stalled a couple of times and on one of these occasions, about 2pm, when we were just to the right of the woods in 21.d, 1,000 yards to the rear of the Blue Line and 500 yards north of the 12th CIB [Canadian Infantry Brigade] right boundary, the enemy began to rush us from the woods near by. Machine gun and rifle bullets were rapping on our tank from all sides and our only hope was to keep all our guns firing and get the tank started if possible. After a great deal of difficulty in cranking the engine, we succeeded in starting the tank again and with our machine guns we wiped out groups of the retreating enemy. We pushed forward about 1,000 yards further on until

---

* I have been unable to establish exactly what the anti-gas tablets and the solution were. The latter could have been the same as used in Vermorel Sprayers to protect dugouts against gas attack. This was a mixture of sodium theosulphate, sodium carbonate and water.

we reached our final objective, where we unloaded our guns and took up positions on some unlevel ground. Our tank was hit and destroyed by a shell before we got all our ammunition and rations out of it. We remained there and held our position against enemy fire until the 72nd Battalion reached us about 6.30pm.[25]

Many of the machine-gun teams did not, however, stay on board the tanks and elected to dismount and walk behind them because of the fumes.

While the Australians had had further to advance between the Green and Red Lines than the Canadians they had a considerably shorter distance to the Blue Line. In the north the 4th and 12th Brigades were to continue to the Blue Line, leaving the 1st Brigade to form a defensive flank on the Somme. Just two battalions, the 12th on the left and 48th on the right, would make the advance to the Blue Line. They paused to wait for Mark V Star tanks to catch up since they had fallen behind, partially because the Australian machine-gun teams, like many of the Canadian ones, elected to walk behind the tanks rather than face the fumes inside. The 12th Battalion, with the German guns on the Chipilly Spur, faced a tough task. Eight Mark V Stars had been allocated to the battalion, but only four made it to the start line on time. Commanding the Australian machine-gunners on board was Captain Bill Lynas of the 16th Battalion, already the holder of the MC and bar and shortly to be gazetted with a further MC and a DSO for actions prior to 8 August. The first task was to pass through the 13th Battalion which was suffering from machine-gun and sniper fire. Lynas, sitting beside the driver, as were the Australian officers in the other tanks, led the tanks onto the knuckle of high ground just south-east of Morcourt. Covered by some trees they surprised some 70 Germans whom they drove back into the waiting arms of the 13th Battalion. The tanks then set off for the Blue line, aiming for Mericourt. They now came under fire from the guns on the

Chipilly Spur. One tank reached the Blue Line, which ran through the outskirts of the village, and dropped off its machine-gun crews before it was hit. Lynas's tank was struck by a shell which did not detonate, but the resultant splinters killed two of the occupants and wounded two others. It also damaged the exhaust which resulted in an increase of fumes inside the tank. Lynas now ordered the machine-gun teams to begin disembarking while the tank was still moving. All, however, became so overcome by the fumes that they could not open the door. The tank was hit again and Lynas managed to scramble out of the top of the tank before collapsing. Men of the 16th Battalion then arrived and extricated those still on board and took all to behind cover so that they could recuperate. As for the other two tanks, they were both hit, but the surviving machine-gunners managed to get into shell holes and helped to shoot the advancing infantry onto the objective. These arrived at about 12.30 p.m., having faced fire in the rear from the Chipilly Spur and from the front, but by fire and manoeuvre managed to capture 200 prisoners and 12 machine guns.

The 48th Battalion did not face the same problem, but to reach the Blue Line it had to cross a valley and then ascend a ridge, on top of which lay its objective, with the village of Proyart beyond. Three Mark V Stars were available. One tank, commanded by Lt M. Brown,* led the attack on the left and got past the old Amiens defence line, which lay just short of the Blue Line, but then came under intense fire. It turned back to drop off its machine-gun teams when it was hit and caught fire. Some of the machine-gunners were killed as they baled out, but the survivors managed to get one Lewis gun into action and this kept the Germans at bay until the lead company of the 48th Battalion arrived. Matters went more smoothly on the right, with both Mark V Stars reaching the Blue Line and one making two trips to bring up further machine guns. Mark Vs of the 8th Tank Battalion also continued on to the Red Line. One was commanded

---

* Bean, *Official History of Australia in the War of 1914–1918* Vol 6 p.586 mistakenly calls him Lt M. Burn.

by Lt Murray. Because of the broken terrain he had been forced at times to guide his tank on foot. Worse:

> ... four of the crew were overcome by the heat & fumes & were unable to serve their guns but I was enabled to keep both 6 Pdr guns in action by serving one myself. From this time onwards the crew of fit men consisted of my driver, one gunner, & myself. Advancing towards the red line we continued to get many excellent targets & captured the Red line without difficulty. I then advanced in front of the infantry's final objective & about 200 yards in front succeeded in rounding up about 50 prisoners. I noticed at this time that the infantry on the left seemed to be slightly behind the line of the general advance; I went to their assistance & succeeded in enabling them to advance. I again advanced towards the Blue line & encountered some dug-outs. A few well directed bursts of fire brought out a number of armed men on whom my driver & myself had some good pistol shooting killing about 9 from 15 yd[s] range. On this the remainder to the no of about 30 surrendered we drove them back towards our infantry. I then proceeded along the front toward some Mark V stars but in doing so received a direct hit which killed one & wounded four. Another hit on the track put us out of action.[26]

In all, out of 36 tanks the 8th Tank Battalion had 9 tanks out of action because of mechanical problems, 1 fell victim to a land mine and 13 were disabled by shell fire. Among the crews themselves 13 were killed, 37 wounded and evacuated, 5 were wounded but remained at duty and 3 were posted as missing.[27]

As for what the battlefield looked like after the attack had passed through, 2Lt Percy Smythe had found time hanging heavy on his hands with the 24th Australian Battalion's Battle Surplus. In the afternoon, and accompanied by his batman, he hitched rides in lorries moving along the Roman road to Warfusée. On the way they passed 'numerous batches of prisoners', as well as ambulances, lorries, and horse drawn transport ferrying back the wounded of both sides. He noted one lorry 'marked with white chalk, "Wounded Diggers and Huns."'

Moving on from Villers Bretonneux, we passed the wrecked aerodrome that we could see from the Villers line at the time of the Hamel stunt, the former front line, and the late No-man's-land, then the old German front line. A few dead Germans lay singly here and there along the way. A couple of supply tanks lumbered noisily across country returning from the fray. Over-head, the 'planes were very busy, many returning from the front and many others going forward.[28]

Throughout the day the brigades which had been holding the line prior to the initial assault had been following up behind the attack. Lt Barton of the 54th Battalion (14th Australian Infantry Brigade):

When daylight had fully come we were up where our front line and attack troops had started from. Many planes were above and many prisoners were moving back and across the open field looking to our left (Villers Brettoneaux [sic] was on our right) could be seen the great forward movement of the many units of war, platoons of advancing reserve infantry, columns of Army Service [Corps], Engineers, Pioneers, Medical Corps, limbers and guns and general service wagons and added to this vast movement on the plain and moving in the opposite direction were squads of prisoners moving back ... All through the day we marched forward with little halts to keep us back into [sic] position.[29]

The 40th Battalion, with the 3rd Australian Division to the north had a similar experience, coming to rest in Reginald Wood just forward of the Green Line and 2,000 yards south-west of Morcourt. There its men did have the opportunity to engage the Germans, as Lt

Thornton Cranswick DCM recounted in a letter to his mother:

Close to us was a battery of German guns, big ones too, & the artillery people were allowing any of our lads the privilege of firing a Fritz shell into Fritz country providing they carried the shell from the dump to the gun. Needless to say there were not any shells left on the dump when we finished.[30]

The Canadian Independent Force had meanwhile been advancing astride the boundary with the French. It was organized in two groups (Nos 1 and 2, each representing the two motor machine-gun brigades), each with five motor machine-gun batteries, two platoons from the Canadian Cyclist battalion, and 20 motor cyclists, another group (No. 3) with two armoured Autocars and four cyclist platoons, an armoured car detachment with four Autocars and one cyclist platoon, and a trench mortar section with two Newton 6-inch mortars mounted on trucks. Led by the armoured car detachment, which had been reinforced by the two cars from No. 3 Group, they began to move down the Amiens–Roye road, passing through Domart two hours later. The armoured cars were then sent forward to make contact with the Germans, while No. 1 Group formed a defensive flank for the Canadian Corps. Shortly before 11 a.m. the armoured cars reached Mézières, which was still held by the Germans and was the responsibility of the French 42nd Division.

In the French sector the second phase of the attack by XXXI Corps began precisely at 7.43 a.m. For the 42nd Division the principal objective was Villers-aux-Erables. Once again a rolling barrage was used, but, in contrast to the first phase, the ground was generally open. Heavy machine-gun and some artillery fire from the village eventually temporarily stalled the advance in the centre and on the right. The 8th Chasseurs had particular difficulties in that the rolling barrage had got too far ahead, eventually over 800 yards in front and was falling behind the village. But on the left, the 2nd Battalion of the 94th Regiment was able to take advantage of the Canadian success and managed to get into the grounds of the chateau just to the north of Villers-aux-Erables. One of the company commanders and his HQ section came across two Germans repairing a telephone line. They were captured and one stated that a colonel and several other officers had been occupying the chateau but had left for Mézières a quarter of an hour before. He then pointed to a cellar, which was found to contain a complete German company, which, under the threat of grenades, quickly surrendered.* This enabled the advance in the centre to continue. It was here that the assistance of the one available tank, a Mark V Female, from Captain Bion's section, was invaluable. This drove through the village, but was unable to suppress German machine guns in houses on the outskirts with Hotchkiss fire, which were still holding up the French advance. Consequently, it drove through these buildings and cleared the village. The French, however, were concerned at one point that the tank did not appear to recognize friend from foe.[31] The capture of Villers-aux-Erables was achieved by 10.30 a.m. and Mézières, from which considerable fire had been coming, was the next 42nd Division objective.

Meanwhile, the 37th Division had advanced in step, while the 66th Division had taken Moreuil. Across in IX Corps the 15th Colonial and 3rd Infantry Divisions had crossed the Avre at 5 a.m. The former had some difficulty in clearing Génouville Wood, south-east of Moreuil, because of the numerous machine-gun nests it contained. Once this was achieved the two divisions swung south-east in line with the main direction of the offensive and by nightfall had reached a line running from the west of Plessier-Rozainvillers to north-west of Contoire.

Returning to the north of the French sector, Mézières proved to be a more complicated operation than was expected. Heavy machine gun fire from the village prevented the French in Villers-aux-Erables and the park to the north of it from immediately continuing the advance. Stokes mortars of the Canadian Independent Force then

* That afternoon a French engineer section went to establish a command post for the 42nd Division in the cellars of the chateau. They discovered the commander of the German 14th Reserve Regiment and his staff sheltering there.

engaged a trench astride the road from Viller-aux-Erables to Mézières from which much of the fire was coming. They forced the Germans to abandon it, but the French company tasked with advancing along this route had by now lost all its section commanders and needed to reorganize before it could continue. Furthermore, Commandant Mesny, commanding 2nd Battalion of the 94th Regiment, was not aware of the success of the Stokes and was preparing to attack Mézières from the north. The problem was overcome by the intervention of elements of the 153rd Division. This had been moving up behind the 42nd and 37th Divisions, the idea being that it should pass between the two and carry on the advance with them. Leading the 153rd Division were the 1st Regiment Moroccan Tirailleurs on the left and the 8th Regiment of Zouaves on the right, with the former moving up through the 42nd Division's sector. Two companies of Renault tanks had been allocated to the Tirailleurs, but had been delayed in its crossing of the Luce. The lead battalion (3rd) made rapid progress, so much so that at 10.15 a.m. the regimental commander, Colonel Cimetière, ordered it not to move along the route Demuin–Moreuil without further orders. When the battalion commander, Captain Messel, a very young officer filled with initiative and drive, received the order his men were already exiting from Moreuil Wood. He himself spoke to the commander of a nearby artillery group who told him that the situation was a little obscure and that the 94th Regiment had probably attained all of its objectives, but had suffered losses. He therefore suggested that an approach via the park north of Villers-aux-Erables might be best. Conscious that his division aimed to be close to Hangest-en-Santerre that evening, Messel did not hesitate. He took one company to the park, while ordering a second to move to the south of Villers-aux-Erables, with a third following up in reserve. He did not bother to wait for the tanks that would support him. Messel and his men quickly got into the park and reached the eastern corner, although he himself was wounded in the shoulder by the fire continuing to come from Mézières. The other company experienced the same problem that had been holding up the 8th Chasseurs, namely a machine-gun nest between Villers-aux-Erables and Dé Wood to its south. The other two companies followed Messel into the park and took up position on its east side and also managed to get into Mouettes Wood just north of the village.

It was now 11 a.m. and Lt Col Détrie, commanding the 94th Regiment, was working out the best way of securing Mézières. He was reassured to receive a message from a liaison officer with the 4th Canadian Division, which was now passing through the 3rd Canadian Division, stating that the Canadians expected to be at Beaucourt and Le Quesnel in the afternoon. This meant that his left flank would be secured. He had also received an offer of six tanks or six machine-gun vehicles from General Brutinel, which he readily accepted to help him take the village. Détrie also asked for artillery fire on Mézières and for the Renaults supporting the Moroccans to be brought up as quickly as possible. He then sent a message to the commander of the 332nd Regiment informing him of what he had done and proposing that he liaise with the Moroccans over the capture of the village. The artillery itself had been proceeding with the original fire plan. This was based on the assumption that Mézières would have fallen very much earlier and that by this time the advance would have reached almost to Fresnoy-en- Chaussée. Hence from just after 11 a.m. fire was concentrated on this village. Nevertheless, it did respond to Détrie's plea and it was arranged that 75mm guns would provide five minutes of neutralizing fire and then lay down a fixed barrage to the east of the village until 12.15 p.m., when it would again turn into a rolling barrage towards Fresnoy. This worked. The fire from the village suddenly ceased and elements of the 94th Regiment and the Moroccans advanced with fixed bayonets and entered its now deserted streets. The reason for the sudden cessation of German resistance appears to have been that one of Brutinel's motor machine gun batteries had managed to get round the flank and forced the defenders to surrender.

At much the same time the situation south of Villers-aux-Erables was also cleared up. This was largely thanks to the deployment of the Renault tank company to help overcome the machine-gun nests, although they did suffer from anti-tank fire from Touffu Wood in the 37th Division's sector to the south. This knocked out one tank and damaged others. The 332nd Regiment now passed through the 94th, while the 16th Chasseurs took over from the 8th Chasseurs in preparation for the attack on Fresnoy. The 3rd Moroccan Tirailleurs had also, by 1 p.m., managed to work their way forward to some 1,000 yards from the village.

In Fresnoy itself the remnants of the 4th Bavarian Regiment had begun to regroup hurriedly just before midday and were joined by elements of the 8th and 25th Regiments. Much of the 14th Bavarian Division's artillery had already been lost, but there were field guns available, as well as plenty of machine guns. The open nature of the terrain also favoured the defence. On the other hand, the Bavarians could expect little help from their neighbours, since both the 225th Division to the north and the 192nd Division to the south were also under intense pressure. Nevertheless, the Germans in Fresnoy were strong enough to prevent efforts to enter it immediately after the capture of Mézières. Indeed, General Goubeau, commanding the 153rd Division and keen to press on to Hangest, tried to send a squadron of the 5th Hussars round the north of the village, but the German machine-gun fire proved too strong. There were even fears that the Germans might launch a counter-attack from the village. It was clear therefore that the 42nd Division would have to make a set piece attack.

There was, however, some confusion between the 42nd and 153rd Divisions. Because of the need to redeploy guns the 42nd Division eventually opted for a Zero Hour of 7.30 p.m., intending that the 332nd Regiment should attack on the left and the 16th Chasseurs on the right. But the Moroccans of the 153rd Division remained impatient to push on and two battalions attacked an hour earlier. Intense machine-gun fire halted them in their tracks and this in spite of supporting fire from the 75s. This, however, did have one favourable result. A small wood just south-west of Fresnoy had been holding up the 16th Chasseurs and this was also engaged by the 75s. The German fire from here noticeably slackened and a company of the Chasseurs took advantage of this and dashed into the wood, capturing some Germans and four machine guns. They were not engaged from Fresnoy and it seemed that the village might have been entered, although this was not so. Consequently, the attack planned by the 42nd Division at 7.30 p.m. would take place. It would, however, be assisted by one of the 153rd Division's Renault tank companies and two motor machine-gun batteries from Brutinel's force. Organized in three sections of five tanks each, with a mix of three tanks armed with a 37mm gun and two with machine guns, the Renaults advanced on the village from the north, west, and south at 7.15 p.m.

The tank section attacking from the west was the first to arrive on its objective:

Versatile, the tanks moved in column, pitching and rolling on the broken ground, but slipping without appreciable effort over the holes created by the shells. After some 400 metres one machine gun tank was left behind with engine trouble and efforts to restart it proved useless. The fuel pipe was blocked .... At 500 metres from Fresnoy, Sourzac [section commander] gave the signal for battle formation and, in two minutes, all the tanks in the section were in line with one another, and one could see the [section commander's] flag in the centre. The right of the line moved parallel to the Mézières road and 200 metres from it.[32]

An ad hoc company made up of two weak platoons from the 1st Moroccan Tirailleurs accompanied the tanks, which were now exchanging fire with the Bavarian defenders. At the same time another Moroccan company had managed to get into the village from the north and another company was working its way round the south of the village. By 7.30 p.m. the western part of the village was in French hands, but it was not until well after dark that the remainder was secured. By then the tanks were low on fuel and ammunition and there was no possibility of pressing on to Hangest until they had been replenished.

It was the end of the 42nd Division's part in the battle. It had suffered 116 killed, 410 wounded and 33 missing during the day, but had captured some 2,200 prisoners and 44 guns of varying calibres. It would now be relieved by the 126th Infantry Division. The 37th Division also succeeded in taking Plessier-Rozainvillers. The night was then largely spent in redeploying the artillery for the next phase.

While the Australians and Canadians were consolidating III Corps had been renewing its efforts to gain Chipilly and the Chipilly Spur. The 58th Division organized a further attack to be carried out by the 2nd/10th Londons during the afternoon but a request for a tank to assist them had to be turned down. The 10th Tank Battalion did have 19 tanks available, but 15 of these were undergoing minor repairs and their crews were exhausted, while the remainder were too far away. Eventually, and with the aid of a preliminary bombardment, the 2nd/10th attacked Chipilly at 7.30 p.m., but were driven back with heavy casualties by numerous machine guns in the village and the high ground beyond.

For the Germans the day had been an unmitigated disaster. The official monograph stated:

As the sun set on the battlefield of the Second Army on the evening of 8 August the greatest defeat which the German Army had suffered since the beginning of the war was an accomplished fact. The line holding divisions between the Avre and the Somme, which had been struck by the enemy attack, were almost completely annihilated. The troops in the front line north of the Somme had also suffered seriously, as had the reserve divisions thrown into the battle during the course of the day.[33]

The divisions facing the Canadians and Australians – 225th, 117th, 41st, 13th – had virtually ceased to exist. North of the Somme, in the British III Corps sector, the 43rd Reserve Division had been in the midst of relief by the 108th Division. The elements which had been relieved immediately found themselves having to help out the 13th Division just south of the river. Six divisions were available to the Second Army as immediate reinforcement, three to the north of the Somme and the other three to the south. Only the latter were to become engaged before nightfall. The 119th Division occupied an area south of Royer, while the 1st Reserve Division was centred on Le Quesnoy-en-Santerre. Both of these were in the French sector and the only reinforcement opposite Fourth Army was the 109th Division which was deployed from Vauvillers in the west to Misery in the east, that is mainly opposing the Canadians.

Thanks to General Eberhard von Hofacker, commanding LI Corps whose 10 mile wide sector lay astride the Anglo-French boundary, these dispositions were changed. Concluding that the main threat lay from the Canadians, rather than the French, he immediately ordered the resting battalions of his two divisions facing the French, 14th Bavarian and 192nd, to be placed in depth in front of the Canadians.* He also arranged with III Corps, his southern neighbour, for the 1st Reserve Division to advance along the Roye– Amiens road and to be prepared to counter-attack. It was then ordered to take up position astride the road and covering from Fresnoy north to Beaucourt and came under artillery and air attack as it did so. In the afternoon Canadian pressure forced it back to the line Le Quesnel– Fresnoy. Von Hofacker also obtained von der Marwitz's agreement for III Corps to surrender the 119th Division to him. It received orders at 8.30 a.m. to move north by lorry to the Vrély – Warvillers area. It began to move two hours later, but because of congestion on the roads and attacks from the air it was not in position until 7.30 p.m. The Division was ordered to mount an immediate counter-attack. Only one regiment was ready to do so, but it had no knowledge of the ground and little artillery support. Consequently the attack was no more than a damp squib. The 109th Division, on the other hand,

---

* The German policy for each forward division was to have all three of its regiments in the line, but with one battalion of each at rest.

being already in place, had an easier task and was merely ordered to take up position around Harbonnières. Of the three reinforcing divisions north of the Somme, the 243rd Division was in the area north-east of Mericourt and moved during the day to the Cappy–Bray area south of the Somme. The 107th Division, positioned in Péronne and south of it, advanced westwards to the old Amiens Outer Defence Line. This left the 26th Reserve Division, which was part of the Seventeenth Army to the north, and it was moved to the Méalte area, north of the battle area. All this meant that there was little reinforcement opposite the French.

Thus, the Germans were left holding the line with a mixture of totally or partially shattered divisions and reserves which had little chance to grasp the situation. The question now was whether they could hold on the following day, especially if the Allied momentum of 8 August was maintained. In the meantime, what had been happening in the skies above the battlefield?

CHAPTER SIX

IN THE AIR

Within the British sector the air space was divided into three sectors –
Northern covering III Corps, Central (Australians), and Southern
(Canadians). In terms of co-operation with the ground forces the air
assets were provided by V Brigade RAF and were allocated as follows:

ROLE	NORTHERN	CENTRAL	SOUTHERN
Corps work	35 Sqn (Armstrong Whitworth)	3 Sqn AFC (RE8)	5 Sqn (RE8)
Tank work	35 Sqn	8 Sqn (Armstrong Whitworth)	8 Sqn
Cavalry/ Armoured Cars	Nil	Nil	6 Sqn (RE8)
Ammunition dropping	9 Sqn (RE8)	9 Sqn	Nil
Smoke laying	Nil	9 Sqn	5 Sqn
Ground strafing	48 Sqn (Bristol fighter) – two flights 80 Sqn (Camel)	41, 84 Sqns (SE5) 201 Sqn (Camel)	23 Sqn (Dolphin) 24 Sqn (SE5) 65,202 Sqns (Camel)

Corps work meant reconnaissance, especially in terms of measuring
the progress of the attack, and artillery co-operation. For working
with the tanks No. 8 Squadron had been specially trained. This
covered a myriad of tasks from helping the tanks keep direction and

reporting on their progress to tank HQs through locating anti-tank guns and ground strafing against targets holding up the advance of the tanks. The same type of role was envisaged for No. 6 Squadron with regard to the cavalry and armoured cars. The ammunition dropping was for machine guns on the objective so that they were better prepared to deal with a counter-attack. It was to be dropped on demand from the ground. The smoke laying aircraft of Nos. 5 and 9 Squadrons would perform this on selected points and at specific times. As far as the ground attack squadrons were concerned all bar No. 65 Squadron, which was to work with the Cavalry, were to send out their aircraft in pairs at half hour intervals from twenty minutes after Zero Hour. In addition, one flight each from Nos. 24 and 84 Squadrons were detailed to attack German observation balloons. While the bulk of No. 48 Squadron was dedicated to ground attack in the Northern Sector its remaining flight was made responsible for reconnaissance at medium altitude throughout the Fourth Army's front.

In terms of communications, each aircraft was to carry distinct markings so that the ground troops could identify its role. Thus aircraft co-operating with the Mark V tanks had a black stripe on either side of the tailplane, while those with the Whippets had a black band on the right tailplane. Corps squadrons had black squares under the wings and ammunition dropping aircraft had the outer two and a half feet of each wing painted black. The machine-gun lorries of Brutinel's Brigade operating on the Amiens–Roye road would have a broad white stripe painted across the bonnet. A variety of signals were to be used. There were to be message dropping centres with distinctive markings on the ground. The infantry were to indicate their position to aircraft by firing red flares, waving metal discs and placing rifles parallel in lines. Aircraft could call on the infantry to indicate their positions by firing white Very lights and using their klaxons. They would also fire parachute flares to indicate German counter-attacks.

The bombers also had an important role to play. These were primarily the province of IX Brigade RAF. It had four day bomber squadrons (Nos. 27, 49, 98, 107), equipped with the DH9, and four night bomber squadrons. Nos. 58 and 83 had the FE2b and Nos. 207 and 215 Squadrons the heavy Handley Page bomber. In addition there were No. 205 Squadron (DH4 – day bombing) and No. 101 Squadron (FE2b – night bombing) from V Brigade. Apart from the Handley Pages of No. 207 Squadron being used during the hours before the attack to drown the noise of the tanks moving up to their assault positions, both day and night bombers were to be used against German airfields, communications (bridges and railway stations) to disrupt the move up of reserves, and known stores dumps. IX Brigade's fighter element, consisting of two SE5 squadrons (Nos. 1, 32) and three of Camels (Nos. 43, 54, 73) would provide protection for the ground attack aircraft and, with Nos. 25 (DH4) and 62 (Bristol fighter) Squadrons, as escorts for the bombers. Finally No. 151 Squadron, with its night fighting Camels, would protect against German night bombers.

The elements of three other RAF brigades were also available. III Brigade had one day bomber squadron (No. 57 – DH4), which was to attack the airfield at Moislans at day break and Etricourt railway station that evening, while No. 102 Squadron (FE2b) would bomb Peronne that night. Its four fighter squadrons (Nos. 3, 56, 60, 87) were to be held in readiness to operate over Fourth Army's front, but were not to be sent out except under the orders of HQ RAF. The Brigade also had a fighter reconnaissance squadron, No 11 with its Bristol fighters. Finally, I Brigade contributed the DH4s of No. 18 Squadron and X Brigade the DH9s of No. 103 Squadron.

The French had also gathered a large air armada consisting of 1,104 aircraft.* This was made up of 180 corps aircraft, six squadrons (65 aircraft) dedicated to reconnaissance and artillery co-operation, two groups of Spad fighters (180 aircraft), two groups of night bombers (52 aircraft), and a complete *Division Aerienne* (432 fighters and 15 day

---

* Wise *Canadian Airmen in the First World War* p.523 gives a figure of 1125 based on the French official history. My figure is taken from Jones *The War in the Air* Vol VI p.435 and Carney *The Western Front: Air Operations May-November 1918*, p.102.

bombers). During the night 7/8 August the French bombers attacked a number of targets and on Z Day itself their day bombers concentrated on places where German reserves were expected to be located and railway stations. The primary mission of the fighters was to ensure air superiority over the First Army's front, but with a significant portion of the *Division Aerienne* being kept in reserve for subsequent days' operations. Fighter ground attack would also be employed and, as with the RAF, attacks against balloons were also emphasized. It was agreed with Fourth Army that neither's aircraft would operate across the inter-army boundary. Furthermore, the French agreed not to attack cavalry because of the difficulty in identifying friend from foe in the air.

It was the day bombers which were first off the ground in the early hours of 8 August. No. 205 Squadron's target was the airfield at Bouvincourt, which lay close to the Roman road some five miles east of Brie. One of the DH4 pilots was Lt William Grossart:

At 3.30am the adjutant woke me. Soon the camp was astir . . . I was soon in the mess in my flying kit drinking my coffee and watching the lads come in in ones and twos, some arm in arm, others giving each other a hearty, more than hearty, 'Good morning!' slap on the back. An air of subdued excitement prevailed. The rumble of distant gunfire broke the silence only to be submerged by the sound of our engines starting up on the aerodrome. Busy mechanics with torches were warming up the engines which this day would never cool.[1]

The DH4s took off at dawn in two formations, a lead one consisting of nine aircraft and the second of eight. Grossart was in the second wave:

The landscape was a mass of flame, the stabs of fire from guns and shells only lighting up a haze of smoke. It was an amazing sight and many were the shells that swept past our planes. The greatest day of the war in the air had begun.[2]

The lead formation arrived over Bouvincourt and dropped a total of thirty-eight 112lb and 25lb bombs, but the observers were unable to see the results. The second wave, however, was not able to locate the target, presumably because of the fog, and attacked Chaulnes railway station instead. They reported that several bombs burst on or close to the target.

Other bomber squadrons also had difficulty in finding their targets. Fourteen DH9s on No. 27 Squadron, escorted by No. 62's Bristol fighters, could not locate St Christ airfield and so dropped their bombs near Peronne. DH9s from No. 98 Squadron were more successful and did manage to drop bombs on St Christ later on in the day. They were attacked by six Pfalzes. Sgts Bush and McDonald, crewing one of the bombers, were forced to fire a Very light at one Pfalz after their gun jammed. McDonald then cleared the stoppage and shot down the German plane. While No. 49 Squadron located Bray railway station and attacked at 500 feet the fog prevented the observers from seeing the results. The same problem beset No. 107 Squadron in its attack on Harbonnières and was aggravated by the smoke of bursting shells. North of the Somme the airfield at Moislains was attacked by ten DH4s of No. 57 Squadron at 8.10 a.m. By now the fog had thinned and the Germans were able to react. The DH4s were attacked by a flight of Fokker DVIIs and by other aircraft which took off from the airfield. The resulting combat saw one German and one British aircraft shot down.

The corps contact squadrons had an even greater problem with the fog. Indeed, the first three Armstrong Whitworths of No. 35 Squadron were forced to land prematurely because of the poor visibility, with one crashing. No. 5 Squadron, which was supporting the Canadian Corps, did manage to get four of its RE8s aloft at 4 a.m. They located some ground targets, which they bombed and machine gunned. It was not, however, until 9 a.m. that the contact patrols were able to achieve anything worthwhile in terms of controlling artillery fire and observing the progress of the attack.

Throughout the morning the ground strafing squadrons were also very active. Each fighter carried four 25lb bombs. It was a role that few pilots enjoyed. The attacks had to be made at very low level, which made them vulnerable to ground fire and to attack by German fighters. One who took part was American Bill Lambert, who had joined the RFC and trained in Canada, and now flying with No. 24 Squadron based at Conteville. He was tasked with ground strafing in the Rosières area:

> The action on the ground is desperate. Debris covers everything below me. Dead horses and men; wagons and gun limbers. Three crashed and burning planes appear, two EA [Enemy Aircraft] and one of ours. Above the noise of my engine I can hear the faint scream of wounded horses. I am on my own and work down to less than 200 feet heading east, looking for trouble. Ground fire is not too bad. Ahead of me, at the edge of a small clump of trees, an enemy machine-gun crew is firing across shell holes at some of our troops about 500 yards away. The nose of 1084 drops and that gun crew appears in my sight. They aim their gun straight at me and I fire a short burst from 100 yards and zoom over the tree tops behind them. A quick turn and back on that gun. No more trouble from them.[3]

Later during the same sortie his fuel tank was holed by ground fire and he was forced to land. After narrowly escaping capture by the Germans he was rescued by a troop of cavalry. Another who was lucky to be able to fight another day was Lt J. M. Mackay of No. 201 Squadron. He was shot down by a Fokker and crash landed 300 yards inside German lines. He made a run for it and met an advancing tank. He climbed into it, but as it was about to go into action Mackay quickly disembarked and made another dash towards his own lines pursued by machine-gun fire and low flying German aircraft. He managed to get through unscathed and eventually got back to his own airfield at Poulainville.[4]

By midday aircraft reports indicated that the Germans were withdrawing and that the roads leading to the River Somme were heavily congested. It was therefore decided to attack the Somme bridges so as to increase the confusion and congestion. The whole of the day bomber force and IX Brigade's scout squadrons were to be involved. Eight DH9s of No. 107 Squadron, accompanied by eleven No. 54 Squadron Camels, took on the bridge at Brie, which carried the Amiens–St Quentin road. The DH9s dropped twelve 112lb bombs and the Camels, operating from low level, dropped nearly fifty 25lb bombs. There were no hits on the bridge and German aircraft were very active, shooting down a DH9 and a Camel. The same two squadrons returned later in the afternoon, but again with no success. Before the onset of darkness two more attacks were made on the bridge. DH4s of No. 205 Squadron claimed one direct hit, but their view was partially obscured by cloud, and then four No. 54 Squadron Camels went in. These two attacks cost another DH4 and four Camels. The road and railway bridges in Peronne were also subjected to repeated attacks by DH9s, Camels and SE5s, but again with little success and in the face of considerable German air opposition.

In the Canadian sector the main targets were the bridges at Bethencourt and Voyennes. Two attacks were made against the former. In the first the German fighters managed to break up the bomber formation before it reached the target and only four out of ten DH9s involved actually attacked it, with two others shot down. The second attempt, again by No. 49 Squadron accompanied by SE5s from No. 32 Squadron, was noteworthy in that the bombers dived to attack from 1,000 feet rather than dropping their bombs from 1,500 feet. As they did so they were attacked by ten Fokkers, which split up the formation. One DH9 was shot down, as was a Fokker, and one direct hit claimed. Interestingly, the SE5s only came across one German scout, which they shot down. The bombers of No. 237 Squadron and No. 73 Squadron's Camels were given the Voyennes bridge as their target. The six bombers actually attacking the bridge came down to 500 feet and below before releasing their bombs, claiming one hit on target. The second attempt saw the bombers attacked by Fokkers when they were at a height of 2,500 feet over the target. Once more the formation was broken up, but the bombers did attack and again at low level. In all some ten tons of bombs were dropped on the bridges, but none were put out of action and a total of eight bombers and eight fighters were lost. Further attacks were made by FE2bs and the night fighters of No. 151 Squadron on the bridges during the night, also with no notable success.

Lack of bombing accuracy, because of the primitive bombsights of the day, and the fact that the bombs themselves were not powerful enough for bridge busting were two reasons why the attacks failed and would continue to fail. The other reason was the German air force. While it had a mere 365 aircraft, including 140 fighters, facing the British Fourth and French First Armies at the beginning of the day, reinforcements were quickly deployed. By the end of it the German Second Army had received almost 300 additional aircraft, including the Richthofen Flying Circus. Its founder, the great ace Manfred von Richthofen (the Red Baron), had been killed on 21 April, and command of it had passed to Hermann Goering. He was on leave when the Allied storm broke and so Manfred's brother Lothar was actually in charge on the day. The Circus arrived during the afternoon and was immediately in action, with Lothar von Richthofen himself claiming three victories. Indeed, honours were about even in terms of aircraft shot down. The RAF suffered 45 aircraft shot down and a further 52 wrecked or badly damaged. Eighty air crew became casualties – 4 killed, 57 missing, and 19 wounded.

The one lesson learned during the day was reflected in the IX Brigade orders for 9 August. The effort against the Somme bridges was to be renewed, but:

It is reported that during today's operations, EA scouts molested our bombers by diving on them from the clouds and preventing them from carrying out their mission effectively. Wing commanders will, therefore, detail scouts for close protection of bombers to ensure that the latter are not interfered with by EA while trying to destroy bridges. This is the sole duty of these scouts who will not, therefore, carry bombs. [5]

The scout pilots would have been relieved to hear this, but whether this would make the bombers any more effective remained to be seen.

CHAPTER SEVEN

WHAT TO DO NEXT?

The Allied media were clear that 8 August was a significant event. The *New York Times* of the following day ran the headline:

HAIG BREAKS FOE'S LINE ON 25 MILE FRONT
GAINS 7 MILES, TAKES 10,000 MEN, 100 GUNS,
GERMAN MAN POWER VISIBLY ON THE WANE

The German press was understandably more muted. The *Freiburger Tagblatt:*

> Between Ancre and Avre the enemy attacked yesterday with strong forces. Assisted by a thick fog, he infiltrated our infantry and artillery lines with his tanks. To the north of the Somme, we threw back the enemy from our positions with our counter-attack. Between the Somme and the Avre we brought the enemy attack to a halt just to the east of the Morcourt – Harbonnières – Caix – Fresnoy – Contoire line. We have suffered losses in prisoners and guns.

On the ground it was clear by the early evening of 8 August that a breakthrough had been achieved, but the question was how it could be exploited. Haig had visited Rawlinson at midday:

> I told Rawlinson . . . to continue to work on the orders already given, namely, to organise his left strongly; if opportunity offers, to advance it to the line Albert – Bray. With his left strongly held he will push his defensive front out to the line Chaulnes –

Roye. Reconnaissance to be pushed forward to the Somme River, while his main effort is directed southeastwards on Roye to help the French. The cavalry should work on the outer flank of the infantry, and move to Chaulnes – Roye as soon as possible.

Later on, at 4 p.m., he saw Debeney and urged him to 'join hands' with Rawlinson at Roye and get his cavalry forward 'as soon as possible' to operate on the right of the Fourth Army.[1]

Fourth Army issued fresh orders that evening. That there was a delay in issuing them was admitted by Rawlinson's chief of staff in a post-war article on the battle: 'What actually happened was that everyone was so busy congratulating everyone else on their share in the victory that valuable time was lost in preparing for an advance next day.'[2] On the other hand, the passage of information was often slow. Thus, not until 8.45 p.m. did HQ Fourth Army receive the news that Cayeux Wood had been secured by Whippets at 4 p.m. and from Monash that his troops were advancing along Warfusée road towards the Red Line. Consequently it took time to establish the true situation.[3] Until this could be done it was difficult to issue meaningful orders. The next day's intention was to establish a line running from Roye in the south through Chaulnes and Bray-sur-Somme to Dernacourt in the north. This represented a further advance of up to 10,000 yards. This time the main role was to be carried out by the Canadian Corps, which was ordered to advance to the line Roye–Hattencourt–Hullu, the last named lying midway between the villages of Chilly and Punchy. Its boundaries were inclusive of the Amiens–Nesle railway on the left and the Amiens–Roye road on the right. General Currie was to decide his own Zero Hour and inform the Australians in good time.

There was, however, a problem. Newly arrived in the Fourth Army area, although still in GHQ Reserve, was the 32nd Division. Brigadier General N. W. Webber, Currie's British Chief of Staff, records:

About 4pm on 8th, Army Commander with ADC only [sic] arrived at Corps Adv. HQ. at Gentelles – Corps Comdr was out on a visit to Div HQ. Plans for 9th were discussed & I asked for 32nd Divn from Army Reserve to be placed at our disposal – Rawly agreed & plans were drafted accordingly.*

On Currie's return situation was explained & he agreed to an advance at 5am: 1st & 2nd Divns on one Brigade front each, 4th Dvn to clean up the corner next to the Roye Road & 32nd Divn then to pass thro' 4th on two Bde front & continue advance.

The necessary orders were on the point of being sent out when at about 6.30pm I got a wire from MGGS [Rawlinson's chief of staff Maj Gen Montgomery] cancelling Army Comdr's order re 32nd Divn & ordering me to return to Dury [Canadian Corps Main HQ] (for which Corps Comdr had already left) for telephone conversation.

Road thro' Boves hopelessly blocked by 32nd Divn, prisoners, lorries of all sorts etc & I didn't reach Dury and the telephone till about 8.30pm.

MGGS very irate with Army Comdr for daring to give away 32nd Divn & with myself for aiding and abetting.

Told him that 3rd [Canadian] Divn would have to be moved up to undertake role proposed for 32nd Divn & that fresh orders would have to be got out. As wires forward were none too reliable orders would have to go by Despatch Rider & motor car & consequently, owing to congestion of roads, impossible to keep to 5am start.[4]

As for the 32nd Division, it had been acting as the reserve to II Corps in Flanders when it received a warning order on 4 August to be prepared for a rail move on the 6th. On 7 August entraining began, by which time the Division knew it was bound for Fourth Army. Indeed, the GOC, Major General Thomas Lambert, had been

* That Rawlinson had released the 32nd Division to Currie is confirmed by an entry in the HQ Canadian Corps war diary (TNA WO 95/1053). This is of a telephone message received from Rawlinson at 7 p.m., in which he stated that the Corps was to 'push on beyond it [the Blue Dotted Line] in the direction of Chaulnes and Roye ... 32nd Division can be brought up as already arranged and is placed at disposal of Canadian Corps.'

ordered to report to HQ Fourth Army on his arrival, which he did on the afternoon of 7 August. He was briefed by General Montgomery, who let in him into the plan for the morrow and said that his division was to be prepared to join the Canadian Corps and would likely become engaged in the battle on the second day. Lambert then went on to the Canadian Corps HQ to learn of the intended role for the Division. Meanwhile, the immediate aim was for the 32nd Division to be concentrated in Boves Wood by midday on the 8th, but this was easier said than done. For a start, the three detraining stations for the division were all more than 20 miles away from the wood. The first train, which had been due at 10 a.m. on the 7th arrived some five hours late and since it was estimated that it would take some 20 hours to detrain the complete division, excluding its artillery, it was clear that to concentrate it by midday on the 8th in Boves Wood was impossible. Although GHQ released it to Fourth Army at 5.20 p.m. on 8 August, according to the 32nd Division's report on the battle[5] it had been decided on the evening of 7 August not to commit it on the 9th and that it should continue to concentrate in Boves Wood. The orders, though, were subsequently changed to the area adjoining Gentelles Wood, probably because Boves Wood lay in the French sector and would have also entailed a much longer subsequent move forward. Not until midnight on the 8th was the 32nd Division, less its artillery, complete there. As for the artillery it did not complete its concentration in the Cagny–Longeau area until 1 p.m. on 9 August. It would therefore appear that when they had their discussion on the afternoon of the 8th neither Rawlinson nor Webber were aware of or had forgotten that the decision had been made the previous evening not to use the 32nd Division on Day 2 of the battle.*

---

* According to Edmonds *1918* vol 4 p.86 Rawlinson had ordered the 32nd Division to move to the Domart area prior to visiting the Canadian Corps HQ. He also ordered the 17th Division to deploy to Daours, just west of Corbie and on the north bank of the Somme, and the 63rd Division to Contay–Rubempré, 15 miles west of Albert. The intention was to give both the Australians and III Corps another division as well, although the positioning of 17th Division indicates that Rawlinson wanted to retain the option of using it to support III Corps.

Be that as it may, Canadian Corps HQ had to do some hurried redrafting of its orders. GOC 1st Canadian Division was summoned to a conference at Corps HQ at 7 p.m., while the 2nd Canadian Division received its orders at 7.55 p.m. Given the communications problems, Zero Hour was postponed until 10 a.m. to allow the orders to be disseminated in reasonable time. The GOC 1st Canadian Division duly reported to Corps HQ and was told of the outline plan. He was to attack in the centre, with the 2nd Canadian Division on his left and the 3rd Division on the right. The Corps objective was to be the line of the road running from Méharicourt in the north through Rouvroy-en-Santerre to Bouchoir in the south. It was hoped that 14 tanks would be available to support the Division. The GOC then decided to attack with two brigades and en route to his Advanced Divisional HQ, which had just opened in Stove Wood, he called in to brief the commander of his 1st Brigade, which would be the right hand assault brigade. After calling in at Stove Wood he set off on horseback to visit HQ 2nd Brigade, the other assault brigade. He then returned to Stove Wood at about midnight and issued confirmatory orders. In the meantime, shortly before 11 p.m., his Rear Divisional HQ received a wire from Corps HQ. This stressed that the time of the main assault was dependent on the 4th Canadian Division gaining the uncaptured section of the Dotted Blue Line in the south, of the Canadian sector, in particular Le Quesnel, which it was to do during the night. There was no telephone communication with Divisional Advanced HQ and so this message had to be sent by despatch rider, who found navigation difficult in the dark and did not arrive at Stove Wood until after 4 a.m. In the meantime the Rear HQ had managed to get a line through to the 1st Canadian Brigade and the Corps message was relayed by hand of officer to the 1st Canadian Division's Advanced HQ at 1.30 a.m. Three quarters of an hour later General Webber telephoned Rear HQ to say that Zero Hour would now be at 10 a.m. At the same time a telephone link was finally established between the 1st Division's Rear and Advanced HQs, but it was not possible to telephone the Corps Report Centre from Stove Wood.

The 1st Canadian Division now faced another problem. It was, of course, holding the line, but the sector held by the 2nd Brigade was to be used by the 2nd Canadian Division for its attack. The GOC of the 1st Division wanted the 2nd Division to relieve the Brigade prior to the attack since otherwise it would have to wait until the former had passed through it. At 2.35 a.m. this request was sent to the Corps Report Centre via Rear Headquarters. The reply came back that this would have to be arranged by the two divisions. The period of darkness was too short for the relief and to carry it out in daylight was not feasible given the exposed nature of the front line defences. Consequently, the divisional attack plan had to be recast. The two 2nd Brigade battalions holding the line would remain in place and in their place the Brigade would take two battalions of the 3rd Brigade, which was in reserve, under command. This took further frantic telephoning to arrange. Thus there was little if any sleep for the divisional and brigade staffs.

The 2nd Canadian Division's communications were in a better state and they received their orders from Corps at 8.55 p.m. The Division would also make its attack with two brigades, the 5th and 6th, but it was not until 12.50 a.m. that Corps stated that Zero Hour would be 10 a.m. There then appears to have been a change of mind, for the 2nd Division issued further orders at 2.35 a.m. stating that the 6th Canadian Brigade was be 'the Advanced Guard', with the 5th Brigade following and prepared to support the left flank, and the 4th Brigade moving behind.

The 3rd Canadian Division issued its orders at 5.25 a.m. on the 9th. It had, however, already received 'Tentative Instructions' late the previous evening to be prepared to advance down the Amiens–Roye road. This, however, was dependent on the capture of Le Quesnel. Arrangements for this had been made on the evening of the 8th and a Zero Hour fixed for 4.30 a.m. The task was given to the 75th Battalion. The Commanding Officer, Lt Col C. C. Harbottle DSO, decided to attack the village from the north while creating a frontal feint. Accordingly, taking advantage of a reverse slope he deployed two companies to make this attack prior to Zero Hour. Meanwhile both field and heavy artillery had been bombarding the village. Promptly at 4.30 a.m. the attack began. The Battalion soon came under heavy fire from Le Quesnel and the high ground to its south and forced it to go to ground. Harbottle then came up and identified a nest of machine guns on the outskirts of the village. Crawling forward with his leading elements, he then led them in a rush and overpowered the guns. This unlocked the defences and by 5.30 a.m. the village was in Canadian hands. It turned out to have been a divisional HQ. Further heavy fighting took place in the woods adjoining Le Quesnel in the south before the 75th Battalion reached the Blue Dotted Line. Harbottle's gallantry and leadership earned him a bar to his DSO and the way was now set for the Canadian Corps to launch its main attack. But, as we shall see, there would be further problems.

Turning now to the Australian Corps, Monash had as early as midday on 8 August warned his divisional commanders that the attack would likely continue on the following day with the emphasis being in the south. The 2nd and 3rd Australian Divisions were put on one hour's notice to move, the former from 4 p.m. that afternoon and the latter from 3 a.m. on the 9th, although no move was expected before 5 a.m. In the meantime both divisions were to continue to reorganize and re-equip. The Fourth Army orders stated that the Australian Corps was to advance on the line Méricourt– Framerville– Lihons. In the north the task was little more than tidying up since the continuing German hold on the Chipilly Spur would make any significant advance very difficult. Otherwise the Australians were to form a strong defensive flank to the Canadian Corps. Zero Hour for the right hand Australian sector would be that of the Canadians, while on the left it would be dependent on that of III Corps, which, like the Canadians, would decide its own.

The plan was for the 5th Australian Division on the left and 1st Australian Division on the right to carry out the initial attack and then for the 2nd Australian Division to pass through the 1st Division and continue with the 5th Division to the final objective. In view of the uncertainty around the Chipilly Spur the 4th Australian Division was ordered not to advance. At midnight the 1st Australian Division, which had remained in reserve, was ordered to move to the Harbonnières area beginning at 8 a.m. on the 9th with its 2nd Brigade, the 1st Brigade following an hour later. During the night the 5th Australian Division had pushed out patrols towards to the Amiens Defence Line, which they reported to be lightly held. They also noted much railway activity in Vauvillers. Indeed, the impression was that the Germans were thinning out as part of a withdrawal operation. Accordingly, the two battalions concerned, the 57th and 59th, were ordered to follow up any withdrawal, which they did, occupying the old Amiens Line by 8 a.m. on 9 August.

Meanwhile, Monash had sent out a further warning order confirming that the attack was to be resumed, but its extent was dependent on how the Canadians got on. While the Zero Hour was not yet known it was unlikely to be before 10 a.m. The divisions involved were to be prepared to move at short notice from 7 a.m. onwards. This created particular problems for the 1st Australian Division. Having been in reserve on the previous day, its HQ had established itself in Villers Bretonneux the previous afternoon. Its two assault brigades (2nd and 3rd) were not, however, complete in their assembly areas in Hamel and Aubigny until midnight. A warning order was sent to these two brigades stating that the 2nd Brigade was to be prepared to advance at 6 a.m., and the 3rd Brigade an hour later. An order then came through to move as planned. The 2nd Brigade, whose HQ was in Corbie, received this at 7.20 a.m. and then had to send out despatch riders to pass the message to its battalions. Consequently it was not until 9 a.m. that the Brigade was wholly on the march and it faced a 10 mile hike to reach its start line. Meanwhile, the brigade commanders were brought by car to divisional HQ to receive their orders and were given a Zero Hour of 11 a.m.

The Cavalry Corps would, in line with Haig's instructions to Rawlinson of the previous day, also be involved. The 1st Cavalry Division would operate on the left with the Australians and the 2nd Cavalry Division on the right. Their instructions were to advance with the infantry and to exploit any opportunity. The Whippets of the 3rd and 6th Tank Battalions would also operate with the cavalry, the idea being that they would be used to clear the cavalry's path of machine guns when the moment for breaking out came. Each battalion was able to provide 24 tanks. As for the heavy tanks, casualties, due both to enemy action and mechanical failures, meant that only 95 were available.

North of the Somme III Corps faced a dilemma. General Butler had a conversation with General Montgomery shortly before 8 p.m. on 8 August. He stated that the 18th Division was not capable, as it stood, of renewing the attack on the morrow. He was, however, deploying reserves, which would give the 18th Division three and possibly four battalions and the 58th Division five battalions available for an attack. In addition he had ordered the 131st US Infantry Regiment to deploy behind the 12th Division as a reserve. He could also deploy the 132nd US Infantry, but this would not be very satisfactory since they had entered the trenches only the previous night for training by platoons under the umbrella of the 47th Division. In summary, General Butler said that if he attacked on the 9th he was concerned that the Germans would immediately counter-attack and regain ground and that he would prefer to wait until the next day. If the attack was being resumed on the morrow then he offered to use two battalions to clear Gressaire Wood. The Fourth Army reply was that the attack would continue on the 9th and that the Americans should relieve the 18th Division. Accordingly, at 10.15 p.m. Butler issued attack orders. The 12th Division would assault on the left and the 58th Division, with the US 131st Infantry on its right, on the right. They were to clear Morlencourt, Gressaire Wood and beyond. The 18th Division would continue to hold its present line, with the 37th Brigade (less one battalion) reverting to the 12th Division for the attack and the 36th Brigade returning to it once the attack had passed through. Just over three hours later there was a change of heart. It had been assumed that the Chipilly Spur had been secured. Indeed, the corps commander had stated in his discussion with Fourth Army's chief of staff that the line in this sector ran just south of Gressaire Wood. The fault appears to lie with a report by a contact aircraft that British troops were on the spur. In any event, once it became clear that the Germans retained both Chipilly and the spur Butler ordered the 58th Division to form a force to capture both. He then postponed the main attack, although the troops were to be prepared to carry it out at short notice.

The Chipilly attack was aimed for dawn, but this proved to be hopelessly optimistic. The 175th was detailed for the attack, but two of the battalions, the 8th Londons (174th Brigade) and 5th Royal Berkshires (37th Brigade) were on loan. The US 131st Regiment would attack on the right of this brigade. The morning of 8 August had found the Regiment with its battalions scattered and astride the Amiens–Albert road. At midday it was put on notice to move and at 4.30 p.m. Colonel Joseph Sanborn, the regimental commander, was informed by III Corps that the 131st were to come under command of the 58th Division and were to concentrate in Heilly and Franvillers astride the Amiens–Albert road and some six miles from the latter. The 1st and 2nd Battalions were in position by about 8.45 p.m. and Colonel Sanborn informed III Corps of this, stating that his third battalion would arrive later that night and the machine-gun company the next morning. He was instructed to go to HQ 18th Division for orders and it was here at 10 p.m. he was ordered by the 58th Division to move his regiment to an assembly area 3,000 yards south of Heilly. They were then to form up facing eastwards and be ready to attack at 1 a.m. Sanborn protested that he was still lacking a good part of his command and that there had been no chance to reconnoitre the ground. Furthermore he had had no opportunity to organize his supplies with his parent formation, the US 66th Brigade. III Corps therefore postponed the attack and instead ordered the Regiment to move further forward to a new assembly area in the steep valley between Vaux-sur-Somme and Sailly-le-See. This took the remainder of the night, with the 18th and 58th Divisions providing guides for the Americans. The remainder of the morning would be spent in preparing for the attack and, for the Americans at least, getting some much needed sleep.

Back to the Canadian sector, on the right, with Le Quesnel now secured, the 3rd Canadian Division was to pass through the 4th Division and proceed with the capture of Folies. It issued orders to this effect at 5.25 a.m. The 8th Brigade, which had spent the night in bivouacs south of Demuin on the original Green Line, was to lead the way, setting off at 8 a.m. and was to be in its assembly area by 10 a.m. The lead battalion was the 5th Canadian Mounted Rifles. The brigade commander met the divisional commander at 9.15 a.m. and was told to pass two battalions through the 11th Brigade, which was holding the line. They were not to stop in the assembly area but were to continue down the Amiens–Roye road. Brigadier General Draper then went off on a reconnaissance with General Brutinel, whose command was continuing to operate along the Amiens–Roye road, with elements helping in clearing the woods immediately south of Le Quesnel. The divisional commander himself ordered the 5th CMR to press on through the designated assembly area. The battalion was then met by the Brigade Major who told them that General Draper would give out his orders once he had returned from his reconnaissance. Consequently it was not until 12 p.m. that the 5th CMR and the 4th CMR, which was also to take part, received their orders. They were to capture Folies, some 3,000 yards beyond Le Quesnel, and, if possible, Bouchoir, 1,000 yards to its south. The 4th CMR was to be on the left and 5th CMR on the right. The southern boundary would be the Amiens–Roye road. The two battalions then pushed on to the start line, which was the Hangest–Le Quesnel road. En route the 5th CMR was told that the French were held up by machine guns to the south-east of Le Quesnel. The 5th CMR arrived at its start line at 1.50 p.m. and the CO, Major W. Rhoades DSO MC, gave out his orders, but at the time no Zero Hour was designated. Then four tanks from the 5th Tank Battalion arrived to support the 5th CMR attack, while another three went to the 4th CMR. Guns of the 9th Canadian Field Artillery Brigade were also to be used. Throughout this time there was considerable scattered shelling and machine-gun fire from the Germans, which did cause some casualties.

Finally, at 2.50 p.m. the attack got underway. Two tanks quickly dealt with the machine guns which had been holding up the French and thereafter the advance proceeded relatively smoothly. By 4.20 p.m. the Canadians had entered Folies and Germans could be seen withdrawing from Arvillers, which lay in the French sector south of the Amiens–Roye road. However, according to the 1st Canadian Battalion (1st Division) it was they who captured Folies since neither of the two CMR battalions had reached it. This makes sense since, as we shall see, its Zero Hour was considerably in advance of that of the 8th Brigade. By 5 p.m. Bouchoir had also been seized by the 5th CMR, but with the French still behind, a defensive flank had to be formed along the main road. It was now clear that the Germans were evacuating Arvillers and so a platoon supported by a tank was sent to occupy it. German transport was seen leaving the village and it was suggested to a British cavalry squadron which had just arrived in the 5th CMR area that they could round it up, but they demurred. Instead an officer, sergeant and two men of the Canadian Light Horse who had reported to the 5th CMR to act as scouts volunteered to carry this out:

The party galloped forward and succeeded in turning back the head of the column (first three wagons) and had returned some 300 yards, when some Huns who had been concealed in a dugout in the vicinity, opened fire on them with machine guns. The Officer and Sergeant, first shooting the lead horses, managed to get back. One of the men was wounded and the other remained out to guard the prisoners and his wounded comrade. As the French were now beginning to move on ARVILLERS and our own situation was well in hand, a platoon of A Coy under Lieut W. H. A. SHORT and one tank were ordered to round up this enemy convoy, and bring in the two CLH men and their prisoners. Subsequently this party had to be recalled before accomplishing their object, on account of the French putting down a rolling barrage on ARVILLERS. This barrage also necessitated the recall of the platoon and tank mopping up ARVILLERS.[6]

The French subsequently occupied Arvillers at 7 p.m., deploying outposts 500 yards to the east. As for the two CLH men, the 5th CMR sent out an officer's patrol that night in an effort to locate them. They found the wounded man, who had succumbed, but there was no trace of the other. In all, though, the 8th Canadian Brigade could feel pleased with itself at accomplishing its objectives at a cost of some 120 casualties.

The 1st Canadian Division had, as we have seen, experienced communication difficulties during the night and had also had to recast its attack plan because of the impossibility of getting the 2nd Division to relieve its 2nd Brigade in the line prior to the attack. Difficulties in getting its other troops forward in time forced a postponement of Zero Hour to 11 a.m. But it was then found that the artillery would not be in position by that time and so there was a further postponement. At 11 a.m. Divisional HQ received news that not only Le Quesnel had been captured by the 4th Canadian Division but Beaufort, 3,000 yards further east, as well. This put a totally new complexion on the attack, for the 1st Canadian Brigade had been ordered to capture Beaufort and then Rouvroy, 3,000 yards further east. Now its start line could be advanced to Beaufort, but this meant redrafting the existing orders. No sooner had this been done than the CO of the 87th Battalion (4th Division) informed the commander of the 1st Brigade that the Germans still held Beaufort and the ground in front of it. Again the orders had to be changed. By this time the two battalions which were to lead the attack, 1st (Western Ontario) and 2nd (Eastern Ontario), were on their way to the assembly area and had to be halted while their COs gave out verbal orders, with Zero Hour now stipulated as 1.15 p.m. No tanks were available and the attack would be supported by two batteries of the divisional machine-gun battalion, as well as the guns of the 1st Brigade Canadian Field Artillery.

At 1.30 p.m. the lead battalions set off from the assembly area in artillery formation but changed to an extended order formation when they began to be fired on by machine guns. The 1st Battalion passed through the 87th Battalion and soon came under further machine-gun fire from the front and from small woods on the high ground to the right near Folies. The latter threatened to disrupt the advance and so A Company was ordered to deal with this opposition, which it did, as well as seizing Folies, which, of course was outside the right hand brigade boundary. Two platoons were then deployed to the southern part of the village to provide a defensive flank and were relieved by the 5th CMR. The advance continued but came up against a strong German position to the east of Folies. The lead companies carried out a double envelopment and some sixty Germans surrendered. The Battalion then consolidated some 1,000 yards west of Rouvroy. The 2nd Battalion's primary objective was Beaufort. This entailed clearing the woods to its west and north, which contained a number of machine guns. With the help of tanks this was achieved. Emerging into the more open country east of the village some Germans were spotted preparing a counter-attack but were dispersed with Lewis gun fire. German artillery and machine-gun fire now began to inflict casualties on the Eastern Ontario Regiment. But by advancing in short rushes they drove the Germans back into Rouvroy. Two more tanks now arrived and helped to drive the German machine guns out of the woods around the north of the village, while a detachment of 11th Hussars entered the southern part of Rouvroy. The 2nd Battalion claimed to have secured the village, but this does not accord with the accounts of the other two battalions in the brigade.

The 4th Battalion (Central Ontario Regiment) was in support and followed 600 yards behind the lead battalions. It initially came under artillery fire from both Folies and Rouvroy, which became more intense when the line Warvillers–Folies was reached and both the support and reserve companies had to deploy in order to keep the momentum going. The left hand forward company then managed to reach Rouvroy and got as far as its church but was then held up. The remainder of the battalion went firm on the Rouvroy–Folies road, machine-gun fire from the high ground running south from Rouvroy bringing the advance to a halt. The 3rd Battalion (Toronto Regiment) was in brigade reserve and took up a position along the eastern edge of Beaufort Wood at 4.15 p.m. Seventy minutes later it received orders from Brigade that the 2nd Battalion was held up in Rouvroy and so the Toronto men were to attack the village. The assault got underway at 7.15 p.m. and was successful, with Rouvroy fully secured after two hours.

The task of the 2nd Canadian Brigade, which was to the north of the 1st Brigade, was to secure the Rouvroy–Méharicourt road. It would mean side slipping to the right to give room for the 2nd Canadian Division's attack. At a conference held at Brigade HQ at 3 a.m. on 9 August it was decided that the 5th and 8th Battalions would lead the way, with the 7th Battalion in support and the 10th Battalion in reserve. One tank company would also be available. But it then became clear that the 7th and 10th Battalions could not be relieved in the line until the 2nd Canadian Division had passed through them. Hence, the 2nd Brigade was loaned the 14th and 15th Battalions. It was now realized that because the Brigade had to move some 3,500 yards south before making the attack the 10 a.m. Zero Hour was too ambitious. Accordingly it was put back to 1 p.m. The lead battalions crossed the start line on time, even though the tanks had not yet arrived. The 5th Battalion (Western Cavalry) was on the right and advanced in 'sectional rushes' in the face of heavy machine-gun fire. Although the ground was flat and open, growing crops provided some concealment. In this way they entered the German front line defences and then paused for 30 minutes to allow units on the flanks to catch up. The next objectives were Warvillers and the wood to its north, both taken with little trouble. Another pause to allow both tanks and the 1st Canadian Brigade on the right to catch up and the Western Cavalry moved on to the Vrély–Rouvroy road and consolidated. By this time, though, the CO, second-in-command, and adjutant had all been wounded.

On the left, the 8th Battalion (90th Rifles) had a much harder time. It faced heavy machine-gun fire from the outset. The fact that the German machine guns were deployed in depth meant that as soon as one nest was subdued fire was continued by other positions in the rear. Even so, the Rifles managed to maintain momentum until reaching a wood 1,500 yards north of Beaufort. Although subjected to intense fire from here, the Battalion managed to overcome the opposition and took some 300 prisoners, as well as a considerable number of machine guns. Having cleared the wood the advance continued, with the German fire not quite so intense, but even so the Battalion continued to suffer casualties, among them their CO Major T. H. Raddall DSO:

When part of the attack was momentarily held up Major RADDALL, with the utmost coolness, walked forward and inquired where the trouble lay. The words had hardly left his mouth when he was hit by a machine gun bullet and instantly killed.[7]

Further serious opposition was met in another wood 1,000 yards further on, but was overcome by encircling it. The Rifles then reached Warvillers, where there was further fighting in the outskirts and woods just to the north-east before it was secured. One company of the 14th Battalion was sent to reinforce the 8th Battalion during the advance but otherwise it and the 15th Battalion were not actively engaged, although the latter suffered considerable casualties from machine-gun fire as it followed the 5th Battalion.

The 2nd Canadian Division was the left hand Canadian assault division. It received orders from Corps HQ at 12.50 a.m. that the advance was to continue towards the Roye–Chaulnes line. At 2.35 a.m. the Division issued its orders to the brigades, stipulating that the 6th Brigade would act as advanced guard, with 5th Brigade following and paying particular attention to the left flank since it was not clear at that stage that the Australians were intending to attack. A later message gave Zero Hour as 10 a.m. and it was then confirmed that the Australians would be advancing. Because the German defences were stronger than originally expected the plan was recast. The 2nd Canadian Division now had the more limited objective of advancing to the line Rosières–Vrély in conjunction with the 1st Australian Division on the left and the 1st Canadian division. The 5th

Brigade would attack through the 2nd Canadian Brigade, with the 6th Brigade on its left. The revised Zero Hour of 11 a.m. was also given. A company of tanks from the 14th Tank Battalion, which was currently leaguered in a gully at Harbonnières, would support the attack, the bulk of them going to the 5th Brigade. Fresh orders were hastily given out to the battalions and the 5th Brigade moved to an assembly area east of Caix. At 11 a.m., however, it was clear to Brigadier General J. G. Ross, the brigade commander, that the 2nd Canadian Brigade was not ready and had been given a new Zero Hour of 1 p.m. In addition, his own brigade was not complete in the assembly area. Hence the 11 a.m. Zero Hour did not appear feasible.

On the other flank, the 6th Canadian Brigade was primarily concerned over the Australian intentions. Therefore the Brigade Major visited HQ 13th Australian Brigade west of Guillaucourt in the company of the Australian liaison officer from that brigade at 9.20 a.m. to find out what could be done if the Australian attack was delayed. At this time Zero Hour was still set at 10 a.m., but the Australians stated that they could not hope to meet this time. The commander of the 15th Australian brigade then asked the GOC 5th Australian Division if he could attack and gain the line of the light railway running south from Harleville. This was agreed and the Brigade Major returned to his HQ, with Zero Hour now 11 a.m. Even though neither the 15th Australian Brigade nor the 5th Canadian Brigade were able to meet this new Zero Hour the 6th Canadian Brigade launched its attack, aware that its flanks would be in the air and that the supporting tanks had not yet arrived. Its battalions were also required to advance across an open plain, which made them easy targets for the German machine guns and artillery. The latter, which had been engaging the Australian artillery deploying in the open near Harbonnières, switched on to the Canadians twenty minutes after Zero Hour, while the machine guns were especially active along the Amiens–Roye railway, which represented the boundary with the Australians, and from the church and other buildings in Rosières. However, by skilful use of fire and movement the attack kept going. The five tanks detailed to support the Brigade then began to appear, although one was directed across the railway to help out the Australians. The 28th Battalion, which was in support, tried to screen the other tanks from view by the German gunners by throwing smoke grenades on the right and windward flank. This proved ineffective and three were knocked out by the German guns before reaching Rosières. The commander of one of these, seeing that one company of the 31st Battalion on the right had lost all its officers, took command of the men and led them forward on foot until he was killed. The final tank did reach Rosières and helped in its capture, but was knocked out in the village. The 9th Cavalry Brigade, which had some Whippets under command, also helped by sending some to help the Australians, thus relieving the pressure on the left flank, while one operated with the 6th Brigade, but was knocked out by a field gun. By 1.30 p.m. Rosières had been cleared, but efforts to advance beyond the village were met by intense machine-gun fire. This brought the advance to a halt and, as a gap had opened between the 29th and 31st Battalions, which were leading the advance, a company from the 28th Battalion was brought up to fill this. The main opposition to a further advance was coming from Lihons and the high ground beyond it, but this lay in the Australian sector. The Germans also attempted to put in a counter-attack, debussing some 1,000 men from lorries, but they were driven back by Lewis gun and rifle fire.

Meanwhile, although it was not complete in its assembly area east of Caix, the 5th Canadian Brigade was told that the 6th Brigade had begun its attack at 11 a.m. and was itself to advance as quickly as possible in order to protect the latter's right flank. The 22nd Battalion therefore moved off at 11.45 a.m., followed by the 25th Battalion. Heavy machine gun fire was encountered from the start, but the attacking battalions were able to overcome it by using scouts to identify dead ground along which Lewis gun teams made their way until they were in a position to engage the machine guns from a flank until they were put out of action or forced to withdraw. The riflemen remained under cover until this had been achieved and then, at a signal, resumed their advance. This tactic prevented heavy casualties and by 3.15 p.m. Vrély had been cleared. It was only now that the tanks caught up. Matters, however, were not helped when a shell wounded the brigade commander and his intelligence officer and killed both the brigade major and the GSO3 2nd Canadian Division, who was acting as liaison officer. The CO of the 22nd Battalion, Lt Col Tremblay, took over command and the advance continued, reaching a line some 500 yards west of Méharicourt by 5.30 p.m. The Brigade then consolidated. This and Australian success on the left enabled the 6th Canadian Brigade to push further forward and the 29th Battalion captured the sugar factory south of Rosières at 4 p.m. The final line reached ran from north of Méharicourt through Rosières and then 700 yards north to the railway embankment. The 9th Cavalry Brigade managed to send patrols east of Méharicourt and towards Chilly, which brought back some useful information. That some 200 machine guns were captured during the day gave indication of the strength of the German defences in this sector.

To the left of the Canadians, the 1st Australian Division had planned a two phase attack. Initially its 2nd Brigade would assault and this would be joined by the 3rd Australian Brigade on its left for the second phase. Fourteen Mark Vs from the 2nd Tank Battalion were to be in support. As we have seen, however, the 2nd Brigade had too far to march to make the original 10 a.m. Zero Hour and it was agreed that the 15th Australian Brigade (5th Division), which was holding the line would attack in conjunction with the Canadians on the right. The two support battalions in this brigade were ordered to make the attack and received their orders at about 9.45 a.m. Both were quickly on the move, but they clearly could not meet the laid down Zero Hour. The brigade commander therefore ordered the 57th Battalion, which was holding the line immediately next to the Canadians to co-operate with them. Zero Hour was then changed to 11 a.m., but the 57th Battalion had already moved. Thus, at 10.50 a.m. the 60th Battalion crossed the start line, passed through the 57th Battalion, and continued the attack. There was initially no supporting artillery fire and again the German machine-gun fire was intense. It took almost two hours to advance 600 yards. On the left the 58th Battalion's first opposition came from the area of the railway station that lay between Harbonnières and Vauvillers. The latter also proved a problem, not only to the 58th Battalion, but also to the 28th Battalion (2nd Australian Division) on its left. The last available tank was called up to deal with the trouble, but it was knocked out by an antitank gun in the village. Nevertheless, the Brigade managed to reach the Green Line which was represented by the road running due south from Vauvillers by 2 p.m.

Meanwhile, the troops of the 2nd Australian Brigade had been making their way to the original start line. This necessitated a five hour march along dusty roads and across broken country on what was a very warm day. The 7th and 8th Battalions eventually crossed the start line at 1.40 p.m. They faced an initial 4,000 yards advance across an open plain which was dominated by Lihons Hill, on which rested the village of that name and which was the ultimate objective. They were subjected to artillery fire from Lihons Hill and also to attacks by low flying German aircraft, but by keeping a very open formation casualties were kept down. The two battalions passed through the 15th Brigade and began their assault.

As far as the 7th Battalion, which was on the left, was concerned:

The ground over which we were to advance was a gentle slope for the first half mile or so, when we passed over a low ridge, then almost flat for the remainder of the distance, rising sharply to the red line – our objective – about 4000 yards off. This last rise gave the enemy a perfect view of our movements during the whole advance, and was, moreover, a difficult spot to attack. It contained a network of trenches and gunpits, and marked the spot where the line had run prior to the German offensive in March. The whole battlefield was covered only by short grass, except for an occasional copse; many old trenches served as cover for the defenders, but gave no assistance to the attackers. The position would be a formidable one to attack at any time, but we were to advance against it with no artillery barrage.[8]

Worse was to come. Two field guns had been made available to support the Battalion, with two Gunner officers attached to Battalion HQ to control their fire. These two individuals apparently vanished thus removing the means of utilizing these guns. Then, as they passed through the 15th Brigade south of Vauvillers they came under heavy machine-gun fire to the front and from the left. This was unexpected since they thought that the forward elements of the 15th Brigade were further forward and that they would provide some covering fire. Worse, it soon became apparent that their left flank was exposed because the 2nd Australian Division had not yet begun to attack. Nonetheless, the 7th Battalion continued to advance and by 4 p.m. had reached the foot of Lihons Hill. The hill itself was riddled with trenches but, with plentiful use of rifle grenades, the Germans were steadily forced back. By 6.30 p.m. the Battalion had reached the crest and within half an hour had linked up with the 8th Battalion on the right. The left flank remained exposed, however, and a company from the 5th Battalion was deployed to cover it. The action had cost the 7th Battalion 238 casualties, including all four company commanders, but 100 prisoners had been made and the captured material included four howitzers of varying calibres, grenade launchers, machine guns and a complete field hospital.

The 8th Battalion also had a tough time. It quickly lost all but one of its supporting tanks and its two supporting guns failed to appear. As the Battalion History put it, 'the battle now developed into a purely infantry operation of a series of section rushes using fire and movement.'[9] At one point the Brigade commander, Brigadier General Heane, asked Lt Col Mitchell whether his battalion was capable of capturing its sector of Lihons Hill. The reply was in the affirmative provided that Mitchell could use his own method of attack. That the assault was successful was largely due to two men, Private Robert Beatham and Lance Corporal William Nottingham. On reaching the main German position the former, assisted by the latter, dashed forward and, with the use of bombs, killed or captured the crews of four machine guns. Once the crest was reached Beatham attacked another machine gun, but fell riddled with bullets. His selfless courage was later recognized by the award of a posthumous VC. Yet, since the Canadian advance had not reached this far the right half of the Battalion was suffering from an exposed flank and was unable reach the final objective.

The 2nd Australian Division's objective was Framerville, where the armoured cars had operated with such success the previous day. The original intention was that the attack should be made by the 5th and 6th Brigades, but the 7th Brigade was then substituted for the 6th. The plan was to attack at 11 a.m. and at 8 a.m. all three brigade commanders were instructed to meet the divisional commander at HQ 7th Brigade at 9.30 a.m. for orders. It was agreed that the 5th Brigade would attack on the left and the 7th Brigade on the right. There would be no artillery barrage, although the guns would engage specific targets. Fourteen Mark V Stars would be available, together with some Stokes mortars. With the brigades some 5 miles distance from the start line an 11 a.m. Zero Hour was an obvious impossibility, especially since the brigade commanders still had to brief their battalion commanders. The commanders of the 5th and 7th Brigades left to deploy their respective HQs in a sunken road north-west of Harbonnières and sent orders for their battalion commanders to meet them there at 11 a.m. This, however, proved to be overly ambitious. The CO of the 20th Battalion did not receive the message until 11 a.m., while that of the 17th Battalion arrived at the spot at 11.20 a.m. but no one else was there. Eventually the orders groups assembled. It was probably at this stage that a revised Zero Hour of 4.30 p.m. was agreed, especially since the orders groups did not break up until 1.30 p.m.

The 5th Brigade's left hand assault battalion, the 18th, was in position at 3.40 p.m., but Lt Col Sadler of the 17th Battalion, which was to attack on the right, had a commanding officer's nightmare. He had left instructions for Captain E. T. Harnett, the next senior officer, to take the battalion to a rendezvous north of Bayonvillers and to be there at midday. This he duly did, but there was no sign of the Colonel. Harnett therefore told the men to have their midday meal, which they did sitting amid tall crops, hiding them from view. Meanwhile, at the conference Brigadier General Martin, commanding the 5th Brigade, told the COs that messages would be sent to their battalions ordering them to move immediately up to the Blue Line. Sadler himself also went there to carry out a reconnaissance and draw up his own orders. When he had finished he looked for his battalion in vain. He then sent his intelligence officer, who had accompanied him to the brigade orders, back to the RV to bring the Battalion to the Blue Line. The IO returned stating that he could not find it. Sadler then spotted a German cavalry horse cropping grass nearby. He sprang into the saddle and galloped back to the RV to look for himself. He was equally unsuccessful and so made for 5th Brigade HQ. En route he met a subaltern attached to Brigade HQ who told him that he was going to the RV and would tell the Battalion to move to the Blue Line. Captain Harnett had meanwhile become aware of other battalions moving forward and, after consulting his fellow company commanders, felt he had better do the same himself. By now it was 3.30 p.m. and the subaltern from Brigade came across the 17th Battalion as it was about to move off. He told Harnett that his objective was Framerville and that Zero Hour was 4.30 p.m. Harnett, realizing that he would have to march for 2 miles to get to the start line, set off immediately while Sadler and his IO continued their search. Sadler's horse foundered and so he borrowed another from the 20th Battalion, whom he came across during his hunt. This animal had been much used and was very tired and so Sadler could only go at a very slow pace as he made his way back to the Blue Line in the hope that his battalion would turn up there. As it happened, and although subjected to air attacks, something which the other battalions suffered during their move up, the 17th Battalion reached its start line ten minutes before Zero Hour and it is difficult to guess who was the more relieved, Capt Harnett or his Colonel.[10]

A minute before Zero there were further air attacks and artillery fire, which wounded Capt Harnett among others. The tanks then rolled forward with the infantry following behind. The German artillery was active, but concentrated mainly on the tanks, although all bar one reached Framerville.* The machine-gun and rifle fire was not intense. The 17th Battalion noted that the Germans appeared to have 'no stomach for fight' and that on approaching Framerville many of them fled and that 'two officers and 150 other ranks surrendered without firing a shot'." The village was secured by 5.30 p.m., with the Germans withdrawing to a ridge 1,000 yards away.

The 7th Australian Brigade on the right attacked with the 27th Battalion on the left and 25th Battalion on the right, also at 4.30 p.m. after passing through the 2nd Australian Division. Again, there was no formal barrage, with the supporting artillery merely engaging selected targets. Tanks led the way, however, although one of the four supporting the 25th Battalion broke down on the start line. There had been no time to brief the tank commanders and those with the 25th Battalion began to veer to the right to keep in touch with the 1st Australian Division's 2nd Brigade. This caused the infantry to do the same. They followed their two remaining tanks to Hill 91, 2,000 yards east of Vauvillers, and, according to the Battalion History, they were met by heavy fire from there. One tank broke its crank-shaft, but the remaining one reached the top of the hill before being knocked out and its crew killed. Thinking that he had now reached his objective, the Commanding Officer of the 25th Battalion now decided to consolidate, although he was in fact 500 yards short and south of it.¹² The 27th Battalion initially made good progress and captured a 4.2-inch howitzer on the north side of the Vauvillers–Frameville road. Its ranks were then engaged by 77mm guns. It also found itself stretched because 5th Brigade, to the north, appeared to

---

*There is a discrepancy in the figures. The 5th Tank Brigade report on the operation (TNA WO 95/112) states that 13 tanks took part and that 12 eventually rallied, but the 15th Tank Battalion's own report (TNA WO 95/103) states that only 12 tanks were involved. One broke down short of the objective and another on the objective, while 3 tanks were knocked out on the objective, leaving 7 to rally. Bean p.638 says that 14 tanks were earmarked but one broke down on the start line.

be veering to the left and the 25th Battalion to the right. This necessitated all four rifle companies being deployed in line, but they reached the high ground south of Rainecourt and linked up with the 25th Battalion.

The 5th Australian Division also originally planned to attack at 10 a.m., using its 8th Brigade to attack from its present position just east of Harbonnières to just short of Vauvillers. Thereafter the 2nd Australian Division would pass through and seize Framerville. The Brigade received its orders at 7 a.m. and the battalion commanders arrived at Brigade HQ near Bayonvillers for their instructions an hour later. According to the 29th Battalion History, these were delayed because of the late arrival of a British artillery officer, although the Australian Official History states that the supporting artillery arrangements were organized with the commander of the 13th Australian Field Artillery Brigade. Vauvillers was viewed as an obstacle to the initial advance and arrangements were made at the orders group for the artillery to fire a barrage on the village at 11 a.m., which was now to be Zero Hour. This would lift after 15 minutes. The assault battalions were to be the 29th and 31st, and the commanding officer of the former, Lt Col J. McArthur, concerned by the wait for the Gunner officer, sent off a warning order to his battalion: 'Bn to be ready to move at 10 a.m. Meal to be served at once.' Then, once he had received his orders, and with the Gunner officer still absent, McArthur wrote out his own orders and sent them by hand of a member of the 13th Australian Light Horse to his adjutant. He finally returned to his battalion at 10.10 a.m. His written orders had not arrived and so he had to give his company commanders a hurried briefing before setting off. Time was now very tight and the Battalion still had to pass through the 57th Battalion and coordinate with the 58th Battalion, which was attacking on the right. It was thus inevitable that the 11 a.m. Zero Hour would not be met, but, with the arrangements already made, the artillery duly launched its fifteen minutes barrage on Vauvillers on time. Five minutes after the bombardment began the seven supporting tanks, from the 8th Tank Battalion, began their advance.

They soon came up against an anti-tank gun located in a shed to the north-west of the village. This knocked out four of the six tanks and a further one was badly ditched. Sgt Wynne was commanding the only tank to survive the action, although it was hit:

> I saw all the tanks knocked out at point blank range, the effect was curious, each Tank when hit raised slightly with the impact and then black smoke issued from the Tanks. I remember as the last Tank was hit the Officer Tank Commander getting out with blood running down the tunic of one arm, and one of the crew helping him run to the safety of the Aussie lines. During this time the Boche was machine gunning them and dust spots were being kicked up on the grass.[13]

Thus, when the 29th Battalion crossed the start line at 11.40 a.m. it was without artillery support and there were virtually no tanks available. The commander of the tanks, Major J. A. Bennewith, agreed to release his one reserve tank after the advance had been held up by a machine gun in Vauvillers cemetery, but this was also knocked out. The 29th Battalion was therefore on its own. Casualties began to mount, including the CO who was rendered unconscious from a wound in the neck. Lt Clayton Davis was commanding the right hand company. His right flank was exposed because the 58th Battalion had not yet come up and he was facing artillery fire over open sights and machine-gun fire from Vauvillers. Noticing that all the officers in the company to the left of him had become casualties, he took command of this as well and decided that Vauvillers, although beyond the Battalion's objective, would have to be captured. Davis was then hit in the neck by a sniper and fell unconscious. Lt Arthur Farmer then took over the two companies and led them in a bayonet charge into Vauvillers. Davis now came to and reassumed command, but then suffered the fumes of a gas shell which exploded alongside him. Even then, he rescued the NCO who was with him when the shell exploded and remained at duty. Thus was Vauvillers secured by 2.30 p.m.*[14] In contrast, the 31st Battalion, which had less far to advance, experienced little difficulty.

North of the Somme, III Corps had been struggling to renew its attack. In the early hours of the morning 58th Division had been ordered to launch another attempt to overcome Chipilly and the Chipilly Spur. A few hours later it warned HQ III Corps that its battalions were now each no more than 200 men strong, casting doubt on its ability to achieve success. III Corps then revamped its plan and issued fresh orders at 1.15 p.m. In the north the 12th Division's principal task was to secure Morlencourt, while in the south the 58th Division, with the US 131st Infantry under command, was to clear the Chipilly Spur and Gressaire Wood, in other words the Red Line of the previous day. Zero Hour was to be 5 p.m. Col Sanborn of the 131st received a warning order at 1.30 p.m. and set off with his battalion commanders to have a look at the ground over which they would attack, with the Chipilly Spur as his initial main objective. This, however, was frustrated by the fact that the Germans were still in Malard Wood. Consequently, they returned and got the regiment in march formation west of Sailly-le-Sec on the road running along the north bank of the river. In the meantime, it would seem that the GOC 58th Division, Major General F. W. Ramsay, realized that the Americans would not be able to make the 'jumping off' point in time. For, at 3 p.m., III Corps sent out a signal that Zero Hour was put back to 5.30 p.m. He then visited the Americans and briefed Sanborn on the plan. He was told that there would be a barrage, which would open at Zero Hour and would be maintained for twenty minutes before lifting and progressing at a rate of four minutes every

---

* Davis was recommended for the VC, but was awarded a DSO. When Monash wrote his own account, *Australian Victories in France*, he stated that Vauvillers had been captured by the 15th Brigade. Lt Col McArthur wrote to Charles Bean explaining the facts, especially that he had ordered his battalion to establish positions on the east side of the village, rather than in it. Thus when the 58th Battalion arrived they initially did not realise that the 29th had already passed through. Bean duly took note when he came to write the official account. (Austin, Ron *Black and Gold: The History of the 29th Battalion 1915–18* p.144 Slouch Hat Publications, Macrae, Victoria, 1997)

100 yards until the final objective was reached. Lt Fred L. Rinkliff of Company C (1st Battalion) recalled that 'our intelligence department came round distributing maps showing our jumping off positions and our parallel lines of advance.' They were then faced with a 4-mile march with full packs in the hot afternoon sun and had to double the last half mile to make the start line on time.[5] Sanborn himself personally went forward on foot to supervise the final deployment of his battalions.[6]

The 12th Division attack was carried out by the 37th Brigade. Initially the 6th Queen's and 6th Royal West Kents attacked north of Morlencourt and the 6th Buffs to the south in order to cut it off. Eight tanks from the 10th Tank Battalion supported the operation. The Buffs initially faced severe opposition, especially from a field gun firing over open sights. This was suppressed by two Lewis gun teams, who skilfully worked their way round to a position from where they could engage the crew. They eventually reached their final objective to the east of Morlencourt. In the north both the Queen's and Royal West Kents also had problems with strongpoints, but with the help of the tanks overcame them. The latter were also inspired by their commanding officer, Lt Col W. R. A. Dawson, already the holder of three DSOs, who led his battalion on horseback, and by Sgt Thomas Harris, who singlehandledly overcame two machine-gun nests before being killed while tackling a third. He was later awarded a post-humous VC. These two battalions also reached the final objective and this meant that Morlencourt was now surrounded. The 1st/1st Cambridgeshires were then sent in with tanks to clear the village, which they did, capturing 77 prisoners, 19 machine guns and four trench mortars.

The 58th Division attacked with the 175th Brigade on the left and the Americans in the centre, and the 173rd Brigade next to the river. But the last named had to sideslip to the right to take up a line from east of Malard Wood to the river and then seize the Chipilly Spur and provide flank protection for the Americans. They were in position at 3.30 p.m. Twelve tanks from the 10th Tank Battalion would also be employed. On the south bank of the river, however, the 1st Australian

Battalion had been monitoring the situation in Chipilly. At 4.30 a.m. it had sent a patrol across the bridge there to establish who was occupying it. It saw Germans by the church and was then fired on by a machine gun. Later that morning two NCOs of C Company, CQMS Hayes and Sgt Andrews, ventured into the western outskirts of the village and found no trace of the Germans. They even picked up a couple of German rifles and a machine gun before returning via the British lines and reporting to their company commander. He informed Lt Col B. V. Stacy, commanding the battalion, of this at midday. Stacy asked the brigade commander if he could send out strong patrols to occupy the village, but was told that he could not because the 58th Division was about to attack it.*

As a preliminary to the main attack and in the knowledge that the Australian patrol had entered Chipilly during the night, the commander of the 176th Brigade, Brigadier General A. Maxwell, gave verbal orders to the CO of the 6th Londons at 2 p.m. He was to concentrate his battalion in the south-east corner of Malard Wood, occupy Chipilly and capture the ridge to its immediate north. There would be no artillery barrage but he would have three tanks from the 10th Tank Battalion and the 7th Londons would cover his left flank. Zero Hour was to be 4.15 p.m. An officer of the 6th Londons:

> We had very little time to sort out our men and explain the business, but we got it done somehow, moved off into the wood and got into position. There were four platoons, each about 40-50 strong ... As soon as we were in position we kicked off and then the fun began.[17]

As the 6th Londons debouched from Celestins Wood they came under heavy fire from both Chipilly Spur and the south-west corner of Celestins Wood. The attack came to a halt, but they were able to provide covering fire for the 2nd/10th Londons on their right, who

---

* This account comes from the 1st Australian Battalion war diary (TNA WO 95/3217). Bean p.650 fn24 states that the two NCOs were unarmed and on a 'souveniring' expedition.

were now ordered to take Chipilly as part of the main attack.[18]

Across on the south bank of the Somme Lt Col Stacy was told by the 1st Australian Brigade commander at 5.50 p.m. to send his two NCOs who had gone into Chipilly that morning to return and find out what the situation was since the British attack on it appeared to have been held up.* The patrol, now of six men and led by CQMS Hayes, set off ten minutes later. They met a company of the 2nd/10th Londons on the road running along the north bank between Sailly Laurette and Chipilly. They spoke to the company commander, Capt J. S. T. Berrell, who agreed that they should go forward and check the village. Berrell then deployed two of his platoons to support the patrol, but as they approached the outskirts they came under machine-gun fire from north of the village. Hayes then split his patrol. Pte Kane went back to guide a Lewis gun team into a good firing position, while Ptes Stephens and Turpin went into and through the village. Sgt Andrews and Pte Fuller proceeded north-east of the village, making use of dead ground. A platoon of the Londons and CSM Haynes joined them, but the British artillery barrage now reached this spot, forcing the platoon to withdraw. The three Australians now spotted some German posts. They overcame one of these, helped by Pte Kane, who had now rejoined them, and then located a much larger post. Crawling to 20 yards from it they threw a grenade. One officer and 31 men surrendered, who were then handed over to the Londons. The Australians then mopped up other posts, achieving a total bag of 73 prisoners and nine machine guns. Their enterprise helped considerably in enabling the 2nd/10th Londons to finally secure the Spur.†[19]

During their escapades the Australian patrol had spotted the US

---

* Curiously, the III Corps war diary (TNA WO 95/680) notes a message received from the Australian Corps at exactly the same time of 5.50 p.m. that one of their patrols operating north of the river had seen no Germans on the Chipilly Spur or in Chipilly itself, except on the bluff overlooking the river approximately 800 yards north-east of Chipilly. It is probable that this referred to the foray by CQMS Hayes and Sgt Andrews.

† The two Australian NCOs were awarded the DCM, and the four privates the MM. Capt Berrell later received the DSO for his performance on this day.

131st Regiment debouching from Gressaire Wood and had been fired
on by them. The Americans had attacked with the 2nd Battalion on
the left, the 1st on the right, and the 3rd Battalion in support. None
of the tanks supporting them crossed the start line, because of ditch-
ing en route, and the battalions were very short of Lewis gun ammunition pans. These were on the ration limbers, which had not been
seen since the previous evening. Lt Rinkliff of the 1st Battalion:

> A considerable amount of minenwerfer fire began to fall on our
> left as soon as the advance started, but executing a movement
> to the right this fire was escaped to a large extent. After the
> attacking troops had advanced through Malard wood coming
> out at the edge along the sunken road looking across the valley
> on the opposite crest the enemy was still present in considerable
> number and held up our advance.

Rinkliff's company commander sent him to see if the sunken road
could be used to connect with a covered approach to the ridge
beyond. He found a large ditch and also a platoon from Company D
in the sunken road. He informed Capt Porter of this and the latter
then deployed the company in one line in the sunken road.

> After extending in line of skirmishers the entire line of troops
> as one man started forward down the slope across the valley,
> increasing their speed and cheering in proportion to the distance
> covered. By this time the remainder of the Germans scattered
> along the crest beat a hasty retreat to the rear except one, who
> evidently had no desire to retreat, but remained in a prone
> position on the crest of the hill until our troops had reached the
> foot, when he came running down with his hands up.[20]

The advance continued to the north of Chipilly and eventually by
9 p.m. had reached a line running from the south-west corner of
Gressaire Wood eastwards to the Chipilly–Etinehem road where it
touched the Somme. The 2nd Battalion meanwhile had reached its

final objective, which represented that of the Regiment and was a line running north-west from the western outskirts of Etinehem to the road running from Corbie to Bray-sur-Somme. It had, however, suffered casualties and was very short of ammunition, as was the 1st Battalion. Both also urgently needed entrenching tools. The ammunition problem was solved by stripping the 3rd Battalion of its stock and replacing it from a dump established at Sailly-le-Sec that evening. The entrenching tools were brought forward by truck and then delivered by carrying parties. Otherwise, the night was spent in tidying up the line, especially gaining touch with the British brigades on the flanks and eradicating pockets of Germans. In spite of their inexperience, especially in administrative matters, the Americans had shown great spirit and dash.

This left the 175th Brigade, which was attacking immediately to the north of the Americans. Matters had not been helped by the fact that the brigade commander, Brigadier General Maxwell-Scott, had been taken ill that morning. His place was taken by the CO of the 9th Londons. But, although not under command of this brigade and remaining under the 174th Brigade, the 7th Londons also joined the main attack, immediately on the left of the Americans. Their objective was the ridge abutting the Somme to the south of Gressaire Wood. But, as the 6th Londons had, they came under heavy fire from Celestin Wood. The Londons continued to advance but by the time they had reached the high ground of the Chipilly Spur all the officers with the attacking companies were down. At this point the CO, Adjutant, and another officer came forward with thirty-five men and five Lewis guns and the Battalion succeeded in reaching the top of the spur. During the reorganization phase the Londons became intermingled with the Americans and at one point a 7th Londons officer led a party of Americans to subdue two German machine-gun posts on the 7th Londons' left flank.[21]

North of the 7th Londons and under the 175th Brigade, the 12th Londons attacked on the right and the 8th Londons (attached from the 174th Brigade) on the left. The principal objective was to clear Gressaire Wood. In spite of the tank support both battalions suffered heavily from machine gun fire. There was also a significant amount of German artillery fire. The advance also began to veer to the right, which meant that the 8th Londons lost contact with the 12th Division on their left. Nevertheless by dusk all objectives had been obtained, although the 5th Royal Berkshires, which had been attached to the Brigade from the 37th Brigade, had to be deployed to cover the gap between the Post Office Rifles and the 12th Division.

In the south the French First Army had also been busy. Debeney's orders merely emphasized the need to protect Rawlinson's right flank and to this end XXXI Corps was given the objectives of Hangest, Arvillers and Erches. Its right flank would in turn be covered by X and IX Corps, while XXXV Corps was to await the order to attack northwards and east of Montdidier. Foch was concerned that these orders were too negative and that Debeney was not displaying sufficient determination to push on. Twice during the morning he emphasized to Debeney that he must reach Roye as quickly as possible. He was not happy about the 42nd Division being withdrawn and ordered that those divisions 'which cannot advance should be leap-frogged, should join the Second Line and be used in support until the result desired by the High Command has been obtained.'[22] As it was, XXXI Corps now had three divisions in line – the 126th on the left, the 153rd in the centre and the 37th on the right. Hangest-en-Santerre was the key initial objective and this fell to the 126th and 153rd Divisions just before 11 a.m. At the same time the 37th Division reached Hill 105 midway along the road running from Hangest southwest to Contoire. Eventually by the end of the day XXXI Corps had reached Arvillers. To its south the 152nd Division was advancing on Contoire and Pierrepont. This had been part of IX Corps, as was the 166th Division to its south. However, this corps now lost its sector of responsibility, which was handed over to X Corps, although its artillery continued to support these two divisions, which became held up by German reserves sent towards Montdidier and its south. Even so, as the Corps advance swung south, the 152nd Division managed to capture Pierrepont and Contoire and reached the area of Davenescourt. The 162nd Division had greater difficulty and was held in the area of Gratrous, some 3 miles north of Montdidier. With Foch's concerns clearly ringing in his ears Debeney had now also employed his XXXV Corps to attack south of Montdidier with the overall aim of taking the town by double envelopment. This fresh attack again took the Germans by surprise, distracted as they were by events to the north. Consequently, on the left the 169th Division reached Assainvillers, which it captured, while the 133rd Division assaulted the heights of Rollot. The 46th Division followed the 169th Division and behind this came two divisions of II Cavalry Corps.*

In the air there had been renewed efforts to take out the Somme bridges. In the Canadian sector Nos. 27 and 49 Squadrons, escorted by Camels from No. 73 Squadron took off at 5 a.m. Such was the intensity of the German air arm, with groups of up to twenty Fokkers and Pfalzes attacking the bomber formations, that few bombs were actually dropped on the bridges. No. 49 Squadron's DH9s were attacked in the target area and the Germans continued to harry them all the way back across the lines, with one crew claiming to have shot down four Fokkers. This aircraft was flown by Lt J. A. Keating of the US Air Service, with 2Lt E. A. Simpson as his observer, and their combat report is worth quoting:

We were persistently attacked by a large number of enemy aircraft; observer fired a good burst into the first enemy aircraft which was only 50 feet from our tail and it turned over on its back and burst into flames: this was over Marchelpot. Another enemy aircraft dived on us and when he got to about 60 or 70 feet distance, observer fired about 100 rounds into him, when a large quantity of flames burst out and machine went down ablaze over Ablaincourt. When over Soyecourt, observer fired a further long burst into another enemy aircraft at very short

---

* On the previous day at 11.30 a.m. Haig had sent an officer to Debeney's HQ to ask him to push forward his cavalry so that it could operate with the British Cavalry. He was told that the French II Cavalry Corps was too far back and, in any event, the routes forward were congested with infantry.

distance which stalled, went into a spin and went down hopelessly out of control, and was seen to crash near Soyecourt.
Immediately after this machine disappeared observer saw
another enemy aircraft diving on our tail, and before he could
change drums the enemy aircraft had approached to within 40
feet of our machine. Observer then fired about 60 rounds
straight into this enemy aircraft which fell over on its side and
spun into the ground west of Soyecourt.[23]

Their own aircraft was so badly damaged that they had to make a
forced landing once inside their own lines. Simpson was awarded an
immediate DFC and Keating was later awarded the same.

No. 107 Squadron sent its bombers across in three waves, each with
a fighter escort. The last of these – five DH9s escorted by four
Camels – took off from their airfield at Ecoivres at 6.20 a.m. Their
target was the bridge at Brie, as it had been for the other two waves.
A large formation of German fighters was patrolling over the target
area. It was Lothar von Richthofen and the Flying Circus. The result
was a disaster, with four of the DH9s and two of the Camels shot
down. In all, No. 107 Squadron lost 9 of its 14 bombers which set out.
One of the survivors, 2Lt George Coles, recorded: 'The few of us
who were left sat down and at mess that night cried like children as
we looked around at the vacant chairs. In two days we had lost
fourteen men out of a complement of twenty-seven.'[24] The story in
the northern sector was much the same with the Germans too often
able to elude the escort fighters. It is significant that three of the
German airfields – Moislans, Ennemain, and Foreste – were within
5 miles of the Somme bridges, Ennemain being the base of von
Richthofen's *Jagdgeschwader* 1, to give the Flying Circus its official
title.

As for the other air activity, the six squadrons concentrating on
ground strafing were detailed to send their aircraft off in pairs at two
hourly intervals beginning at 4.30 a.m. It would seem that they were
not kept abreast of the changes to the various Zero Hour, since

they operated according to the original stipulation. They, too, were harassed by German planes, as were the Corps squadrons carrying out their artillery and reconnaissance work. Aircraft casualties were not as bad as the previous day, though, with 45 aircraft destroyed and 47 air crew casualties.

The Germans had welcomed the pause on the Fourth Army front during the morning. The Second Army had received substantial reinforcements during the night in the form of six divisions. Three further divisions appeared during the 9th in front of the British sector and further divisions in front of the French. Most travelled by train, bus, and lorry and often became divorced from their artillery and were deployed piecemeal. This made it almost impossible to co-ordinate counter-attacks and is the reason why so few took place. Even so, the reinforcement did enable some of the more shattered divisions to be withdrawn from the line. Their main concern was in the south, where indications were that the French Third Army was about to join in by attacking in the area Montdidier–Noyon, which represented the southern face on the German salient. The right hand part of von Hutier's Eighteenth Army was therefore pulled back some 4 miles, leaving just strong rearguards to defend the existing line. Their intelligence was to be proved right.

CHAPTER EIGHT

DAYS THREE AND FOUR

The Germans were still reinforcing. (See Map 6.) The 38th Division, which had been in the Cambrai area, arrived at Chaulnes on the evening of the 9th. They noted a high degree of disorderliness among the troops who were withdrawing. Some drunken Bavarians shouted out to them: 'What do you war-prolongers want? If the enemy were only on the Rhine – the war would then be over.' The Divisional staff found it impossible to obtain clear information on the situation. It was thought that remnants of the 117th and 119th Divisions might still be holding out, but there was a wide gap between them. The 38th Division set out to fill this and did so during the night. The Alpine Corps, which had come from the Tourcoing area and was deploying to the Hallu–Hattencourt sector, experienced similar confusion on arrival. Its History records:

> There was general excitement and fear of renewed air attacks . . . In the early hours of the 10th August no one could give a clear idea of the actual position at the front; no one knew anything about the troops on right or left, or about the divisions in position, . . . individuals and all ranks in large parties were wandering wildly about, but soon for the most part finding their way to the rear . . . only here or there were a few isolated batteries in soldierly array, ready to support the reinforcing troops.[1]

The prospects for an Allied breakthrough therefore still appeared good, but organizing a continuation of the assault would once again not be smooth.

On the evening of 9 August Rawlinson wrote a eulogistic entry in his diary, praising the achievements this far of his army. He considered the Australian and Canadian infantry as 'probably the decisive factor'. He also recorded that that afternoon he had been to see Haig in his train and that Debeney had also been present. The main concern now, according to Haig, was that the Fourth Army's rapid advance meant that the resultant expanded frontage was comparatively thinly held. He therefore wanted Debeney to extend his sector to include Roye and 5 kilometres to the north of it. The French First Army commander was initially resistant to this stating that it would upset his plans. He then relented and agreed to seize Roye by enveloping it from the north.[2]

The Fourth Army's orders for 10 August stated that the advance was to continue to the line Roye–Chaulnes–Bray–Dernancourt. Its boundary with the French First Army was to continue along the Amiens–Roye road, until short of Roye, where it looped to the north to give the French space in which to capture this town. The Canadian Corps' left boundary would continue along the Amiens–Wesle railway line. The Cavalry Corps was to operate on its right to both assist the Canadians and the French. It was confirmed that the 32nd Division was now under Canadian command, as was the 13th Tank Battalion. The Australian Corps was, as on the previous day, to conform with the advance of the Canadians and reach the line Lihons– Framerville–Méricourt. In order to overcome the problem of co-ordination with III Corps astride the Somme the Australians were to extend their northern boundary to include the Bray–Corbie road and take under command the 131st US Regiment and some artillery north of the river, including that of the 58th Division. III Corps, 'if not already in possession of it', was to establish itself on a line running from Dernancourt, some 2,500 yards north of Morlencourt, to a point 2,000 yards north-west of Bray. This was the subject of a separate order, which also amended the Australian objective to the line Lihons–Chuignolles and across the river to the west of Bray to link up with III Corps to its north-west.[3]

So again the Canadians were taking the lead. Currie decided to renew the assault with just two divisions. The 4th Canadian Division would relieve the 1st and 2nd Divisions and the British 32nd Division the 3rd Division. But first there was some tidying up to be done. The village of Le Quesnoy-en-Santerre, which lies just north of the Amiens–Roye road and 2,000 yards east of Bouchoir, had been an objective on 9 August and it was necessary that it be secured before the main attack on the 10th began. The task was given to the 2nd Canadian Mounted Rifles, which had been the reserve battalion of the 8th Brigade. A reconnaissance party went out on the evening of the 9th to study the ground, but en route was fired on by machine guns situated south of the Amiens–Roye road. The officer commanding the machine-gun company supporting the attack was wounded in the hand. It turned out that it was a party of 45 Germans whom the French had failed to mop up, but later captured. Brigadier General Brutinel heard of the attack and offered motor transport to move the battalion up to Bouchoir. This was gratefully accepted. The attack itself was mounted at 4.20 a.m. and was supported by four tanks, although these did not arrive until 6 a.m. and initially made slow progress in the face of heavy machine-gun fire. Even so, they enabled the 2nd CMR to clear the village and occupy trenches to the east of it by 7.30 a.m. In the meantime, the 1st CMR had been ordered up and they occupied what was the old British front line to the north-west of Parvillers.

Currie had originally laid down that the main attack should begin at 8 a.m. The 32nd Division was informed at 8.15 p.m. on 9 August that it had been released to the Canadian Corps and that it would be required to pass through the 3rd Canadian Division and continue the advance, the Corps objective being the line Roye–Hattencourt–Hallu. The Division was ordered to send a staff officer to Corps HQ to receive orders. He arrived there at 9 p.m. and was given the interdivisional boundaries and told that besides its integral artillery the 32nd Division would also have some Canadian artillery and an RGA brigade. Twenty-four tanks would also be available. Meanwhile General Lambert, realizing that it would take time to disseminate written orders, went round his brigades to give them initial verbal orders. His plan was for the 97th Brigade to attack on the left, with the 96th Brigade on its right. The 14th Brigade would be in support 1 mile to the rear. The infantry would advance in front of the tanks and call them forward to deal with obstinate strongpoints. Divisional confirmatory written orders were sent out to the brigades by car, mounted officer or motor-cycle despatch rider at 12.30 a.m., although as the roads were clogged and the night was very dark they took time to reach their destination. Even so, thanks to the efficient Canadian movement control organization the 32nd Division was at the start line by the planned Zero Hour of 8 a.m.*

Apparently the 96th Brigade only learned about the Canadian attack against Le Quesnoy when it reached Bouchoir.[4] The 15th Lancashire Fusiliers were accordingly sent straight to the village and helped the Canadians with its mopping up. They then passed through the Canadians, but now came under heavy machine gun fire, which temporarily stalled the advance. The 16th Lancashire Fusiliers came up and this enabled Wood 101, 1,000 yards south-east of Le Quesnoy, to be taken. German artillery fire now began to increase in intensity and casualties mounted. Nevertheless the two battalions pressed on and by 10.30 a.m. had captured the Bois de la Intaie and, to its south and on the Amiens–Roye road, La Cambuse, where physical contact with the French First Army was made. This represented an advance of 2,500 yards from Le Quesnoy, with a German artillery battery being captured. German resistance now became very fierce. This was not helped by the fact that the attackers were now crossing the trenches that marked the front line prior to the German March 1918 offensive. Even so, the Lancashire Fusiliers rushed Square Wood, just to the east of the Bois de la Intaie, capturing a pillbox, which had been

---

* According to the Canadian Official History (Nicholson p.415) 32nd Division's own artillery did not arrive until 10.30 a.m., having been delayed by German night bombing, and it had to be supported by the 5th Canadian Divisional artillery. This had, in fact, already been allocated to the 32nd Division and there is no mention in its report on the battle (TNA WO 95/2372) of any delay to its own artillery, although during the early stages of the attack the 3rd Canadian Division's artillery was employed to allow time for the 5th and 32nd artillery to deploy behind their respective brigades.

known by the French in 1917 as the *Tour de Défiance*. The Germans now fired an intense barrage and counter-attacked. The Lancashire Fusiliers were forced to withdraw to the western edge of Square Wood, but managed to cling on to the pillbox. Once this attack had been repulsed the Fusiliers, supported by four tanks, pushed on towards Damery. All four were knocked out within ten minutes of crossing the March 1918 German front line. The infantry did make further progress, but found themselves exposed on both flanks. Consequently the 96th Brigade withdrew once more to the western edge of Square Wood.

The 97th Brigade had also initially made good progress, passing through the Canadians at Rouvroy-en-Santerre and reaching the old British front line by 9.30 a.m., albeit with heavy casualties. The infantry continued to press forward towards Parvillers in the face of machine-gun fire of increasing intensity and reports received at Divisional HQ indicated that the leading troops had reached the outskirts of the village before the advance stalled. It was now about 3 p.m. and General Lambert concluded that Parvillers and Damery could only be taken if a fresh and coordinated attack was made by both brigades supported by artillery and tanks. Four reserve tanks from the 4th and 5th Tank Battalions were therefore sent forward. However, when General Lambert visited HQ 97th Infantry Brigade he found that the situation was not as rosy as he thought. He was told that only three companies from the reserve battalion were available for the attack and that the line was not as far forward as originally thought and was still 1,000 yards short of Parvillers. The fact, too, that the 96th Brigade's right flank would be exposed, since the French had been unable to progress beyond La Cambuse, led General Lambert to conclude that a further attack with merely his existing assets was not practicable and that it would have to be delayed until the following day when fresh troops could be gathered. Consequently, both brigades remained where they were.

What, though, of the 4th Canadian Division to the north? It received verbal orders at 8.30 p.m. on 9 August. General Watson planned to attack with his 10th Brigade on the right and 12th Brigade on the left. The brigades were to move from their present positions on the line Beaufort–Caix and pass through the 2nd Canadian Division on the line Warvillers–Vrély–Rosières at 8 a.m. He had been promised the assistance of the 1st Tank Battalion, together with one and a half companies from the 13th Tank Battalion and the possibility of a further company from the 14th Tank Battalion. He also had additional artillery assets in the form of two Australian field artillery brigades and one of mobile heavy artillery. The divisional commander became unhappy, however, over the number of tanks physically available for the 8 a.m. Zero Hour. He therefore obtained permission from the Canadian Corps HQ to delay the attack until sufficient tanks could be gathered. Eventually ten tanks from the 1st Tank Battalion and nine from the 13th Tank Battalion reached the assembly area and Zero Hour was reset for 10.15 a.m.

The 10th Canadian Brigade set off with the 44th and 46th Battalions in the lead, the idea being that the 47th and 50th Battalions would pass through them once the Fouquescourt–Maucourt road was reached. They were passing through the old French defences and these slowed the advance. The supporting tanks, too, were unable to make much progress because of the terrain and did not get further than the Maucourt–Rouvroy road. On the right the 44th Battalion managed to get into Fouquescourt, but then the supporting artillery opened fire on the village, forcing it to pull back. This encouraged the Germans to re-enter it. In the meantime, three tanks from the 14th Tank Battalion had been called up to support the 47th Battalion, which was now ordered to retake the village. While one tank was left in reserve behind Warvillers Wood the other two were ordered to clear the village. It meant traversing the old 1916 British front line, which now consisted of collapsed trenches, dug-outs that caved in as the tanks passed over them, and much wire. As a result one tank ditched some 300 yards short of the village. The Germans now shelled it, but by putting up a smokescreen to provide cover the crew were able to unditch it. Later it ditched again and caught fire some 1,000 yards east of Fouquescourt. The other tank got into the village, with the infantry following. The tank commander had led it in on foot and then went back to confer with the CO of the 47th Battalion. On his return to the tank, which was now surrounded by Germans, he was shot in the back by a sniper. This tank was also lost, but by 6.30 p.m. the Canadians had succeeded in securing the village in the face of heavy artillery fire and were holding the high ground to the east. They could not progress any further, however. In contrast, the 46th Battalion, although initially discomforted by fire from Maucourt, seized this village, capturing two field guns and a number of machine guns, and by early afternoon had reached the Maucourt– Fouquescourt road. The 50th Battalion then took over and reached the Chaulnes–Roye railway line. The 12th Brigade initially faced fire from the east of Méharicourt as it exited from the village and from Maucourt. But its advance was so rapid that the German defenders were soon withdrawing rapidly towards Chilly. Here they put up a fight, but the village was in the hands of the 72nd Battalion by 12.30 p.m. The 78th Battalion then passed through and by 2 p.m. Hallu was in its hands. The left hand battalion, the 85th, experienced heavy machine-gun fire from the Chaulnes–Lihons ridge to the north, but reached its objective. The 38th Battalion then continued the advance and reached the Lihons–Chilly road.

The 4th Canadian Division might understandably have felt satisfied at what it had achieved this far, but this was not so. On the right flank it had made no contact with the 32nd Division, which was now to the rear because of the resistance it had met. The 38th Battalion continued to be troubled by machine-gun fire from Lihons and the 78th Battalion at Hallu had both flanks in the air. There was also a gap between it and the 72nd Battalion at Chilly. In addition, there was a strong body of Germans in Hattencourt and to its south. Indeed it was from there that the first counter-attack was launched south-westwards towards the 72nd Battalion at 3.30 p.m. Advancing in short rushes the Germans got to within 15 yards of the Canadian positions but were beaten back by rifle and Lewis gun fire and with the help of a 6-inch Newton mortar. A second counter-attack took place at 7.30 p.m. This time the Germans skirted round the left flank of the 78th Battalion and struck at Chilly from the north. This brought them up against Battalion HQ and the CO had to hastily organize a defence using his signallers, runners, pioneers, scouts and other headquarters details. This checked the attack and then Germans were taken in the flank, which forced them to withdraw. The Canadians had managed to hold on to their gains, but, as the 4th Canadian Division's report stated:

It was evident that the enemy's reserves were beginning to have their effect and here, as on the right, the attacking troops were confronted with the enemy's old trench system. Progress was naturally slow and casualties were beginning to increase. The ground was impracticable for Cavalry and the tanks were seriously handicapped.* There was an unwelcome reversion to Trench Warfare, and it was evident that further progress could not be made without serious risk and unwarranted losses, unless, as in a 'set-piece' offensive, the attacking troops were to be adequately supported by Heavy Artillery and an increased number of tanks.[5]

The last sentence certainly echoed the conclusions of General Lambert of the 32nd Division. As for sufficient tanks, the number of those, and their crews, which were still fit for battle was continuing to rapidly decline.

For the Australian Corps Lihons remained unfinished business. Monash conformed to the Canadian Zero Hour of 8 a.m. for renewing the attack in this sector. The task was given to the 1st Australian Division, which had battled gamely to get to Lihons the previous day. The attack would be made by the 2nd and 3rd Brigades, with the 1st Brigade, which had been overwatching the Chipilly Spur being

---

* In fact the 1st Tank Battalion claimed that its tanks reached all their objectives, although one was burnt out by machine-gun fire, two were hit by shells and burnt out, while another was also hit but managed to rally, together with the other six (report on operations in TNA WO 95/109). Of the nine 13th Battalion tanks, three were disabled by artillery fire while on the move, one hit by bombs and set on fire while stationary and another ditched and could not be recovered (*History of the 13th Tank Battalion* TNA WO 95/115).

returned to the Division during the night to become the reserve and deployed near Rosières. As for the attacking brigades, the 2nd Australian Brigade was on the right. Its selected assault battalions were the 5th and 6th, with the latter on the right. There would be a creeping barrage which would open 15 minutes before Zero Hour on a line 700 yards ahead of the Red Line. The artillery fire would then move forward at 100 yards every two minutes until the Blue Line, where it would continue to assist consolidation of the objective. Although HQ 1st Australian Division had initially been promised tanks, it seems that none could be made available. Very sensibly the CO of the 6th Battalion sent a liaison officer to the Canadian battalion on his right. The brigades now duly deployed, but at 7.50 a.m., just ten minutes before Zero Hour, the 6th Battalion's liaison officer returned to say that the Canadians would not be attacking at 8 a.m. and that their left flank would remain midway between Vaux and Rouvroy until they received orders to attack. Neither Divisional nor Brigade HQ appear to have been aware of this and it came as a bombshell. It was too late, however, to postpone the attack.

Almost as soon as the 5th and 8th Battalions crossed the Red Line they came under heavy machine-gun fire. It was the same with the 3rd Australian Brigade on the left and matters here were made worse by the fact that the existing front line was not as far forward as indicated in the orders. Hence its two lead battalions, the 9th and the 11th, came under machine-gun fire before they reached the Red Line. A German aircraft also strafed the 11th Battalion with machine-gun fire. That the barrage had commenced so far ahead of the Red Line meant that the infantry lost much of its protection and had to deal with the machine-gun fire on their own. On the right, the appearance of a tank, which was due to support the Canadians, enabled the 6th Battalion to reach the hamlet of Halt, some 1,500 yards west of Lihons. Then, at about 11 a.m. came news that the 3rd Australian Brigade had reached the Blue Line. What had actually happened was that the 9th Battalion, which was attacking on the right, had got as far as Crepey Wood. Efforts to clear it resulted in heavy casualties and, after patrols had been sent out to try to establish contact with the flanks, the survivors withdrew to trenches on the west side of the wood. Unfortunately, the commanding officer made a map reading error and claimed that his men were west of Auger Wood, just north of Lihons. The mistake was realized when the 5th Battalion stated that it was under heavy fire from this wood. The Canadians now came up on the right, but while efforts were made to continue the attack the troops were becoming very tired and, with casualties continuing to mount, little progress was made. By 4 p.m. the attack had ground to a halt, with Lihons remaining tantalizingly out of reach. Once again, the deployment of the German reserves and the dominance of old trench systems had caused a loss of momentum.

To the north the 25th Battalion from the 2nd Australian Division was also to attack to conform with the 1st Australian Division. Although it, too, was scheduled to attack at 8 a.m., it claimed that the 11th Battalion on its right attacked at 7.45 a.m., presumably to take advantage of the opening of the barrage, and so its two lead companies, led by Lt Col Davis in person because he was short of officers, also attacked. With no artillery or tank support available they were soon under heavy fire from their objective, which was Hill 91, 2,000 yards east of Vauvillers. This pinned down the left hand company, but that on the right, advancing in short rushes, managed to get up the slope of the hill. By this time the 11th Battalion on the right had advanced well ahead and contact had been lost with it. Considering that a further attempt to advance without supporting fire was fruitless, Col Davis ordered his men to halt, while he sent for trench mortars. These eventually arrived, but by then it had been decided to resume the Australian attack at 4 a.m. the following morning. The mood in the 25th Battalion by this stage was not good:

We are feeling exhausted, annoyed and rebellious, for we have had practically no sleep since the night of the 7th, and have had very little food and water, and hard continuous fatigues. It would only need a determined leader, and quite a number would, without permission, leave the line and return to some spot where they could get some rest behind the line.[6]

It was a clear indication that the strain was beginning to tell.

The other Australian task involved the reorganization of the forces astride the Somme. The 4th Australian Division duly took over the north bank of the Somme up to and including the Corbie–Bray road to the north of Etinehem. The US 131st Regiment, which was now under Australian command, spent the day tidying up its line. Its 2nd Battalion now covered the north flank, holding the Bray–Corbie road to a double telegraph post lying 2,000 yards west of Corbie, while the 1st Battalion faced east, linking up with the 2nd Battalion at the double telegraph post and then covering the eastern edge of Gressaire Wood and thence down to the river. The Germans sent some machine-gun teams down the road from Bray, but the Americans drove them off. There was, however, persistent shelling, including gas, by the Germans, which aggravated the growing American fatigue. This was not helped by the fact that when they came under Australian command at 8 a.m. on the 10th they had been without food and water for 48 hours.[7]

A conference had, however, been held at HQ 4th Australian Division at which Monash, the GOC 3rd Australian Division and the commander of the 10th Australian Brigade were present. The purpose was to plan a night operation to clear the Germans from the high ground around Proyart and from Etinehem. For this purpose the 3rd Australian Division would pass its 10th Brigade through the 4th and 12th Brigades. This brigade would go on to tackle Proyart, while the two 4th Australian Division brigades were relieved. Etinehem would be tackled by the 4th Australian Division's other brigade, the 13th, which would cross the river and then pass through the Americans.* The Proyart operation was an imaginative one conceived by Monash himself. He conceived the idea of literally boxing in the Germans by advancing along the old Roman road running east from Warfusée–Abancourt to the crossroads south-east of Proyart and then turning north via Chignolles to the Somme. The 13th Bri-

* The 50th Australian Battalion was already north of the river, having crossed the previous night and taken up position astride the Chipilly Spur.

gade's battalions would occupy this right-angled line and hold it, thus containing all the Germans in the boxed-off area. The other two 3rd Australian Division brigades would then help to mop it up. There was to be no supporting barrage, although the heavies would intermittently take on targets in the Froissy valley and bridges beyond it. Monash also intended to use tanks for the initial advance, the very first time that they had been employed at night, as well as armoured cars to drive up and down the Roman road during the second phase to persuade the Germans that the attack was coming along this axis.

Although the Brigade commander, Brig Gen Gillibrand, thought that the plan could work there was a high degree of disbelief and astonishment at the lower levels of command. Lt Col Knox-Knight, commanding the 37th Battalion, which was to lead the advance, remarked to the commander of the six tanks that had been allocated from the 8th Tank Battalion: 'There'll be a train load of VCs waiting for us when we get back, but we won't want them if we get through with our lives.'[8] As for his platoon commanders:

> ... one of whom remarked: 'To me this stunt is either a "cinch" or it is a blasted impossibility. If there are no Fritzes there, it is a "cinch," but if they are watching, then God help us!' Another one joined in. 'There's no end of the darnn-fool ideas that some of our military heads get. Talk about bees in their bonnets! They've got a whole hive.'[9]

The tanks themselves were to operate in two groups of three. The first group was to lead the way, with one tank actually on the Roman road and the other two in the fields on either side. The 37th and 38th Battalions would follow them and then would come the second group of tanks similarly deployed as the first. The 40th and 39th Battalions would follow up. Vickers machine guns and mortars were also to be used. Zero Hour was set off 9.30 p.m., but this was postponed by half an hour when it was realized that German observation balloons were covering the approach route.

At the last moment, on the recommendation of Capt D. E. Hickey who was commanding the tanks, it was decided that all the tanks should proceed down the road since it was realized that the Germans had camps and other obstacles on both sides of it. In the meantime the 37th Battalion had arrived in position at 8.30 p.m. and then waited for darkness to fall. At 10.00 p.m. the column set off, led by the 37th Battalion's scout officer and a small patrol which was responsible for ensuring that the correct turn to the north was made. He was also accompanied by the tank section commander and then the first tank.

> Except for the rumbling of this monster all remained quiet – for a minute. Suddenly a flare went up, and another, and then a thousand flares and rockets floated in the sky, and the great main road with its fringing line of tall trees stood out in bold relief. In a moment out crashed machine-gun fire on the leading tank, and all along the road. But the column pressed on.[10]

Casualties began to mount and in the front Lt N. G. McNicol, the scout officer, and his men were forced to take cover behind the lead tank. The tanks themselves, in the words of the 8th Battalion's History 'were unable to cope with this in the dark', although their 6-pdr guns were able to neutralize fire coming from a derelict Mark V Star on the north side of the road.*[11] After progressing some three quarters of a mile the battlefield illumination enabled McNicol to spot the clump of trees which marked the turn off to the north. Soon afterwards a runner from the lead company brought a message from its commander. It stated: 'The battalion is cut to pieces. It is no use going any further.' McNicol therefore got the lead tank to halt and open fire with all its guns. At that moment he and his patrol were caught by a burst of machine-gun fire and became casualties. The tank commander was also seriously wounded. By now the Germans were firing an artillery barrage further down the column and their aircraft also joined in, dropping some 50 bombs on the 40th and 39th

---

* The German machine guns had anti-flash devices fitted, which made it very difficult to identify the sources of their fire.

Battalions. Gas shells, too, added to the growing confusion. Worse, Lt Col Knox-Knight was killed by a fragment of an anti-tank shell which had hit a tree by him. The tanks themselves had got well ahead of the infantry and Capt Hickey decided to turn them round, especially since many of the crews were now wounded:

> I felt rather like a wild animal trainer with huge beasts to control. In the dark the tank crews could not easily understand my directions nor hear my voice above the noise. Every time the tanks moved the enemy machine-guns simply went mad, and there was a terrific fusillade of bullets.[12]

The tanks moved back some 150 yards and then ran into elements of the 40th Battalion, together with the three reserve tanks. The infantry demanded that the tanks remain halted, since every time they moved they drew German fire. It became clear that an impasse had been reached and that nothing could be gained by continuing the operation. At 3.30 a.m. the tanks were withdrawn* and the Brigade began to prepare a defensive line which linked up with the 2nd Australian Division on the Roman road north of Rainecourt and the 4th Australian Brigade in the existing front line 1,500 yards south-west of Proyart. Monash's plan had been highly imaginative but overly ambitious, especially given a clearly alert enemy. As for the use of tanks at night, the 5th Tank Brigade report on operations commented: 'Against a determined enemy Tanks are little value in a Night Attack owing to their inability to locate machine guns. Only their moral effect can be relied upon.'[13]

In contrast the 13th Infantry Brigade's attack against the Etinehem pocket proved a much more straightforward affair. The 49th and 51st Battalions joined the 50th Battalion on the north bank of the Somme on the morning of 10 August. The plan was to advance from the Chipilly Spur across the base of the Etinehem peninsula and occupy

---

* All managed to get back to their rallying point, although the lead tank had been riddled with armour piercing bullets.

the heights overlooking Bray. To this end the 49th Battalion was to advance along the Corbie–Bray road to the high ground overlooking Bray and form a protective flank facing northwards. Simultaneously the 50th Battalion would advance on an axis 1,000 yards to the south. It would then turn and face south. Behind the 50th came a company from the 51st Battalion. This was to seal off Etinehem and then at dawn secure the village. Again, there would be no supporting barrage, but there would be tanks, in this case three from the 2nd Tank Battalion. Two would support the 49th Battalion, while the other was held in reserve.* It was agreed with the tank commander that the tanks would be best employed in driving down the Bray–Corbie road making as much noise as possible and then cruise around for half an hour before returning. This was on several grounds. They could not distinguish between friend and foe in the dark if they opened fire and would have to keep to the roads because of the extreme difficulty in navigating over rough ground at night. They also only had fuel sufficient for half an hour's action.[14] The attack kicked off at 9.30 p.m. with the two tanks, one behind the other and at an interval of 200 yards, leading the way along the road. There was some wild firing from German machine-gun posts, but the tanks pressed on regardless and were soon some distance ahead of the infantry. They themselves easily suppressed the positions from which the surprised Germans had not fled and soon achieved their objective. The 50th Battalion met no opposition until it had advanced some 400 yards when there was a brief burst of machine-gun fire, but nothing more. Half a mile from their start line some twelve machine guns opened up and a flare was fired, which fell behind the Battalion. The fire then ceased and there was no further discernible opposition. Apart from a delay in turning south at the wrong point, the Battalion reached its objective. The company from the 51st Battalion also had a problem when it turned south in that one of its platoons went missing. Scouts were sent out to try to find it:

---

* Monash had hoped that four could be made available, in which case one would have been allocated to the 50th Battalion. Unfortunately there were insufficient fit tanks.

The scouts returned to B Company stating that the only troops they could find were Scottish. Lieutenant Earl declared to the scouts that there were no Scottish troops in the vicinity. The scouts assured the officer they had spoken to the troops and could not understand their guttural accent. Lieutenant R. Earl sent troops to investigate, with the result that the party returned with several German prisoners.[15]

The platoon was then found and the company dug astride the road running east from Etinehem and awaited the dawn, as did the other two battalions.

In the north of Fourth Army's sector III Corps's operation principally concerned the 12th Division. From early morning the 58th Division and the 131st US Regiment had been sending out patrols to establish whether the Germans had withdrawn from the Old Amiens Defence Line, which ran to the east of Tailles Wood (to the north of Gressaire Wood) and then ran north-west across Hill 105 to Dernancourt. By midday it was clear that the Germans had withdrawn, but that there was a strong concentration of gas in Tailles Wood which made it difficult to enter. On the 12th Division front to the north the picture was different in that the Germans were still holding on. Accordingly III Corps issued orders for an attack by both divisions for 6 p.m. However, the 9th Londons reported that they had succeeded in reaching the Amiens defence line beyond Tailles Wood and so the attack would merely be mounted by the 12th Division and more specifically its 37th Brigade. Four tanks from the 8th Tank Battalion were allotted. The attack was launched on time and the Amiens defence line quickly gained. One of the four tanks received a direct hit in its right sponson and according to the section commander, Lt G. Garnham: 'The remaining 3 Tanks cruised about in front of the first objective dealing with heavy machine gun fire from the right and finally patrolling the ground on the left flank and returned safely to their respective coys.'[16]

In the morning of the 10th Foch had visited Haig and told him that he wanted the advance to continue to the line Noyon–Ham– Péronne and to attempt to secure bridgeheads across the Somme. Haig warned that this could only be done if the Germans were wholly demoralized. He also discussed with Foch his ideas for an offensive to liberate the Béthune coal mines, as well as others towards Bapaume and Monchy-le-Preux. Haig expected the German reserves to soon arrive in strength on the Fourth Army front, in which case the offensive would inevitably have to be closed down and he would need to launch his Bapaume and Monchy-le-Preux attacks with Byng's Third and Horne's First Armies respectively. Foch, however, apparently asserted that the French First and Third Armies were not meeting 'serious opposition' and so the German morale must be low. Haig accordingly issued orders for the advance to continue and also ordered Byng 'to raid, and if situation favourable to push forward advance guards to Bapaume.' The British commander-in-chief went on to visit Currie at his headquarters. The latter told him that he feared a German counter-attack and wanted to keep two divisions in reserve to deal with this. Haig impressed upon him the value of pursuing the Germans over the Somme rather than allow them to reorganize and thus ensure a more costly assault across the river later on. A message from the Cavalry Corps that the German opposition was diminishing and that cavalry divisions were being sent to the high ground north-east of Roye and to Nesle appeared to reinforce his argument.[17]

While Haig was with Currie, Rawlinson arrived and so Haig was able to give him his orders face-to-face. Rawlinson was conscious that the old Somme battlefield was acting as a brake on progress, but agreed to attempt to achieve bridgeheads over the Somme. Haig then went on to the headquarters of the 32nd Division, where Lambert explained to him his reasons for halting his attack and trying again on the morrow with fresh troops and more tanks. This and Rawlinson's reservations began to give Haig doubts.

The main event for the French First Army was the capture of Montdidier. During the night the Germans had begun to withdraw from it fearing that they were in danger of being surrounded. They deployed machine-gun teams to act as a rearguard. At midday on 10

August the French troops entered the town, now reduced to a mass of ruins. In the hope that a decisive breakthrough might still be possible Debeney ordered the 6th Cavalry Division to follow behind XXXI Corps and the 2nd and 4th Cavalry Divisions to do the same behind XXXV Corps. The commander of the latter decreed: 'It is no longer a case of methodical, slow and carefully mounted attacks with a debauch of artillery fire, but of strong reconnaissances working by encirclement and pushing forward rapidly.'[18] The First Army then managed to advance to a line La Boissière–Fescamps–Remangies but by now, like the British Fourth Army, it had come up against the old 1916 defences.

The French, however, expanded the offensive still further. At 4.20 a.m., and without any preliminary barrage, General Georges Humbert's Third Army attacked towards the River Matz. The direction of the attack was initially north-east and across the high ground cut by deep valleys which made up the Boulogne-la-Grasse massif. Yet by 7 a.m. his troops were across the river and driving the Germans back. They penetrated to a depth of 5 miles by the end of the day.

Recognizing that the air attacks on the Somme bridges were proving too costly, the emphasis changed on 10 August to railway stations to disrupt the deployment of German reserves. Twelve bombers from Nos. 27 and 49 Squadrons attacked Péronne railway station with a large escort of 40 SE5s and Bristol fighters. There was a fierce battle with some fifteen Fokkers over the objective. One German fighter went down in flames, but one RAF bomber and four SE5s were also shot down. An attack was also made on the station at Equancourt, but was frustrated by heavy cloud. Subsequent attacks were made on Péronne station later in the day and FE2bs and Handley Pages continued them during the night. Otherwise the day bombers were rested. The constant presence of German fighters over the battle area resulted in ground strafing being much reduced, with a consequent increase in offensive patrols. Indeed, the energy displayed by the Germans had already resulted in a considerable RAF reinforcement on the Fourth Army front.

★

Haig's instructions to Rawlinson and Debeney for 11 August reiterated the requirement to achieve bridgeheads over the Somme. While the French Third Army was not under Haig's command, his orders stated that it would be exploiting the success achieved by Debeney and that its intention was to clear the Noyon area. The British Third Army was also to carry out minor operations on its front to test German reactions. Byng was to 'take immediate advantage of any favourable situation which the main operations may create and push advanced guards in the general direction of Bapaume'.[19] Rawlinson's own orders for resuming the advance were to 'press on to the Somme between Ham (exclusive) and Péronne and establish bridgeheads on the right bank of the river.' Again, it was the Canadians who would take the lead, with the Cavalry Corps being ordered to spearhead their advance and Currie again allowed to select his own Zero Hour, although Fourth Army's orders stipulated that it should be 'as early as possible'.[20] When HQ Cavalry Corps received these orders at 8 p.m. on 10 August there was immediate concern. Attempts to get forward to Nesle and Roye that afternoon had been stopped in their tracks and it was certain that the same would happen on the 11th. Accordingly, Brigadier General Home, the chief staff, went in person to HQ Fourth Army to explain the Cavalry's strong reservations in that the Germans were now in strength and that the ground was impassable to large numbers of horsemen. He did not get back until 3 a.m., but revised orders had meanwhile been telephoned through. The 1st Cavalry Division was ordered to send out patrols with the infantry so that if a further breakthrough became likely the division could be deployed. Apart from one brigade, which was detached to support the Australians in accordance with the original orders, the other two cavalry divisions were to remain in their bivouacs at one hour's notice to move.[21]

As far as the Canadians were concerned, Currie issued his orders late on the evening of the 10th. The advance was to be resumed with the 32nd Division attacking on the right and the 4th Canadian Division on the left. The objective was given as the Somme between Offoy and St Christ. The 32nd Division needed to carry out some reorganization as a result of its initial attack. Consequently, its attacking troops were to be the 14th Brigade, with a company from the 96th Brigade attached, and a battalion less one company from the 97th Brigade. The initial objective was given as the line Bois de Damery–Damery–Parvillers–La Chavatte, with the 14th Brigade then going on to capture Fresnoy-les-Roye. Because Damery and Parvillers were known to be strongly held it was planned to initially bypass them, relying on artillery fire to contain them, and then capture them from the flanks and rear. The infantry would also have the protection of a creeping barrage, with fire being opened at Zero Hour on a line 300 yards beyond where the existing front line was thought to be. Thirty minutes after Zero it would begin to advance 200 yards every eight minutes, a much slower rate than had been the case up until now. Eight tanks from the 5th Tank Battalion and eight from the 4th Tank Battalion would also be available. The original plan had been for Zero Hour to be between 8 a.m. and 9 a.m., but it became apparent that the attackers would be very exposed to hostile fire as they moved down the slopes towards the German lines. Zero Hour was therefore brought forward to 4.20 a.m. with the agreement of the Canadian Corps HQ. Subsequently, the brigades reported that it would be impossible to have their troops deployed by this time and so the time of the attack was put back to 9.30 a.m.

The 4th Canadian Division did not issue confirmatory orders until 4.20 a.m. on 11 August. The 10th and 12th Brigades would carry out the attack and their objective was given as the line Forchette–Fuzeaux–Chaulnes. At least twelve tanks from the 1st, 13th and 14th Tank Battalions were expected to be available, but the orders stressed that the attack would not take place without their presence and Zero Hour would be dependent on their arrival, although prior to this the infantry were to gain as much ground as possible through infiltration. No divisional fire plan was laid down. Instead brigade commanders were invited to arrange fire support directly with their artillery liaison officers. The artillery was exhorted, however, to detail its forward sections to support the tanks and to be prepared to engage anti-tank guns. What is curious is that there appears to have been no attempt to co-ordinate its attack with that of the 32nd Division. As for the other three Canadian divisions, they were ordered merely to consolidate, with the 3rd Canadian Division placed in Corps reserve.

For the Australian Corps it was a question of unfinished business on the flanks and its men were in action early to complete it. In the south Lihons remained in German hands and the 1st Australian Division was tasked with another attempt to take the village. Zero Hour was set for 4 a.m. to conform with operations by the 2nd and 3rd Australian Divisions to the north. The 2nd Brigade, with four tanks, would take Lihons itself, while the 3rd Brigade would attack on the left with just two tanks. The morning itself was foggy and very dark and only one tank was in position at Zero Hour to support the 3rd Brigade. The troops attacked behind a creeping barrage, although at 100 yard lifts every three minutes this proved to be too quick for the infantry who were faced with crossing a network of trenches. Heavy machine-gun fire was experienced from the outset. Because of the poor visibility it was random rather than aimed and the advance pressed onwards. But it also caused touch to be lost between the two brigades. Even so, the attack was successful, with lately arrived tanks being used to mop up Lihons itself. As the Divisional report put it:

> We were now in a secure position, on a commanding ridge looking well over the Canadians on the right and well over the enemy's country in all directions. We were in touch on both flanks, for though the Canadians had not advanced we had thrown back a defensive flank along the railway.[22]

The Germans, however, were not prepared for this situation to continue.

Taking advantage of the continuing fog, at 6 a.m. came the first of a series of counter-attacks. It struck the weakest point in the 11th Battalion's line, which was held by a platoon a mere seventeen men strong. They managed, with rifles, Lewis guns and grenades to beat it off and another which followed almost immediately. At 8.30 a.m. a party of Germans succeeded in breaking through towards Crépey Wood, but were eventually repulsed after heavy fighting. These counter-attacks continued for much of the day, with the Germans taking advantage of the numerous trenches to infiltrate through the defences. Ammunition began to run short and exhaustion grew. Lt Col J. W. Mitchell of the 8th Battalion observed:

> During a lull in the fighting when the heat of the sun was greatest, a reaction had set in and signs of intense drowsiness and fatigue were very apparent. The poor lads dozed as they stood at their posts.[23]

True, Major General Glasgow still had his 1st Brigade available, but he wanted to keep it intact and was not prepared to commit it piecemeal to bolster his defences.

To support the attack of the 1st Australian Division the 2nd Australian Division's 7th Brigade attacked, also at 4 a.m., on its left flank. The assault was carried out by the 26th and 28th Battalions. Their objective was the high ground to the west and south-west of Harleville. The barrage proved very effective and the objective was secured at a cost of just over 100 casualties. Some 70 Germans were captured, together with 18 machine guns. The only problem was that the 26th Battalion on the right found itself with a gap of 700 yards between its right flank and the neighbouring 1st Australian Division battalion, the 11th. Consequently it had to form a defensive flank. The 5th Australian Brigade conformed to the attack of the 7th Brigade, its objective being the remainder of the high ground west of Harleville and that north of Rainecourt. The fog made navigation difficult and the Germans responded to the opening barrage with gas and HE shells. There was also heavy machine-gun fire from the Proyart area on the left flank. The objective was gained within the hour, however. The Germans did launch a counter-attack at 5.30 a.m., but this was easily dealt with and included the use of recently captured machine guns.

As soon as the 5th Brigade was firm on its objective the 3rd

Australian Division astride the Somme ordered its 38th Battalion to gain touch. This entailed filling a 700 yard gap which now existed between it and the 20th Battalion of the 5th Brigade. The 38th Battalion's A Company carried out this task amid the still lingering fog. When it lifted A Company discovered that they had dug in within 20 yards of a German strongpoint. Two members of the company opened fire on it until a white flag was raised. They rushed the post and took the surrender of an officer and twenty other ranks, another officer having been killed. The same happened with another German machine-gun post a little later on and it was significant that German machine guns from Proyart opened fire on the surrendering members of the post, presumably to discourage others from doing the same.[24]

Aross the river the 3rd Australian Division still needed to tidy up the situation in front of Bray and at Etinehem. The 13th Brigade at dawn was positioned in a box-like posture, with the 49th Battalion facing north, the 50th Battalion covering Bray to the east, and B Company of the 51st Battalion poised to take Etinehem. The Americans provided the fourth side of the box from the positions along the eastern edge of Gressaire Ridge. Finally, the remainder of the 51st Battalion was situated behind the US 131st Regiment and covering the river bank. There was not much that could be done by the 50th Battalion facing Bray. Daylight found it with its positions very exposed on the east side of the Etinehem spur and the Germans began to subject them to artillery fire. It could do little more than send out reconnaissance patrols, as did the 49th Battalion to the north. As for Etinehem, B Company of the 51st Battalion attacked at dawn, supported by Vickers machine guns and Stokes mortars. To the surprise of the attackers only one German was in residence, the remainder of the 150-strong garrison having withdrawn across a footbridge over the Somme during the night. The Company then dug in south of the village in a position from which it could cover the crossings over the river. The Division, however, was left in an unsatisfactory position with the Germans still holding a salient based on Proyart just south of the Somme.

Eyes were now turned south to the 32nd Division's attack. The attacking troops (1st Dorsets, 5th/6th Royal Scots and the 2nd King's Own Yorkshire Light Infantry (KOYLI)) managed to reach their jump off positions without being spotted. The barrage opened on time at 9.30 a.m. Unfortunately it came down 500 yards instead of 300 yards ahead of the existing front line, which was thought to be the old German front line rather than the British one. Consequently, forward German machine-gun posts were untouched by it and were quick to get into action against the attacking infantry. There were also dense belts of wire to cross. Even so the Dorsets managed to clear the Bois en Equerre and by 11 a.m. had reached the Bois de Milieu on the left and close to the western outskirts of Damery on the right. Undeterred by heavy officer casualties the Royal Scots got into Parvillers, in spite of their four supporting tanks being knocked out, but were too weak to maintain their hold on it. On the extreme left the 97th Brigade's 2nd KOYLI was similarly held up. In the meantime, just after 10 a.m., General Lambert received a telephone call from the Canadian Corps commander. Currie told him not to push the attack too hard if there was a danger of suffering heavy casualties. Lambert immediately went forward to the headquarters of the two attacking brigades to obtain a closer feel for the situation. He decided that there was nothing to be gained in pursuing the attack on Parvillers, but that there were indications that the German hold on Damery was weak. He therefore told the commander of the 14th Brigade to deploy his reserve battalion, the 15th Highland Light Infantry, to this end but only if there was a good chance of capturing the village without heavy loss. In the light of increasing German artillery and machine gun fire, Brigadier General L. P. Evans VC DSO concluded that it was not worth the effort and informed Lambert of this at 4.50 p.m. Accordingly Lambert issued orders for the line to be consolidated as it stood.

The attack of the 4th Canadian Division on the left of the 32nd Division would not be mounted until the tanks allocated had arrived. The 10th and 12th Brigades were responsible for carrying it out and were provided with the same artillery. Six were to be provided by the

13th Tank Battalion and six from the 14th Tank Battalion. The account of the former states that the tanks motored 14,000 yards in some two and a half hours from Cerisy to Méharicourt, which was found to be under intense German bombardment. Accordingly, the tanks lay up in a former German artillery emplacement some 400 yards to the south-west. Because of the uncertainty of the situation on the north flank around Lihons and problems in gathering sufficient artillery support the attack was three times postponed.[25] But at 10 a.m. came a further problem. The previous day's attack had left the 78th Battalion holding Hallu, but with both its flanks in the air. A company from the 38th Battalion had been sent up on the morning of the 11th to help secure the left flank, but the right remained vulnerable. Now the Germans put down a heavy barrage on the village and then counter-attacked from Hallu Wood. This also fell on the 50th Battalion, the left hand unit in the 12th Brigade to the south. This finally put paid to the prospects of the 4th Canadian Division's attack and at 12.30 p.m. Currie ordered it to be cancelled. After bitter fighting the 78th and 50th Battalions were forced to withdraw to the Chilly area.

The delays in mounting the Canadian Corps attacks had an effect on the French 126th Division to its immediate right. The French were intending to attack at dawn, but learned the previous evening that the British 32nd Division could not attack until 7 a.m. The French liaison officer with the 32nd Division apparently waited most of the night for a copy of its attack orders and eventually arrived with them at the 126th Division's HQ at Arvillers shortly before dawn. To their horror the French realized that the British would not now attack until 9.30 a.m., which would mean that the French left flank would be in the air for at least four hours. It was too late to halt the French attack, which went ahead on time. Initially progress was good, but the attack became held up by Z Wood, which lay south of Damery and just north of the Amiens–Roye road. The cause of this was machine-gun fire from Damery, which was in the 32nd Division sector. The Germans then counter-attacked and General Matthieu, commanding the 126th Division, considered that there was no point in trying to progress further until the British had captured Damery.

Capt Cyril Falls was now the British liaison officer with the Division and he went across to the 32nd Division HQ to find out what was happening:

> ... the GSO1 asked me what General Mathieu now proposed to do, and there was almost a row, which would have been my fault, for I very wrongly (and truly) said:- 'I don't think he proposes to budge, sir. He thinks he has been let down.' Naturally the GSO1 was annoyed. He answered: 'I presume he does not hold me responsible.' I said: 'No, sir, but you must admit there has been a hopeless lack of coordination, and as this battle is being fought under the orders of British GHQ, he holds the British responsible for that.'

Falls found that the British staff had little idea of how the 32nd Division's attack was progressing. When he returned to HQ 126th Division he heard that General Mathieu was planning to renew his attack at 4.30 p.m., but needed to know precisely the line the British had reached. He decided that the only answer was to see for himself. Accompanied by a French staff officer and amid increasing German shell fire he managed to get within a few hundred yards of Damery and rightly concluded that it was still in German hands. Just before 4 p.m. a staff officer from the 166th Division on the right arrived with a copy of orders for a local attack which it was mounting at 5.30 p.m. and requested that the 126th Division co-operate. General Mathieu ascertained that he had twenty minutes to stop his own barrage and then, after some difficulty, got through to the 166th Division. The two commanders agreed to mount a joint attack at 6 p.m. The 166th Division was successful, but the further attempt against Z Wood failed.[26] In the rest of the XXXI Corps sector the story was much the same and gains were few, as was the case with X Corps. Since the prospect of a breakthrough now appeared slim II Cavalry Corps returned to the Avre valley. The French Third Army did make better progress, in spite of broken ground, its advance being an average of 2 miles throughout its sector.

On the air side the main targets during the day were Cambrai, Péronne and Equancourt railway stations. Twelve DH9s of No. 98 Squadron and eight from No. 107 Squadron set off to attack the latter at 7.30 a.m. There was heavy cloud over the target and the two squadrons failed to meet up. Only three bombers from No. 107 Squadron reached the target and bombed and No. 98 Squadron was intercepted by Pfalzes before it could reach the target and so it dropped its bombs and turned for home, two DH9s being shot down. The fighter escort from Nos. 1 and 43 Squadrons failed to make contact. Better success was had against Cambrai and Péronne stations, which were attacked by twelve DH9s and one DH4 from Nos 27 and 49 Squadrons. Several hits were observed on the sidings of both places and there was no German interference. DH4s of No. 205 Squadron carried out three further attacks against Péronne station during the day and did meet some German planes, one of which was shot down when it appeared in the middle of the bomber formation. Attempting an attack from below the formation a Pfalz was actually struck by a bomb, which tore off one of its wings before continuing on to explode close to the station. Remarkably, No. 205 Squadron had no aircraft casualties. Indeed it had only one aircraft written off during the four days and that had been able to land after being badly shot up. The DH9 squadrons, on the other hand, all had a number of aircraft shot down and others having to abort because of mechanical problems. The official historical monograph covering this period concluded that the excellence of the DH4's Rolls-Royce engines, as opposed to the BHP engines of the DH9, was a major reason for this discrepancy between the two aircraft types. [27]

The slower aircraft used by the Corps squadrons and the fact that they often had to fly in a more predictable fashion than the scout aircraft made them particularly vulnerable to air and ground attack. One crew who suffered was that of Capt Ferdinand ('Freddie') West, a flight commander in No. 8 Squadron, and his observer Lt William Haslam. On 8 August they had crash landed in fog on return to their airfield and the following day they had been shot down by ground fire, but had survived. On 10 August, having written off two Armstrong

Whitworths, they took off in yet another Big Ack, as the aircraft was fondly called by its crews. Their task was to monitor the progress of the tanks in the Rosières area. Soon after they crossed over the lines they noted a formation of Fokker D.VIIs in the vicinity, but believed that there was sufficient cloud about to provide them cover. West then spotted what appeared to be German troops gathering for a counter-attack near Roye. He went to check this out and also attacked with bombs and strafed them with machine-gun fire. They then turned for home, but found their way blocked by the Fokkers. The leader attacked from below and his first burst struck home. Haslam suffered a flesh wound to his leg, but West was much more badly wounded, his left leg all but severed and his right leg also hit, and their aircraft was diving towards the ground. Semi-conscious, West managed to pull the joystick back enough to get the plane in level flight once more, while Haslam engaged the German aircraft with his machine guns. He hit the leader and this appears to have deterred the others from continuing their attacks. They managed to get back across the lines and, spotting an open field, West put the aircraft down, suffering agony as he did so. Luckily, there were some Canadian medics close by and these helped Haslam to extricate his pilot from the cockpit. Both men were then taken to a field dressing station where West had his leg amputated, but not before he had given details of the German concentration around Roye. For his extraordinary courage and determination, coming on top of his experiences of the previous two days, Freddie West was later awarded the Victoria Cross.*

Just before 1 p.m. on 11 August Rawlinson summoned his corps commanders to a conference at HQ 2nd Australian Division at Villers Bretonneux. The reason for this location was that he had heard that Monash had convened a meeting with his divisional commanders

---

* Many accounts state that this event took place on 12 August, largely because an account of it appeared in the RAF daily communiqué of that date. However, no tanks were in action that day and so this cannot be so. West himself (he had already been awarded the MC) remained in the RAF, being fitted with an artificial leg and rose to be an Air Commodore.

there for 2.30 p.m. Rawlinson therefore laid down 3 p.m. for his own conference. Monash had, in his own words,

> ... selected a place on the western outskirts of the town, suitable for the Conference, under a bunch of trees. All around was a scene of the greatest activity. On one side of the main road was a large wired-in prisoners cage, in which over 3000 Boche prisoners, who had been captured during the last twenty-four hours ... An immense stream of traffic was pouring up the road towards the Front ... the first railway train which had succeeded in getting through Amiens since the battle was actually steaming through the cutting at 2.30.[28]

No sooner had his subordinate commanders gathered than the CIGS, Sir Henry Wilson, arrived, followed by Haig, who gave the assembled Australian audience a complimentary speech, praising Monash in particular. Then came Rawlinson followed by his other corps commanders, as well as Hugh Elles of the Tank Corps and Lionel Charlton the commander of VIII Brigade RAF. Haig insisted that Rawlinson's conference not be delayed and he began by asking the view of his corps commanders on the present situation, but the flood of visitors had not ended. A short while later another three cars arrived with French Prime Minister Georges Clemenceau, his finance minister, and Ferdinand Foch on board. Monash recalled:

> Of course there was no thought of serious work or discussion for some twenty minutes, while everybody was being presented to everybody else, and I was personally, naturally – with General Currie – the leading figure in the show, for everybody was highly complimentary and marvelled at the completeness of our success.[29]

When serious discussion resumed Rawlinson announced that he was temporarily halting the offensive, while Byng and his Third Army took up the torch. In the meantime more artillery and tanks would be gathered with a view to resuming the offensive on 14 or 15 August.

CHAPTER NINE

THE IMPACT OF AMIENS

On 11 August 1918 there was a conference presided over by the Kaiser at von Hindenburg's headquarters at Avesnes. At it the Kaiser uttered: 'I see that we must strike a balance. We have nearly reached the limit of our power of resistance. The war must be ended.'[1] Two days later there was a further high level conference at Spa. Ludendorff stated that Germany no longer had the means to launch another offensive 'to force the enemy to sue for peace by an offensive' and 'as the defensive alone could hardly achieve that object . . . the termination of the war would have to be brought about by diplomacy.'[2] Von Hindenburg, according to his memoirs, took a slightly different view:

If the enemy repeated these attacks with the same fury, in view of the present constitution of our army, there was at any rate some prospect of our powers of resistance being gradually paralysed. On the other hand, the fact that the enemy had once more failed to extract all possible advantages from his great initial success gave me the hope that we should overcome further crises.

He also reminded those present that 'we were still standing deep in the enemy's country'. He argued that peace feelers should not be put out until there had been an improvement in the military situation.[3] All this implied that he hoped that the Allies would allow the Germans a respite before they attacked again. This was not to be so.

On 12 August King George V and Queen Mary, who had been in France during the Amiens attack, visited the Fourth Army. The King inspected elements of the US 33rd Division, although the 131st Regiment was not present, being still in the line, and conferred on Pershing and General Tasker Bliss, the US representative on the Supreme War Council, the Knight Grand Cross of the Order of the Bath. Their Majesties then went on to visit III Corps, Amiens, and finally the Australians at Bertangles, where he knighted Monash. Rawlinson was present only part of the time. Haig came to his HQ in the afternoon to brief him, Debeney, and Byng on the next phase. He stated that the immediate objective for the Fourth Army was the line from Chaulnes to the high ground east of Roye and that the advance was to be generally north-east. The Third Army was to break through and aim for Bapaume, the idea being to turn the flank of the Germans in front of Rawlinson. Haig stated that Rawlinson should renew the offensive on the 15th and that Byng, reinforced with two cavalry and four infantry divisions, together with 200 tanks, was to attack on the 20th. (See Map 7.)

Rawlinson noted that the attack would be continuing across the old Somme battlefields, and the trenches would be 'full of MG nests so I fear we will have a higher casualty list'.[4] When he went through the plan with Sir Arthur Currie, the latter was aghast. He produced air photographs of the German defences and also warned of the likely high casualty bill. He was therefore opposed to the attack. Rawlinson forwarded Currie's views to Haig, who cancelled the attack the day before it was due to take place. Next day he had a somewhat acrimonious interview with Foch, who was angry at the cancellation. Haig replied that he alone was responsible for the operations of the British Army and Foch calmed down.

Meanwhile, Ludendorff had authorized a slight withdrawal by the Seventeenth Army in front of Byng in order to remove a salient south of Bucquoy and thus save on manpower. Byng reported this on 14 August and followed up, although the Germans pulled back little more than a mile and it did not affect their main defensive position. Byng launched his main attack on 21 August, again with fog to assist him. On the first day the attack reached the Arras–Amiens railway, an advance of about 2 miles, but the main German defences had not been reached and hence there was no opportunity for the cavalry and armoured cars to exploit as they had done on 8 August. Byng, cautious by nature, now ordered a pause on the grounds that his men were suffering from the heat and the artillery needed to redeploy. This made his opponent, Otto von Below, the Seventeenth Army commander, believe that he had shot his bolt and he began to prepare a counter-attack. All this was in contrast to what was happening in the French sector. On 20 August the tough General Charles Mangin launched his Tenth Army from the Aisne to the Oise and in two days advanced some 5 miles. On his left Humbert resumed his assault on the following day and advanced in step with Mangin. In the light of this Haig was not best pleased when he heard of Byng's decision. On 22 August he issued a note to his army commanders. It stated in part:

> The methods which we have followed, hitherto, in our battles with limited objectives when the enemy was strong, are no longer suited to the present conditions.
>
> The enemy has not the means to deliver counter-attacks on an extended scale, nor has he the numbers to hold a position against the very extended advance which is now being directed upon him.
>
> To turn the present situation to account the most resolute offensive is everywhere desirable. Risks which a month ago would have been criminal to incur, ought now to be incurred as a duty.
>
> It is no longer necessary to advance in regular lines and step. On the contrary, each division should be given a distant objective which must be reached independently of its neighbour, and even if one's flank is thereby exposed for the time being.[5]

With 8 August clearly echoing in his ears, Haig could sense that ultimate victory lay just around the corner.

On the same day of 22 August von Below launched a series of counter-attacks against the Third Army, but they were poorly coordinated and repulsed without too much difficulty. To the south Rawlinson's III Corps attacked, its objectives Albert and high ground between the Somme and the Ancre. It was almost totally successful, apart from a counter-attack against the 47th Division, which drove one of its brigades from ground it had just captured. Pressured by Haig, Byng resumed his attack on 23 August. It began in the early hours of the morning with preliminary attacks. VI Corps in the north launched its main attack at 4.55 a.m., while that of IV Corps began at 11 a.m. The tanks played their part, as did the RAF, and by the end of the day the River Sensée had been reached in the north, while in the centre it came to a halt just 3 miles west of Bapaume. Some 5,000 German prisoners were also taken, an indication that German morale was slipping.

After Amiens Ludendorff had refused to sanction any significant withdrawals in order to shorten the front but he did agree to a construction of an extension to the Hindenburg Line (called the Siegfried Line by the Germans), which the Germans had built in winter 1916–17 and withdrawn to in the spring of 1917. Known as the Wotan Position by the Germans it ran from south of the River Scarpe up to just east of Armentières, and was called Drocourt–Quéant Switch Line by the British. On 26 August Ludendorff relented and gave orders for the Second Army, still facing Rawlinson, and the Eighteenth Army to its left to begin withdrawing to this line. But, driven on by Haig, Byng and Rawlinson had continued to attack, with the Australian Corps being particularly aggressive. General Sir Henry Horne's First Army joined in on 26 August. The Canadian Corps, which had been returned to Horne, advanced 4 miles down the Arras–Cambrai road, outflanking the northern extremity of the Hindenburg before coming to a short halt in front of the Drocourt–Quéant Line two days later. Then, on the night of 30/31 August, in the Fourth Army sector, the Australians crossed the Somme and Somme Canal between Clery and Péronne and turfed the crack 2nd Guards Division off the dominant Mont St Quentin to the north of Péronne.

The Germans were still fighting hard, sufficient to inflict some

120,000 casualties on the BEF during August, but this had to be balanced against the 63,000 prisoners and 870 guns that had fallen into British hands. In truth they were being stretched on the rack. As the Bavarian Official History described it:

> ... the German front ached and groaned in every joint under the increasing blows delivered with every fresh and increasing force [sic]. Heavy losses in men, horses and material had been suffered, and the expenditure of man-power had reached terrifying proportions. The German divisions just melted away. Reinforcements, in spite of demands and entreaties, were not forthcoming. Only by breaking up further divisions and regiments in the field could the gap be more or less filled.[6]

Ludendorff was forced to sanction further withdrawals to the main Hindenburg defences, as well as accept the loss of the territory the Germans had gained during their April 1918 Lys offensive. This was followed up by the British Armies and the French First, Third, and Tenth Armies.

But if Foch and Haig, and the other senior commanders, increasingly had their tails up, the British government was becoming concerned. Lloyd George instructed Sir Henry Wilson, the CIGS, to send Haig a note 'warning him that the War Cabinet would not approve attacks on the Hindenburg Line involving heavy casualties whether to British or American troops.' Wilson sent it marked 'HW personal', writing that 'the War Cabinet would become anxious if we received heavy punishment in attacking the Hindenburg Line WITHOUT SUCCESS [sic].' Haig not surprisingly took umbrage, considering the Cabinet to be 'underhand' in their interfering, and 'do not dare openly to say that they mean to take the responsibility for any failure though ready to take the credit for every success!' He replied to Wilson: 'What a wretched lot! How well they mean to support me! What confidence!' Wilson responded with a placatory note saying that it was not that the Cabinet had lost confidence in them, but that they were still deeply concerned over manpower and were also 'curiously hostile' to the Americans and the French.[7] This is probably because it appeared in London that during August the BEF had been doing most of the fighting, but this would change.

September opened with the British First Army assaulting and breaking through the Drocourt–Quéant Line, again achieved by the Canadians. Then, on 3 September, Foch issued a fresh directive. The British, supported by the adjoining French armies, were to press on towards Cambrai and St Quentin, while the French would push beyond the Aisne. The Americans, now given the opportunity to operate as a distinct entity, were to first remove the German salient at St Mihiel and then advance with the French Fourth Army towards Mézières. As Foch explained to Colonel Charles à Court Repington, the London *Morning Post* war correspondent, it was a question of 'Tout le monde va à la bataille . . . We hammer them everywhere. This will go on for six weeks . . . In the end they'll be worn out.'[8] Haig was imbued with the same spirit. He returned to London on 9 September, after agreeing an attack in Flanders with the Belgians, and saw the Secretary of State for War, Lord Milner. He sought to impress upon him how much the situation had changed on the Western Front in recent weeks:

> The discipline of the German Army is quickly going, and the German officer is no longer what he was. It seems to me to be the beginning of the end . . . What is wanted now at once is to provide the means to exploit our recent successes to the full. Reserves in England should be regarded as Reserves for the French front, and all yeomanry, cyclists etc. now kept for civil [home] defence should be sent to France *at once* [sic]. If we act with energy now a decision can be obtained in the very near future.[9]

This should be set against the backdrop that at the time the Supreme War Council was looking to finish the war with a final offensive in summer 1919. It was called Plan 1919 and orders had already been placed for the production of a new tank, the Medium D, with the aim of having 1,000 of them ready for the offensive. The British and French governments were therefore bent on building up strength for this, rather than incurring heavy casualties during autumn 1918. In spite of this Lord Milner agreed to give Haig all the support he could.

Pershing's First US Army duly attacked the nose of the St Mihiel Salient on 12 September, assisted by the French Fourth Army on the left. In the space of a week the salient had been eradicated, with 15,000 prisoners and 250 guns taken. On that same day of 12 September the 56th (London) Division (Third Army) captured Havrincourt and, aided by two other divisions, threw back a counter-attack by four of Germany's best divisions. It was the last significant counter-attack to be made in the British sector. It also marked the beginning of the closing up to the Hindenburg Line phase.

While this was going on two further blows were struck. The Americans had extended to their left to take in most of the Argonne Forest. With Henri Gouraud's Fourth French Army again on their left they struck northwards between the Rivers Suippe and Meuse on 26 September. The following day the British First and Third Armies resumed their advance towards Cambrai. On 27 September the Belgians and British Second Army joined in, with an offensive north of the Lys. Finally, on 29 September the British Fourth and French First Armies ruptured the Hindenburg Line, with the 46th Division crossing the Canal du Nord at a stroke, and began to fight their way through the rest of the German defensive belt. Ludendorff, who had been forced to take a short rest at the beginning of the month because of nervous exhaustion, looked at the situation map, and with Bulgaria already about to sue for peace, declared at a Council of War with the foreign secretary that Germany must seek an immediate armistice.

On 5 October the British armies finally fought their way through the complex of defences that made up the Hindenburg Line, with the Canadians fighting their way across the old Cambrai battlefield and into the town itself. In the north the Flanders offensive initially progressed well, but the ground which had been so fought over during the late summer and autumn of 1917 became almost as boggy as it was then. This time it was resupply that became badly affected, so much so that no less than 15,000 rations for Belgian and French troops taking part had to be dropped by air. This forced a pause. In the centre of the Allied line the French were advancing steadily across the Aisne and northwards, while the Americans had cleared the Argonne Forest and were now about to form a second army. In the meantime the Germans had appointed a new chancellor, Prince Max of Baden, to handle the negotiations for an armistice. He made a request to President Woodrow Wilson for an armistice based on the Allied terms issued under Wilson's Fourteen Points at the beginning of the year. His reply was not that which von Hindenburg wanted. Wilson demanded the agreement to the evacuation of all occupied territory in the West as a precondition. Von Hindenburg, on the other hand, clearly hoped for an armistice with the German forces holding their present positions. As he wrote to his wife:

> The armistice is militarily necessary to us. We shall soon be at the end of our strength. If the peace does not follow, then we shall at least have disengaged ourselves from the enemy, rested ourselves and won time. Then we shall be more fit to fight than now, if that is necessary. But I don't believe that after two – three months any country will have the desire to begin war again.[10]

In that case Germany would be left with a bargaining chip in the French and Belgian territory that she still held. Prince Max sent a conciliatory reply to Wilson offering to introduce democratic government, but Wilson became ever stiffer in his demands as October wore on, demanding the abdication of the Kaiser and insisting that the armistice must be a surrender, with no question of any possible resumption of activities.

The fighting continued. Von Hindenburg and Ludendorff now believed that if they could show that the German Army could not be broken more favourable peace terms might be negotiated. And fight on the German Army did, but now it was very much a question of skilful rearguard actions, with their machine-gunners, as ever, playing a lead part. The Allies, however, were not to be denied. The Flanders offensive was renewed and the other British armies continued to push steadily forwards, as did the French. It was, however, in the American sector that German resistance was at its fiercest, helped considerably by the advantageous nature of the terrain to the defence. American progress at one point ground virtually to a halt, with Foch wanting to remove Pershing from command. But behind the German front line the situation was worsening by the day. Left wing agitators had infiltrated the ranks of the Army and Navy and discipline began to crumble, resulting in a naval mutiny. Eventually, as Turkey and then Austria–Hungary bowed out, armistice negotiations began in earnest. On 9 November Germany was proclaimed a republic and the next day the Kaiser fled across the border to neutral Holland. An armistice Agreement was eventually reached at 5 a.m. on 11 November. Shortly afterwards Canadian troops entered Mons, where for the BEF it had all first started 51 months earlier. Six hours later the guns fell silent.

That, in brief, is the story of the Hundred Days, although in fact it was only ninety-six. Yet, it was the opening day, 8 August, which really set the pattern for what was to follow. In the space of a few hours the British Fourth Army, assisted by the French First Army, demonstrated that tactics had been evolved which were as effective, if not more so, than the German stormtroop approach that had produced such crises in the Allied ranks during the spring and early summer. It was the culmination of what military historians have termed the 'learning curve'. First was the ability to achieve complete surprise. In this context tribute must be paid to the high quality of staff work, something which has been so often lambasted, especially that of the British Army during 1914–18. That the complete Canadian Corps, the Cavalry Corps, two brigades of tanks and a large amount of extra artillery could be deployed from elsewhere in the British sector in such a short space of time, and without the Germans knowing about it, was an extraordinary achievement, although the part the RAF played in preventing German air reconnaissance from operating successfully over the lines cannot be ignored. It was highly efficient staff work which also ensured that all elements involved in the attack were in the right place for Zero Hour.

The attack itself also showed how much the understanding of the all arms battle had evolved. Artillery, tanks, armoured cars, machine guns, trench mortars, infantry, and airpower combined as never before. True, not everything worked as hoped, notably the co-operation between the cavalry and Whippet tanks, but this had not been tried before. Neither had the use of the Mark V Stars as armoured personnel carriers. The Germans tended to blame just the tanks for the disaster they suffered, but this was largely because they had so few themselves. In truth, no one weapon was dominant. The infantry showed that they were able to cope when their tanks were knocked out or did not appear. Indeed, the quality of low level infantry tactics in terms of fire and movement, especially those practised by the Australians, was most marked. The artillery was invaluable, but in contrast to the mistaken 1915–17 belief that it could win battles on its own, its growing flexibility to adapt to rapidly changing situations stood out. As for the air side, first fog, and then the rapid reaction by the German air force meant that it is very questionable whether the Allies had achieved anything more than air parity over the battlefield on the day itself. This makes the achievements on the ground during 8 August all the more impressive.

It is true that in one respect the British did copy the German tactic of infiltration. It was not, however, by specially trained infantry, but something much more appropriate to what was becoming an increasingly technological war. The Medium tanks and, even more especially, the sixteen Austin armoured cars of the 17th Battalion of the Tank Corps caused confusion in the German ranks out of all proportion to their numbers. What was not possible, given the speed of the Mark V tank and infantry on their feet, as well as the vulnerability of horsed cavalry to machine guns, was immediate exploitation of their success. There was another reason as well –

communications. Fourth Army had done everything possible in its planning to ensure that communications worked, applying 'belt and braces'. Every existing method – line, pigeon, wireless, air-ground, liaison officer, despatch riders (motor-cycle and mounted), heliograph, and the so often much used last resort, the runner – was employed, but the fog of war still reigned. Information still took too long to arrive at the relevant headquarters and this made it difficult to gauge the actual situation on the ground in a timely way.

The delay in the passage of information was one reason for the delay in Fourth Army organizing operations for the following day. The other was that everyone in authority was almost in a state of shock at what had been achieved, as Rawlinson's chief of staff admitted. In their defence it is worth restating that this was the first major attack that the British Army had carried out since Cambrai in November 1917 and that had been carried out by the Third Army and not the Fourth. The 'bite and hold' policy which had evolved during 1915–17 in which a piece of ground was seized and then there was a pause while the artillery was moved forward to support the next phase had become somewhat inbred. There was also a deep respect for the fighting qualities of the German Army, especially its ability to mount immediate counter-attacks. This is why the Mark V Stars had been used to bring machine guns forward and No. 9 Squadron RAF to drop ammunition for them on the objective. The expectation was that the Germans would inevitably counter-attack before nightfall on 8 August and so consolidation was the priority, rather than immediately preparing to push on eastwards.

This is excusable, but when HQ Fourth Army had finally realized that the Germans were in trouble the orders issued were too loose in that they did not lay down a Zero Hour, but left it to the Canadian Corps, which was now to take the lead role, to decide. Currie allowed this flexibility to his subordinate formations and this impacted on the Australians and III Corps. In the end, virtually every brigade attacked at different times, indicating that corps and divisions were as surprised by the success as Fourth Army was. Few brigades were in the position to attack early, if nothing else because they were at a distance from their start lines. This gave the Germans a valuable breathing space and, although very shaken, they were able to shore up their defences to a degree. There was, too, the problem of tank availability. Battle casualties, mechanical breakdowns and crew exhaustion meant that the number of available tanks was sharply reduced. On 8 August 421 had gone into action, but only 143 were available on the following day. Seventy-nine were fit on 10 August, but only 38 on the last day of the attack.[11] By this time, faced with traversing the old Somme battlefield against a now coherent German defence, it was clear that further progress could only come at the cost of heavy casualties, something which the commanders of 1918 were not prepared to countenance any more.

It was this that set the pattern for the rest of the Hundred Days, apart perhaps from the Americans during the Meuse-Argonne battle. Once an offensive had begun to run out of momentum the policy was to halt it and attack elsewhere. This also kept the Germans off balance in that they were never able to commit what reserves they still had to any particular sector. But the nature of the ground fighting had changed in another way. This was increasing decentralization. It did not apply so much to the Americans, who were still on a very steep learning curve, as to the French and the British, whose senior commanders were now so experienced that they could be allowed to operate on a very much looser rein than had been the case. It is a charge that has been levelled against Haig that he delegated operations too much to his army commanders. Yet, they too, and the corps and even the divisional commanders below them found that they could not exert tight control over events in this more open form of warfare, which was often a case of Allied advanced guards tussling with German rearguards and having to use their own initiative. Only when they reached a serious obstacle were higher commands able to take control once more. Otherwise it was more a question of merely giving guidance as to objectives and the shape of the battle.

Beginning with von Hindenburg in his 1919 memoirs, the Germans claimed that their army was not defeated in the field and the idea of the 'stab in the back' was eagerly seized on by the political right wing in Germany, if nothing else to combat the Communists, who came close at one point to taking over the country during the civil war that broke out in the immediate aftermath of the Armistice. The fact was that the German Army in the West was defeated in the field and this was the reason why Ludendorff, and von Hindenburg, wanted an armistice. That the terms were not in the end what they desired was because the German people had had enough and no longer had any belief that the Army could do anything to avert defeat. That 8 August 1918 was the day that the Allies won the war was because it opened the door to ultimate victory. From then onwards the Germans accepted that they could no longer win. It was, indeed, the 'Black Day', to quote Ludendorff, and a 'Catastrophe', as reflected in the title of the German official monograph on the battle. Amiens also provided a blueprint for land warfare in the future. Just over twenty years later, with infinitely better performing armoured vehicles, aircraft and radio communications, the same tactics would be replicated in the German *Blitzkrieg* which would so devastate Europe during the years 1939–41.

THE MAN WHO WON THE WAR?

The London *Sunday Express* of 8 November 1931, three days before the thirteenth anniversary of the Armistice, had a lead story bearing the headlines:

THE MAN WHO ENDED THE WAR.
Subaltern's Capture of the Hindenburg Line Defence Plans
GREAT WAR SECRET OUT AFTER 13 YEARS
GERMAN PLANS FOUND BY YOUNG OFFICER
WHERE IS HE?
FORGOTTEN HERO OF RAID ON ENEMY HQ

The story was that on the evening of 28 September 1918, just before the assault on the Hindenburg Line, Major D. P. (actually D. F.) Stevenson DSO MC commanding No. 35 Squadron RAF briefed his officers and men on what was about to take place. One of those present was a mechanic, who knew shorthand, and noted down exactly what the squadron commander said. Major Stevenson pointed out the gun flashes of the artillery bombarding the German positions and went on to say:

A subaltern took some papers from a German staff officer. They were found to contain a complete plan of the defences of the Hindenburg Line. Every machine-gun, trench-mortar, and battery position were marked; the places where troops were to be billeted and the places where they were to draw rations were marked.

He said that this information had to be confirmed by air reconnaissance, including by No. 35 Squadron, which was equipped with
Armstrong Whitworths and Bristol Fighters. The defences appeared
to match up with the captured plans in every respect.

The *Sunday Express* decided to find out more and interviewed
Rawlinson's chief intelligence officer in August 1918, Lt Col Valentine
Vivian, who was now, although naturally the newspaper did not
know it, head of MI6's counter-espionage section. He related that he
'gave each officer taking part in the battle near Arras [sic] that started
on August 8, 1918 – Ludendorff's Black Day, as he himself called it –
a small map of every German divisional and brigade headquarters
known to us.' The officers were instructed to visit these HQs and
search for documents, killing or capturing any staff they found. He
went on to relate that cavalry and armoured cars had 'raided a
German corps headquarters at Wancourt, south-east of Arras [sic]'.
They entered a room littered in 'torn up papers'. The subaltern in
charge 'stuffed all the papers in empty sand bags'. He brought them
back and they were passed to the Cavalry Corps HQ. Once examined,
it was realized that they were a gold mine of information, which was
confirmed by air reconnaissance. 'Foch decided to attack at once –
and the war was over.' So, asked the newspaper, 'WHERE IS THE
SUBALTERN WHO ENDED THE WAR? The "Sunday Express"
invites him to come forward and take his place in history.'

The following Sunday the newspaper was able to report that the
officer in question had come forward. He was none other than Lt
Ernest Rollings of the 17th Armoured Car Battalion Tank Corps, who
had led the raid into Framerville on 8 August. On discharge from the
Army he had returned to being a policeman and was now a Sergeant
with the Neath Police in South Wales. Several other 'young officers'
had also claimed to be the mystery subaltern, but Rollings was the
only one who matched up and to confirm it the paper took him to
see his old commanding officer, Colonel E. J. Carter, who is reported
to have said 'There is no doubt about it, he is your man.' Rollings
himself recalled that he had been briefed at the Australian Corps HQ
to search for German HQs and seize documents. The tanks towed

two cars for about two and a half miles until the roads were clear of shell holes.

Framerville was now about seven and a half miles away. In the distance we could see the German rearguard still retreating but fighting desperately to make a stand. I knew that if the break in the line was filled that would be the end of us, but I decided to make a bid for it, and we raced at top speed along the Amiens – St Quentin road ... By noon we had fought our way through to Framerville, with the rearguard behind us being dealt with by the Australians. We found the German corps headquarters in an old farmhouse. I remember there were three steps leading to the door, because I mounted them slowly, revolver in hand.

But the German staff had fled a few minutes before, apparently, and so complete was their panic that they had not stopped to burn their papers. Some of the documents were torn up, but I packed every scrap into sandbags. I could not read German, and in any case I had no time to read any of the documents, so every little torn up scrap went into the sandbags.

When Rollings got outside he found his crew holding up four German staff officers. They stripped them of their papers and side-arms, but all four were then killed by a burst of machine gun fire. The cars eventually got back and Rollings passed over his sandbags filled with paper to his company commander. He heard nothing more about the matter, but did receive a bar to his MC.

The story now took another turn. Lady Houston, the wealthy widow of shipping magnate Sir Robert Houston, was a well known philanthropist. She was best known for the gift of £100,000 that she had made in January 1931 to the aircraft company Supermarine to enable Britain to enter the Schneider Trophy, the international air speed competition, after the Air Ministry, because of shortage of funds, had declined to provide any backing. Britain did win the Trophy that year and, having also won the two previous competitions, was allowed to keep the Trophy in perpetuity. This made

Lady Houston a national heroine and now, after reading about him in the *Sunday Express*, she said that she would like to give Rollings a cheque for £5,000 in recognition of his part in winning the war and as 'a tribute to his courage and a little nest-egg for the future.' The presentation, arranged by the newspaper, took place in the Empire Cinema, Neath on the evening of Saturday 21 November in the presence of a number of local dignitaries. Lady Houston herself could not make the presentation in person as she was ill and it was done by the Mayor of Neath. The Editor of the *Sunday Express* was present and made the point that it was not Rollings himself who had come forward, but one of his brother officers, Lt J. T. Yeoman. Although his armoured car section was not involved in the Framerville action, he had told the newspaper that Rollings was the man they were after.

In the meantime there had been a further twist. The *Manchester Evening Chronicle* of 17 November 1931 carried a piece concerning a local Manchester man, Cecil Rhodes, who owned a radio shop. He claimed to have been a Corporal and the commander of the other armoured car in Rollings's section and to have been awarded the Military Medal. Certainly his MM was gazetted on 21 January 1919, with his rank shown as Lance Corporal, and his account did tally in some respects with that of Rollings:

We swept right into Framerville. The place was full of Germans. Those who could ran for shelter, but many of them never reached it. In the village there was a biggish house with a notice 'Korps Kommander' or something like that over the door. I jumped out and ran inside. There was nobody there, and I didn't wait to look round and rushed out again. A German orderly was just running away with either a box or a basket, I am not sure which. My gunner shot him and I grabbed the basket and threw it in the car.

It apparently turned out to be full of pigeons which were later used to send false messages to the Germans. Rhodes then took his car out to the other side of the village and came across a field gun in action and so despatched the crew. He returned to the village, spotted four German staff officers on horseback and shot them. He then grabbed a leather case from one of the bodies and handed it in on reporting back to his company HQ. As for Rollings, Rhodes says that he did not see him in Framerville after they entered it, although he conceded that his section commander may have gone into the HQ later on and searched it. In another account, given to *The Western Mail* of the same date Rhodes stated that when they entered the village Rollings turned left while he entered the HQ, with one of his gunners fixing a flag bearing General Rawlinson's signature above the door. He also said that he handed the case he had taken from the dead German officer to Rollings on their return. The paper also carried a report on an interview with Rollings about Rhodes' claims. Rollings remembered that there was a man called Rhodes in his section, but he did not think that he was an NCO. He was adamant that only he entered the headquarters. 'I was in charge of the section and did not want to expose my men to any undue risk. They sat in the cars to cover me while I went in.'

Apart from the statements made to the newspapers, there is no documentary evidence still existing as to what information the papers that Rollings seized contained. There is also no evidence on the German side of any formation headquarters being in Framerville on 8 August. It was in the LI Corps sector, but its HQ was at Misery, well to the east. There were three divisional HQs – 117th, 225th and 14th Bavarian – situated just to the west of Vauvillers, some 2 miles south-west of Framerville. The village itself was held by elements of the 2nd Battalion 227th Reserve Regiment and there was a battery positioned just south of the village. Yet Rollings had sent a message by pigeon timed at 11.15 a.m., which stated: 'Have toured round Framerville and upset all their transport, etc. Australian flag hoisted at 11.15am on German Corps HQ.'[1] The only conclusions that can be drawn is that either it was a forward HQ for LI Corps or, bearing in mind Rollings's mention of transport, some form of logistics HQ. Regardless of that, General Sir Archibald Montgomery-Massingberd,

Rawlinson's chief of staff and now Adjutant General to the forces*, confirmed the detail that was learned of the German defences as a result of Rollings' find: 'It has fallen to the lot of few commanders to be provided with such detailed information as was furnished by the German memorandum.'[2]

Ernest Rollings himself, surprised at being so suddenly thrust into the limelight as a hero, continued to serve in the Neath police. He was made a Freeman of the town in 1932 and was acting Chief Constable of Glamorgan when he retired from the Force in 1943. Thereafter he worked in the investigation department of the Board of Trade and died in February 1966 aged 73.[3] While he may not literally have been 'the man who won the war', there is no doubt that the documents he brought back from that farm house in Framerville on that exhilarating August day did provide the key to unlocking the greatest obstacle that the Allies faced during their final victorious advance.

* He had added 'Massingberd' to his name in 1926 and was later CIGS 1933–36.

ORDERS OF BATTLE

8 AUGUST 1918

BRITISH

FOURTH ARMY (Rawlinson)

Army troops consisted of two 12-inch railway guns, four anti-aircraft batteries, and six searchlight sections RE

Cavalry Corps (Kavanagh)

Each cavalry brigade included a 13-pdr RHA battery, apart from the Canadian Cavalry Brigade, which had two batteries, and a machine gun squadron

IST CAVALRY DIVISION (MULLINS)
1st Cavalry Brigade – 2nd Dragoon Guards, 5th Dragoon Guards, 11th Hussars
2nd Cavalry Brigade – 4th Dragoon Guards, 9th Lancers, 18th Hussars
9th Cavalry Brigade – 8th Hussars, 15th Hussars, 19th Hussars

2ND CAVALRY DIVISION (PITMAN)
3rd Cavalry Brigade – 4th Hussars, 5th Lancers, 16th Lancers
4th Cavalry Brigade – 6th Dragoon Guards, 3rd Hussars, 1st/1st Oxfordshire Hussars
5th Cavalry Brigade – 2nd Dragoons (Royal Scots Greys), 12th Lancers, 20th Hussars

3RD CAVALRY DIVISION (HARMAN)
6th Cavalry Brigade – 3rd Dragoon Guards, 1st Royal Dragoons, 10th Hussars
7th Cavalry Brigade – 7th Dragoon Guards, 6th (Inniskilling) Dragoons, 17th Lancers
Canadian Cavalry Brigade – Royal Canadian Dragoons, Lord Strathcona's Horse, Fort Garry Horse
3rd Tank Brigade – 3rd and 6th (Light) Battalions (Whippets)

III CORPS (Butler)

Each Division had two field artillery brigades, two medium trench mortar batteries, and a machine-gun battalion. Each brigade had a trench mortar battery

Corps troops – 1st/1st Northumberland Yeomanry, 10th Tank Battalion, Corps Cyclist battalion, three 8-inch howitzer brigades, one 9.2-inch howitzer brigade, three mixed brigades (60pdr guns, 8-inch & 9.2-inch howitzers), one mobile brigade (60pdrs, 6-inch howitzers), one 12-inch howitzer battery, one heavy trench mortar battery

12TH DIVISION (HIGGINSON)
35th Brigade – 7th Royal Norfolk, 9th Essex, 1st/1st Cambridgeshire
36th Brigade – 9th Royal Fusiliers, 7th Royal Sussex, 5th Royal Berkshire
37th Brigade – 6th Queen's (Royal West Surrey), 6th Buffs (East Kent), 6th Royal West Kent

18TH DIVISION (LEE)
53rd Brigade – 10th Essex, 8th Royal Berkshire, 7th Royal West Kent
54th Brigade – 11th Royal Fusiliers, 2nd Bedfordshire, 6th Northamptonshire
55th Brigade – 7th Queen's (Royal West Surrey), 7th Buffs (East Kent), 8th East Surrey

47TH (LONDON) DIVISION (GORRINGE)
140th Brigade – 1st/15th London (Civil Service Rifles), 1st/17th London (Poplar and Stepney Rifles), 1st/21st London (Surrey Rifles)
141st Brigade – 1st/18th London (London Irish Rifles), 1st/19th London (St Pancras), 1st/20th London (Blackheath and Woolwich)
142nd Brigade – 1st/22nd London (The Queen's), 1st/23rd London, 1st/24th London (The Queen's)

58TH (LONDON) DIVISION (RAMSAY)
173rd Brigade – 2nd/2nd London (Royal Fusiliers), 1st/3rd London (Royal Fusiliers), 2nd/4th London (Royal Fusiliers)
174th Brigade – 6th London, 7th London, 8th London (Post Office Rifles)
175th Brigade – 9th London (Queen Victoria's Rifles), 2nd/10th London (Hackney), 12th London (The Rangers)

US 33RD (ILLINOIS) DIVISION (BELL)
122nd Machine Gun Battalion
65th Brigade
129th Regiment (3rd Illinois) – three battalions

130th Regiment (4th Illinois) – three battalions
123rd (5th Illinois) Machine Gun Battalion
66th Brigade
131st Regiment (1st Illinois) – three battalions
132nd Regiment (2nd Illinois) – three battalions
124th (5th Illinois) Machine Gun Battalion

AUSTRALIAN CORPS (Monash)

Divisional and brigade supporting arms as per III Corps

Corps troops – 13th Australian Light Horse, Corps Cyclist Battalion, three 8-inch howitzer brigades, RGA, two 9.2-inch howitzer brigades, two mixed brigades, two mobile brigades, four 6-inch gun batteries, one 12-inch howitzer battery

5th Tank Brigade – 2nd, 8th, 13th, Tank Battalions with Mark Vs, 15th Tank Battalion (Mark V Star), 17th Armoured Car Battalion

1ST AUSTRALIAN DIVISION (GLASGOW)
1st Australian Brigade – 1st, 2nd, 3rd, 4th Battalions (New South Wales)
2nd Australian Brigade – 5th, 6th, 7th, 8th Battalions (Victoria)
3rd Australian Brigade – 9th (Queensland), 10th (South Australia), 11th (Western Australia) , 12th (Tasmania) Battalions

2ND AUSTRALIAN DIVISION (ROSENTHAL)
5th Australian Brigade – 17th, 18th, 19th, 20th Battalions (New South Wales)
6th Australian Brigade – 21st, 22nd, 23rd, 24th Battalions (Victoria)
7th Australian Brigade – 25th (Queensland), 26th (Queensland), 27th (South Australia), 28th (Western Australia) Battalions

3RD AUSTRALIAN DIVISION (GELLIBRAND)
9th Australian Brigade – 33rd, 34th, 35th, 36th Battalions (New South Wales)
10th Australian Brigade – 37th (Victoria), 38th (Victoria), 39th (Victoria), 40th (Tasmania) Battalions
11th Australian Brigade – 41st (Queensland), 42nd (Queensland), 43rd (South Australia), 44th (Western Australia) Battalions

4TH AUSTRALIAN DIVISION (SINCLAIR-MACLAGAN)
4th Australian Brigade – 13th (New South Wales), 14th (Victoria), 15th (Queensland/Tasmania), 16th (Western/South Australia) Battalions
12th Australian Brigade – 45th (New South Wales), 46th (Victoria), 48th (South /Western Australia) Battalions

13th Australian Brigade – 49th (Queensland), 50th (South Australia), 51st (Western Australia) Battalions

5TH AUSTRALIAN DIVISION (TALBOT-HOBBS)
8th Australian Brigade – 29th (Victoria), 30th (New South Wales), 31st (Queensland), 32nd (South/Western Australian) Battalions
14th Australian Brigade – 53rd, 54th, 55th, 56th Battalions (New South Wales)
15th Australian Brigade – 57th, 58th, 59th, 60th Battalions (Victoria)

CANADIAN CORPS (Currie)

Divisional and brigade supporting arms as per III Corps

Corps troops – Canadian Light Horse, Royal North-West Mounted Police, three 8-inch howitzer brigades, one 9.2-inch howitzer brigade, two mixed brigades, three mobile brigades, three 6-inch gun batteries, one 12-inch howitzer battery

4th Tank Brigade – 1st (Mark V Star), 4th, 5th, 14th Tank Battalions (Mark V)

CANADIAN INDEPENDENT FORCE (BRUTINEL)
1st Canadian Motor Machine Gun Brigade – three motor machine-gun batteries, one machine-gun company
2nd Canadian Motor Machine Gun Brigade – two motor machine-gun batteries, one machine-gun company
Canadian Cyclist Battalion
Trench Mortar section (truck mounted)

1ST CANADIAN DIVISION (MACDONELL)
1st Canadian Brigade – 1st (Western Ontario), 2nd (Eastern Ontario), 3rd (Toronto), 4th (Central Ontario) Battalions
2nd Canadian Brigade – 5th (Saskatchewan), 7th (British Columbia), 8th (Manitoba), 10th (Alberta) Battalions
3rd Canadian Brigade – 13th (Royal Highlanders of Canada), 14th (Royal Montreal), 15th (48th Highlanders of Canada), 16th (Canadian Scottish) Battalions

2ND CANADIAN DIVISION (BURSTALL)
4th Canadian Brigade – 18th (Western Ontario), 19th (Central Ontario), 20th (Central Ontario), 21st (Eastern Ontario) Battalions
5th Canadian Brigade – 22nd (French Canadian), 24th (Victoria Rifles of Canada), 25th (Nova Scotia Rifles), 26th (New Brunswick) Battalions

6th Canadian Brigade – 27th (Manitoba), 28th (Saskatchewan), 29th (British Columbia), 31st (Alberta) Battalions

3RD CANADIAN DIVISION (LIPSETT)
7th Canadian Brigade – Princess Patricia's Canadian Light Infantry, Royal Canadian Regiment, 42nd (Royal Highlanders of Canada), 49th (Edmonton) Battalions
8th Canadian Brigade – 1st, 2nd, 4th, 5th Canadian Mounted Rifles
9th Canadian Brigade – 43rd (Manitoba), 52nd (Manitoba), 58th (Central Ontario), 116th (Central Ontario) Battalions

4TH CANADIAN DIVISION (WATSON)
10th Canadian Brigade – 44th (New Brunswick), 46th (South Saskatchewan), 47th (Western Ontario), 50th (Calgary) Battalions
11th Canadian Brigade – 54th (Central Ontario), 75th (Central Ontario), 87th (Canadian Grenadier Guards), 102nd (Central Ontario) Battalions
12th Canadian Brigade – 38th (Ottowa), 72nd Seaforth Highlanders of Canada), 78th (Nova Scotia Highlanders), 85th (Winnipeg Grenadiers) Battalions

NB – the 17th, 32nd and 63rd Divisions were en route to join the Fourth Army.

FRENCH

FIRST ARMY (Debeney)

No details could be found of artillery and other supporting arms under direct army or corps command. There were two battalions of light tanks (Renault).

Each division had four groups of 75mm guns and two of 155mm, two trench mortar batteries, and a cavalry squadron.

II Cavalry Corps (Robillot)

2ND CAVALRY DIVISION (LASSON)
17th, 18th Chasseurs à Cheval
4th, 8th, 12th, 31st Dragoons

4TH CAVALRY DIVISION (LAVIGNE-DEVILLE)
3rd, 6th Cuirassiers

28th, 30th Dragoons
2nd, 4th Hussars

6TH CAVALRY DIVISION (MESPLE)
13th Chasseurs à Cheval
2nd, 14th, 17th, 26th Dragoons
12th Hussars

IX Corps (Garnier-Duplessir)

3RD DIVISION (DE BOURGON)
51st Infantry Regiment – three battalions
87th Infantry Regiment – three battalions
272nd Infantry Regiment – three battalions

15TH COLONIAL DIVISION (GUÉRIN)
2nd Colonial Infantry Regiment – three battalions
5th Colonial Infantry Regiment – three battalions
6th Colonial Infantry Regiment – three battalions

152ND DIVISION (?)
114th Infantry Regiment – three battalions
125th Infantry Regiment – three battalions
135th Infantry Regiment – three battalions

X Corps

60TH DIVISION (RÉVEILHAC)
202nd Infantry Regiment – three battalions
225th Infantry Regiment – three battalions
248th Infantry Regiment – three battalions

166TH DIVISION (?)
170th Infantry Regiment – three battalions
244th Infantry Regiment – three battalions
19th Battalion Chasseurs á Pied
26th Battalion Chasseurs á Pied

169TH DIVISION (?)
13th Infantry Regiment – three battalions
29th Infantry Regiment – three battalions
39th Infantry Regiment – three battalions

XXXI Corps (Toulorge)

37TH DIVISION (SIMON)
2nd Regiment Zoauves – three battalions
3rd Regiment Zoauves – three battalions
2nd Battalion Moroccan Tirailleurs
3rd Battalion Moroccan Tirailleurs

42ND DIVISION (DEVILLE)
94th Infantry Regiment – three battalions
332nd Infantry Regiment – three battalions
8th Battalion Chasseurs á Pied
19th Battalion Chasseurs á Pied

66TH DIVISION (BRISSAUD DESMAILLET)
2nd, 6th, 12th, 17th, 24th, 27th, 28th, 64th, 67th, 68th Battalions Chasseurs
    Alpins
5th Battalion Chasseurs á Pied

126TH DIVISION (MATHIEU)
55th Infantry Regiment – three battalions
112th Infantry Regiment – three battalions
173rd Infantry Regiment – three battalions

153RD DIVISION (?)
418th Infantry Regiment – three battalions
1st Regiment Moroccan Tirailleurs – three battalions
9th Regiment Zoaves – three battalions

GERMAN

Each division had four artillery battalions, a cavalry squadron and a trench
mortar company. No detail could be found on army and corps artillery

SECOND ARMY (von der Marwitz)

XI Corps (Kühne)

13TH DIVISION (VON BORRIES)
26th Infantry Brigade
13th Infantry Regiment (1st Westphalian) – three battalions

15th Infantry Regiment (2nd Westphalian) – three battalions
55th Infantry Regiment (6th Westphalian) – three battalions

41ST DIVISION (GRASER)
74th Infantry Brigade
18th Infantry Regiment (1st Posen) – three battalions
148th Infantry Regiment (5th West Prussian) – three battalions
152nd Infantry Regiment (1st Alsatian) – three battalions

43RD RESERVE DIVISION (KNOCH)
85th Reserve Infantry Brigade
201st Reserve Infantry Regiment – three battalions
202nd Reserve Infantry Regiment – three battalions
203rd Reserve Infantry Regiment – three battalions

107TH DIVISION (HAVENSTEIN)
213th Infantry Brigade
52nd Reserve Infantry Regiment – three battalions
227th Reserve Infantry Regiment – three battalions
232nd Reserve Infantry Regiment – three battalions

LI CORPS (von Hofacker)

14TH BAVARIAN DIVISION (VON KLEINHENZ)
8th Bavarian Infantry Brigade
4th Bavarian Infantry Regiment – three battalions
8th Bavarian Infantry Regiment – three battalions
25th Bavarian Infantry Regiment – three battalions

109TH DIVISION (VON BEHR)
174th Infantry Brigade
2nd Grenadier Regiment (1st Pomeranian) – three battalions
376th Infantry Regiment – three battalions
26th Reserve Infantry Regiment – three battalions

117TH DIVISION (HOEFER)
233rd Infantry Brigade
11th Reserve Infantry Regiment – three battalions
22nd Reserve Infantry Regiment – three battalions
157th Infantry Regiment (4th Silesian) – three battalions

192ND DIVISION (LÖFFLER)
192nd Infantry Brigade

183rd Infantry Regiment – three battalions
192nd Infantry Regiment – three battalions
245th Reserve Infantry Regiment – three battalions

225TH DIVISION (VON WODTKE)
173rd Infantry Brigade
18th Reserve Infantry Regiment – three battalions
217th Reserve Infantry Regiment – three battalions
373rd Reserve Infantry Regiment – three battalions

LIV CORPS (von Larisch)

27TH DIVISION (VON MAUR)
53rd Infantry Brigade
120th Infantry Regiment (2nd Württemberg) – three battalions
123rd Grenadier Regiment (5th Württemberg) – three battalions
124th Infantry Regiment (6th Württemberg) – three battalions

54TH RESERVE DIVISION (KÖHLER)
107th Reserve Infantry Brigade
246th Reserve Infantry Regiment (Württemberg) – three battalions
247th Reserve Infantry Regiment (Württemberg) – three battalions
248th Reserve Infantry Regiment (Württemberg) – three battalions

233RD DIVISION (VON DEWITZ)
243rd Infantry Brigade
448th Infantry Regiment – three battalions
449th Infantry Regiment – three battalions
450th Infantry Regiment – three battalions

243RD DIVISION (VON SCHIPPERT)
247th Infantry Brigade
122nd Fusilier Regiment (Württemberg) – three battalions
478th Infantry Regiment (Württemberg) – three battalions
479th Infantry Regiment (Württemberg) – three battalions

SELECT BIBLIOGRAPHY

Those titles marked with an asterisk can be read on the internet.

PRIMARY UNPUBLISHED SOURCES

Narney, J. C. *The Western Front: Air Operations May – November 1918* RAF Historical Section monograph, the National Archives AIR 1/677/21/13/1887

Rawlinson, FM Lord *War Journal 11 May 1918 – 22 November 1919* and associated loose documents Churchill Archives Centre, Cambridge RWLN 1/11 and 1/12

OFFICIAL HISTORIES

Bean, C. E. W. *Official History of Australia in the War of 1914–18 Vol 6 Angus & Robertson, Sydney, 1942**

Bean, C. E. W. *Anzac to Amiens* Australian War Memorial, Canberra, 1983 edition*

Bose, Major Philo von *Die Katastrophe des 8.August 1918* Verlag von Gerhard Stalling, Berlin, 1930

Cole, Christopher ed *Royal Air Force 1918* William Kimber, London, 1968

Edmonds, Brig Gen Sir James E. CB CMG *History of the Great War: Military Operations France and Belgium 1918* Vol III Macmillan, London, 1939

Edmonds, Brig Gen Sir James E. CB CMG ed *History of the Great War: Military Operations France and Belgium 1918* Vol IV HMSO, London, 1947

Jones, H. A. *The War in the Air* Vol VI HMSO, London, 1937

Nicholson, G. W. L. *Official History of the Canadian Army in the First World War: Canadian Expeditionary Force 1914-1919* Queen's Printer and Controller of Stationery, Ottawa, 1962*

Wise, S. F. *The Official History of the Royal Canadian Air Force Volume 1: Canadian Airmen and the First World War* University of Toronto Press, 1980

PERSONAL ACCOUNTS

Bion, Wilfred R. *The Long Weekend 1897–1919: Part of a Life* Fleetwood Press, Abingdon, 1982

Dinesen, Thomas VC *A Dane with the Canadians* Jarrolds, London, 1930 (recently republished by the Naval and Military Press)

Downing, W. H. *To the Last Ridge: The War Experiences of W H Downing* Grub Street, London paperback edition, 2002

Foch, Ferdinand, trans Colonel T Bentley Nott *The Memoirs of Marshal Foch* Heinemann, London, 1931

Hankey, Lord *The Supreme Command 1914–1918* Vol 2 Allen & Unwin, London, 1961

Hickey, Capt D. E. *Rolling into Action: Memoirs of a Tank Corps Section Commander* Hutchinson, London, 1936

Hindenburg, Field Marshal von *The Great War* Greenhill Books, London, 2006

Lambert, Bill DFC *Combat Report* Corgi paperback edition, London, 1973

Livesay, J. F. B. *Canada's Hundred Days: With the Canadian Corps from Amiens to Mons, Aug 8 – Nov 11, 1918* Thomas Allan, Toronto, 1919*

Ludendorff, Erich *My War Memories 1914–1918* Vol II Hutchinson, London, 1919

Scott, Canon Frederick George CMG DSO *The Great War as I saw it* F. D. Fairchild, Toronto, 1922*

Sheffield, Gary and Bourne, John ed *Douglas Haig: War Diaries and Letters 1914–1918* Weidenfeld & Nicolson, London, 2005

FORMATION AND UNIT HISTORIES

The Adjutant *The 116th Battalion in France* E. P. S. Allen, Toronto, 1921*

Anglesey, The Marquess of FSA *A History of British Cavalry 1816–1919 Volume 8: The Western Front, 1915–1918, Epilogue, 1919–1939* Leo Cooper, London, 1997

Bennett, Capt S. G. MC *The 4th Canadian Mounted Rifles 1914–1919* Murray Printing Co, Toronto, 1926*

Brumwell, P Middleton MC CF *The History of the 12th (Eastern) Division in the Great War, 1914–1918* Nisbet & Co, London, 1923

Carne, Lt W. A. *In Good Company: An Account of the 6th Machine Gun Company AIF in search of Peace 1915–1919* 6th Machine Gun Company (AIF) Association, Melbourne, 1937

Dean, Arthur & Gutteridge, Eric W. *The Seventh Battalion AIF: Resumé of Activities of the Seventh Battalion in the Great War – 1914–1918* Abb-typesetting Pty Ltd, Melbourne, 1986 (original edition 1933)

Farndale, Gen Sir Martin KCB *History of the Royal Regiment of Artillery: Western Front 1914–18* Royal Artillery Association, Woolwich, 1986

Godfrey, Capt E. G. MC *The 'Cast Iron Sixth': A History of the Sixth Battalion London Regiment (City of London Rifles)* Stapleton, London, 1938

Grafton, Lt Col C. S. *A History of the Canadian Machine Gun Corps* Canadian Machine Gun Corps Association, 1938*

Green, F. C. *The Fortieth: A Record of the 40th Battalion AIF* John Vail, Hobart, 1922

Grasset, Col A. *Montdidier: Le 8 Aout à la 42e Division* Berger-Levrault, Paris, 1933

Liddell Hart, Capt B. H. *The Tanks: A History of the Royal Tank Regiment and its Predecessors: Volume 1 1914–1939* Cassell, London, 1959

Longmore, Capt C. *The Old Sixteenth: Being a Record of the 16th Battalion AIF During the Great War, 1914–1918* History Committee of the 16th Battalion Association, Perth, 1929

Mackenzie, Lt Col K. W. MC *The Story of the Seventeenth Battalion AIF in the Great War 1914–1918* privately, Sydney, 1946

Messenger, Charles *Terriers in the Trenches: The Post Office Rifles at War 1914–1918* Picton Publishing, Chippenham, 1982

Montgomery, Maj Gen Sir Archibald KCMG CB *The Story of the Fourth Army in the Battle of the Hundred Days, August 8th to November 11th, 1918* Hodder & Stoughton, London, 1931

Nichols, Capt G. H. F. *The 18th Division in the Great War* Blackwood, London, 1922

Rutter, Owen ed *The History of the Seventh (Service) Battalion the Royal Sussex Regiment 1914–1919* Times Publishing Company, London, 1934

Sanborn, Col Joseph B. *The 131st US Infantry (First Infantry Illinois National Guard): Narrative – Operations – Statistics* Chicago, Illinois, 1919

Wanliss, Newton *The History of the Fourteenth Battalion AIF: Being the Story of the Vicissitudes of an Australian Unit during the Great War* Arrow Printery, Melbourne, 1929

Williams-Ellis, Maj Clough MC & Williams-Ellis, A. *The Tank Corps* George Newnes, London, 1919

SECONDARY SOURCES

Bilton, David *Images of War: The German Army on the Western Front 1917–1918* Pen & Sword, Barnsley, 2007

Clayton, Anthony *Paths of Glory: The French Army 1914–1918* Cassell, London, 2003

Coffman, Edward M. *The War to End All Wars: The American Military Experience in World War 1* Oxford University Press, New York, 1968

Falls, Cyril *The Great War 1914–1918* Capricorn Books edition, New York, 1961

Fuller, Bt Col J. F. C. DSO *Tanks in the Great War* John Murray, London, 1920

Harris, J. P. with Barr, Niall *Amiens to the Armistice: The BEF in the Hundred Days Campaign, 8 August – 11 November 1918* Brassey's, London and New York, 1998

Hart, Peter *Aces Falling: War Above the Trenches, 1918* Weidenfeld & Nicolson, London, 2007

Jones, Ralph E., Rarey, George H., Icks, Robert J. *The Fighting Tanks since 1916* National Service Publishing Co, Washington DC, 1933

Kabisch, Maj Gen Ernst *Der Schwarze Tag: Die Nebelschlacht von Amiens (8/9 August 1918)* Verlag Otto Schegel, Berlin, 1938

Lee, John *The Warlords: Hindenburg and Ludendorff* Weidenfeld & Nicolson, London, 2005

Livesey, Anthony *The Viking Atlas of World War 1* Viking, London & New York, 1994

Matrix Evans, Martin *1918: The Year of Victories* Arcturus Publishing, London, 2002

McWilliams, James & Steel, R. James *Amiens 1918* Tempus, Stroud, 2004

Messenger, Charles *Call to Arms: The British Army 1914–18* Weidenfeld & Nicolson, London, 2005

Nash, D. B. *Imperial German Army Handbook 1914–1918* Ian Allan, London, 1980

Palmer, Alan *Victory 1918* Weidenfeld & Nicolson, London, 1998

Pedersen, P. A. *Monash as Military Commander* Melbourne University Press, 1985

Prior, Robin & Wilson, Trevor *Command on the Western Front: The Military Career of Sir Henry Rawlinson 1914–18* Blackwell, Oxford, 1992

Schreiber, Shane B. *Shock Army of the British Empire: The Canadian Corps in the Last 100 Days of the Great War* Vanwell paperback edition, St Catherine's, Ontario, 2004

Serle, Geoffrey *John Monash: A Biography* Melbourne University Press, 1982

Simpson, Andy *Directing Operations: British Corps Command on the Western Front 1914–18* Spellmount, Stroud, 2006

Terraine, John *To Win a War: 1918 The Year of Victory* Sidgwick & Jackson, London, 1978

Travers, Tim *How the War was Won: Command and Technology on the Western Front 1917–1918* Routledge, London & New York, 1992

Wilson, Trevor *The Myriad Faces of War: Britain and the Great War, 1914–1918* Polity Press, Cambridge, 1986

Woodward, David R. *Lloyd George and the Generals* Associated University Presses, London and Toronto, 1983

WEBSITES

1914-18.net: Eine Projekt von Malt Znaniecki http://www.1914-18.info/erster-weltkrieg.php?u=17&info=Home (potted German formation histories)

Australian War Memorial Collections http://cas.awm.gov.au/TST2/cst.acct_master?surl=1993037855ZZSDPAELDBQP34908&stype=4&simplesearch=&v-umo=&v_product_id=&screen_name=&screen_parms=&screen_type=RIGHT&bvers=4&bplatform=Microsoft%20Internet%20Explorer&bos=Win32

Canadian Expeditionary Force Study Group http://www.cefresearch.com/matrix/index.html

Histoire des divisions de l'armée française http://fr.wikipedia.org/wiki/Cat%C3%A9gorie:Histoire_des_divisions_de_l%27arm%C3%A9e_fran%C3%A7aise

Library and Archives Canada – http://www.collectionscanada.ca/archivianet/020152_e.html

The Long, Long Trail http://www.1914-1918.net/ and associated forum

The National Archives, Kew, UK http://www.nationalarchives.gov.uk/default.htm

NOTES

AWM – Australian War Memorial
TNA – The National Archives, Kew, London

Chapter 1 Setting the Scene

1 4th Australian Division Intelligence Summary of 13 July 1918 TNA WO 95/3446
2 Clayton *Paths of Glory* p.169
3 The censor report is found as an annex to a volume of the Haig diary under TNA WO 256/33
4 Bean *Anzac to Amiens*, p.447
5 Haig diary entry, 1 June 1918
6 http://www.firstworldwar.com/source/additionalusforces_pms.htm
7 *Reports of Commander-in-Chief AEF: Staff Sections and Services* Historical Division, Department of the Army, Washington DC, 1948, p.5
8 *Ibid.*, p.14
9 Rawlinson diary entry, 1 July 1918
10 *Ibid.*, 30 June 1918
11 Haig diary entry, 1 July 1918
12 Beaumont, R. A. *Hamel, 1918: A Study in Military-Political Interaction* Military Affairs Vol. 31, No 1 (Spring 1967), p.14
13 Bean *Official History*, Vol. 6, p.263
14 Longmore *The Old Sixteenth*, p.180
15 This account is taken from Bean, *op. cit.*, pp.277–9, and Haig and Rawlinson diary entries. That of Rawlinson does not reflect his discussion with Monash on the early evening of 3 July.
16 Bean, *Official History* Vol. 6, pp.284, 285
17 Edmonds, *Military Operations France and Belgium 1918*, Vol. III, p.207fn
18 TNA WO 95/3324
19 The German viewpoint is taken mainly from information collected by

Capt J. J. W. Herbertson from the German archives in the early
1920s for the Australian Official History and found under TNA
CAB 45/172
20 Roskill, *Hankey: Man of Secrets*, p.570
21 11th Australian Brigade War Diary TNA WO 95/3429, which has the
full text of the speech.

Chapter 2 Planning

1 Haig diary entry, 5 July 1918
2 TNA WO 158/72
3 A translation of Directive No 3 is found in Edmonds *1918*, Vol. 3, Appendix
II
4 Haig diary entry, 17 May 1918
5 Bean, *Official History of Australia in the War of 1914–18*, Vol. 6, pp.466–7
6 Rawlinson diary entry, 13 July 1918
7 Haig diary entry, 16 July 1918 TNA WO 256/33
8 TNA WO 158/24 gives the full plan
9 Edmonds, *1918* Vol. 3, pp.313–14
10 Rawlinson diary entry, 21 July 1918
11 TNA WO 158/20 *Situation on the British Front and Proposals for Counter-offensive Operations*
12 TNA WO 158/83
13 Foch, *The Memoirs of Marshal Foch*, pp.425–30
14 Haig diary entry, 24 July 1918
15 Rawlinson diary entry, 24 July 1918
16 TNA WO 158/241
17 TNA WO 158/29 contains Foch's original letter and directive. That
Debeney had been placed under Haig's command is confirmed by a
letter written by Lawrence on that same day, 28 July, to Rawlinson and
Debeney. It also confirmed the aim of freeing up Amiens and the Paris–
Amiens railway (see WO 158/241).
18 Rawlinson diary entry, 28 July 1918
19 The full text of all these orders is given in Edmonds, *1918*, Vol. 4, pp.524–7.
20 Pedersen, *Monash as Military Commander* p.244
21 Bean, *op. cit.* pp.504–5, Haig diary entry, 31 July 1918
22 Rawlinson diary entry, 31 July 1918
23 Diary entry, 3 August 1918 from Briscoe, Diana ed., *The Diary of a World
War I Cavalry Officer* (Costello, Tunbridge Wells, 1985)
24 Sheffield & Bourne, *Douglas Haig* p.434 for Haig's letter to Wilson,

Jeffery, Keith ed. *The Military Correspondence of Sir Henry Wilson 1918–1922* (Bodley Head for Army Records Society, London, 1985) pp.47–8 for Wilson – du Cane letters, Hankey, Lord, *The Supreme Command 1914–1918*, Vol. 2 (Allen and Unwin, London, 1961) pp.829–30, Roskill, Stephen, *Hankey: Man of Secrets – Volume 1 1877–1918* (Collins, London, 1970) pp.584–6, Woodward, David R., *Lloyd George and the Generals* (Associated University Presses, London and Toronto, 1983) pp.324–6.

Chapter 3 Preparation

1 The full text of this notice is given in Edmonds, *Military Operations France and Belgium 1918*, Vol. 4, p.16, Note 2
2 HQ Canadian Corps G Branch War Diary TNA WO 95/1053
3 TNA WO 95/1052, 1053 HQ Canadian Corps G Branch War Diary
4 The logistical problems are based on Schreiber *Shock Army of the British Army*, pp.37–9
5 Livesay, *Canada's Hundred Days*, pp.21–2
6 1st Can Div report on Amiens attack in G Branch war diary TNA WO 95/3730
7 Bennett, *The 4th Canadian Mounted Rifles*, p.112
8 This account is based on *Ibid.*, pp.111–14
9 Canadian 27th Infantry Battalion war diary, TNA WO 95/3831
10 Nerney, *The Western Front: Air Operations May –November 1918*, p.65 fn TNA AIR 1/677/21/13/1887
11 Drawn largely on a report on the Battle of Amiens found in HQ Tank Corps War Diary TNA WO 95/94
12 Doneley, Bob *Black over Blue: The 25th Battalion at War 1915–1918*, pp.141–2 USQ Press, Toowoomba, Queensland, 1997
13 Haig and Rawlinson diary entries
14 TNA WO 95/3446
15 A copy of the German interrogation report was later captured and a translation of it is found at Appendix 15 to the 13th Australian Infantry Brigade war diary TNA WO 95/3520
16 Letter dated 18 November 1918 AWM 2DRL/1298
17 Sample load is taken from Appendix E to HQ 5th Tank Bde's report on operations with the Australian Corps 8–15 Aug, TNA WO 95/112
18 From the 102nd Infantry Battalion history, Ch 10 www.102ndbattalioncef.ca
19 TNA WO 95/3866
20 AWM PR 86/341
21 Rawlinson diary entry 4 August 1918

22 Report of Conference at HQ Fourth Army 5 August 1918 TNA WO 158/241

23 Haig and Rawlinson diary entries, 5 August 1918

24 Edmonds, *op. cit.*, pp.31–4

25 *Cavalry Corps Instructions No 2* TNA WO 95/575

26 Full orders are given in Edmonds, *op. cit.*, pp.574–5

27 TNA WO 158/20

28 Edmonds, *op. cit.*, p.28

29 This detail on 5 Tank Bde is taken from its report on operations 8–15 Aug, *op. cit.*

30 Bion, *The Long Weekend*, pp.229–240

31 TNA CAB 45/203 and also quoted in Falls, Cyril *The Great War 1914–1918* (Capricorn Books paperback edition, New York, 1961) p.374

32 Bennett, *op. cit.*, p.114

33 The Adjutant, *The 116th Battalion in France*, p.65

34 Dinesen, *A Dane with the Canadians*, pp.214–15

35 Rutter, *History of the Seventh (Service) Battalion The Royal Sussex Regiment*, pp.221–3

36 Messenger, *Terriers in the Trenches*, p.118

37 *Recollections of the "Push" of 7th–8th August* http://members.ozemail.com.au/~imcfayden/finney.htm

38 Bion, *op. cit.*, pp.241–4

39 1st Canadian Division report on the operation p.7 TNA WO 95/3730

40 Green, *The Fortieth*, p.149

41 Edmonds, *op. cit.*, p.38

42 *My War 1917–18* AWM PR00420.

43 Scott, *The Great War as I saw it*, p.275

44 Diary entry AWM PR01463712

Chapter 4 The Green Line

1 Mackenzie, *The Story of the Seventeenth Battalion AIF in the Great War*, p.259

2 http://www.canadianletters.ca/collectionsSoldier.php?collectionid=115&warid=3

3 Diary entry AWM 83/155

4 Godfrey, *The 'Cast Iron Sixth'*, pp.222–3

5 Rutter, *The History of the Seventh (Service) Battalion the Royal Sussex Regiment*, pp.223–4

6 Longmore, Capt C. *Eggs-a-Cook: The Story of the Forty-Fourth: War – As the Digger Saw it* p.106 Colortype Press Ltd, Perth, 1921

7 Brahms, Vivian *Cede Nullis: The History of the 42nd Battalion, 11th Infantry Brigade, Third Division, Australian Imperial Force during the Great War of 1914–1918* Smith and Patterson, Brisbane, 1938 and http://www.firstaif.info/42/spirit42/c6-enterprise.htm

8 Carne, *In Good Company*, p.331

9 Mackenzie, *op. cit.*, p.261

10 Bryce, Lt Col E. D. DSO *2nd Tank Battalion: Report on Operations of 8th August, 1918* TNA WO 95/3549

11 19th Canadian Battalion war diary August 1918 Appendix 2 TNA WO 95/3816

12 1st Canadian Division report on operations, war diary TNA WO 95/3730

13 *Narrative of Action in Front of Amiens, August 8th, 1918* 16th Battalion war diary TNA WO 95/3781

14 Rawlinson diary entry, 7 August 1918

15 The Adjutant, *The 116th Battalion in France*, p.64

16 43rd Battalion war diary TNA WO 95/3878

17 *Ibid.*

18 Grasset *Montdidier: Le 8 Aout à la 42e Division* p.82

19 *Ibid.*, pp.96–7

20 *Ibid.*, p.104

21 Falls diary TNA CAB 45/203

22 Grant diary TNA WO 106/1456. Du Cane letter is in Jeffery *The Military Correspondence of Sir Henry Wilson 1918–1922*, p.48

Chapter 5 To the Blue Line and Beyond

1 *My War 1917–1918* AWM PR00420

2 Wurtele, *Amiens – August 1918* http://thercr.ca/history/1914-1919/amiens_1918_wurtele.htm

3 Downing, *To the Last Ridge*, p.143

4 5th Australian Division *Report on Operations* TNA WO 95/3549

5 Freeman, Roger *Second to None: A Memorial History of the 32nd Battalion AIF 1915–1919*, pp.226–7 Peacock Publications, Norwood, South Australia, 2006

6 *The Victory of August 8, 1918* Reveille Vol. 9, No 12, 1 August 1936, p.21

7 *History of the 13th Tank Battalion*, p.35 TNA WO 95/115

8 Wanliss *History of the Fourteenth Battalion AIF*, p.320

9 *Ibid.*, p.323

10 Bean, Vol. 6, p.569

11 Longmore, *The Old Sixteenth* p.187

12 Lee, Maj J. E. DSO MC *The Chronicle of the 45th Battalion AIF* pp68–69 Australian Defence League, Sydney, 1926

13 Letter to Brig Gen Edmonds, the Official British Historian, 20 May 1939 TNA WO 95/1053

14 *2nd Tank Battalion: Report on Operations of 8th August, 1918* TNA WO 95/3459

15 Marix Evans, *1918: The Year of Victories*, p.165

16 *History of the 15th Tank Battalion* TNA WO 95/103

17 *Narney The Western Front Air Operations May –November 1918*, p.121

18 Bean, Vol. 6, p.576

19 http://www.awm.gov.au/1918/battles/amiensgun.htm

20 Lt Arnold's full account dated 1 Jan 19 originally appeared in *Weekly Tank Notes* in Jan 19 and is reproduced in Williams-Ellis, *The Tank Corps*, pp.201–6

21 Greenhous, Brereton, *Dragoon – The Centennial History of the Royal Canadian Dragoons*, p.233 Guild of the Royal Canadian Dragoons, Belleville, Ontario, 1983 (originally published in the *Canadian Defence Quarterly* Vol. IV No 2 January 1927)

22 *Ibid.*, p.234

23 The account of the 17th Battalion's activities is drawn from its war diary WO 95/116 and that of 5th Australian Division (WO 95/3549), which also includes reports by the individual section commanders. A copy of that by Lt Rollings is also found in the Tank Museum, Bovington under reference 04216.

24 *Report on Operations in Conjunction with Tanks August 8th 1918* 4th Canadian Machine Gun Battalion war diary

25 Grafton, *A History of the Canadian Machine Gun Corps*, pp.139–40

26 Travers, Tim *Could the Tanks of 1918 have been War-Winners for the British Expeditionary Force?* Journal of Contemporary History Vol. 2 No 3 (July 1992), pp.400–401

27 8th Tank Battalion report on operations TNA WO 95/114

28 Diary entry AWM PR01463/12

29 St Clair, Ross *Our Gift to Empire: 54th Australian Infantry Battalion 1916–1919*, p.202 the author, Sydney, 2006

30 Letter No 66 dated 22 August 1918 Cranswick Letters held in the Army Museum, Western Australia under reference PD605

31 Grasset, *Le 8 Aout 1918 à la 42e Division*, p.143

32 *Ibid.*, pp.219–220

33 Bose *Die Katastrophe des 8.August 1918*, p.196

Chapter 6 In the Air

1 Hart, *Aces Falling*, p.212
2 *Ibid.*, p.213
3 Lambert, *Combat Report*, p.219
4 Narney, *Western Front Air Operations*, p.128 TNA AIR 1/677/21/13/1887
5 *Ibid.*, p.127

Chapter 7 What to Do Next?

1 Diary entry, 8 August 1918
2 Montgomery-Massingberd, Gen Sir Archibald, *August 8, 1918*, Reveille, Vol. 6, No 1, 1 September 1932 (reprinted from the Royal Artillery Journal)
3 HQ Fourth Army war diary TNA WO 95/437
4 Letter to Brig Gen Edmonds, the official historian, dated 8 May 1939 TNA WO 95/1053
5 *Report on Operations of 32nd Division August 10th & 11th 1918* TNA WO 95/2372
6 *5th CMR Battalion Summary of Operations period Aug 8th, 1918 to August 10th, 1918, inclusive* 5CMR war diary TNA WO 95/3873
7 1st Canadian Division report war diary TNA WO 95/3730
8 Dean & Gutteridge, *The Seventh Battalion AIF*, p.121
9 Austin, Ronald J., *Cobbers in Khaki: The History of the 8th Battalion 1914–1919*, p.201 Slouch Hat Publications, McCrae, Victoria, 1997
10 This account is taken from Bean, p.637 and Mackenzie, *The Story of the Seventeenth Battalion AIF*, pp.266–8
11 Mackenzie, *op. cit.*, pp.268–9
12 Doneley, Bob, *Black Over Blue: The 25th Battalion at War 1915–1918*, p.146 USQ Press, Toowoomba, Queensland, 1997
13 Travers, *How the War was Won*, p.126
14 Bean, pp. 624–6, Austin, Ron, *Black and Gold: The History of the 29th Battalion 1915–18*, pp.141–4, Slouch Hat Publications, Macrae, Victoria, 1997, 5th Australian Division War Diary TNA 95/3549
15 Sanborn, *The 131st Infantry in the World War*, p.212
16 *Ibid.*, p.60
17 Godfrey, *The 'Cast Iron Sixth'*, p.226
18 175th Brigade *Report on Operations August 8th to 10th 1918* TNA WO 95/2990
19 Patrol report in 1st Australian Bn War Diary TNA WO 95/3217, Bean pp.651–2, Stacy, B. V., Kindon, F. J., Chedgey, H. V., *The History of the First Battalion AIF 1914–1919*, pp.104–5

20 Sanborn, *op. cit.*, pp.212–13
21 175th Brigade Report, *op. cit.*
22 Edmonds, *1918*, Vol. 4, p.110
23 Jones, *War in the Air*, Vol. 6, p.447
24 Hart, *Aces Falling*, pp.222–3

Chapter 8 Days Three and Four

1 Edmonds, *Military Operations*, Vol. 4, p.139
2 Haig diary entry, 9 August 1918
3 Both orders are given in TNA WO 158/241
4 32nd Division report on operations, TNA WO 95/2372
5 4th Canadian Division report on operations, TNA WO 95/3882
6 Doneley, Bob *Black over Blue: The 25th Battalion at War 1915–1918*, p.147 USQ Press, Toowoomba, Queensland, 1997
7 HQ 4th Australian Division report on operations TNA WO 95/3446
8 Bean, p.687
9 McNicol, N. G., *The Thirty-Seventh: History of the Thirty-Seventh Battalion AIF*, pp.219–220 Modern Printing Co, Melbourne, 1936
10 *Ibid.*, p.220
11 p.41TNA WO 95/114
12 Hickey, *Rolling into Action*, p.246
13 TNA WO 95/112
14 13th Australian Brigade report, TNA WO 95/3520
15 Browning, Neville *For King and Cobbers: The History of the 51st Battalion AIF 1916–1919* p.297 the author, Perth, 2007
16 8th Tank Battalion report on operations TNA WO 95/103
17 Haig diary entry, 10 August 1918
18 Edmonds, *1918*, Vol. 4, p.138
19 TNA WO 158/241
20 HQ Canadian Corps War DiaryTNA WO 95/1053
21 HQ Cavalry Corps war diary TNA WO 95/575 and Home, *The Diary of a World War I Cavalry Officer*, p.180
22 TNA WO 95/3166
23 Austin, Ronald J., *Cobbers in Khaki: The History of the 8th Battalion 1914–1919*, p.208 Slouch Hat Publications, McCrae, Victoria, 1997
24 Fairey, Eric, *The 38th Battalion AIF: The Story and Official History of the 38th Battalion AIF*, pp.65–6 Bendigo Advertiser and Cambridge Press, Bendigo, Victoria, 1920
25 *History of the 13th Tank Battalion*, p.40 TNA WO 95/115
26 Falls Diary TNA CAB 45/203

27 Narney, *The Western Front: Air Operations*, p.149
28 Serle, Geoffrey, *John Monash: A Biography*, pp.349–50
29 *Ibid.*, p.350

Chapter 9 The Impact of Amiens

1 Edmonds, *1918*, Vol. 4, p.140
2 Ludendorff, *My War Memories*, Vol. II, pp.684–7
3 Hindenburg, *The Great War*, pp.202–3
4 Diary entry, 12 August 1918
5 TNA WO 158/241
6 Terraine, *To Win a War*, p.130
7 Woodward, *Lloyd George and the Generals*, p.331, Sheffield & Bourne, *Douglas Haig*, p.453, Jeffery, *The Military Correspondence of Field Marshal Sir Henry Wilson*, p.50
8 Terraine, *op. cit.*, p.143
9 Diary entry, 10 September 1918
10 Lee, *The Warlords*, p.179
11 Figures taken from TNA WO 153/24

Postscript: The Man Who Won the War?

1 Bean, *Official History of Australia*, Vol. 4, p.578
2 Montgomery, *The Story of the Fourth Army*, p.149
3 This account is largely drawn from Rollings's personal file in TNA WO 339/73494 and an article about him on the website of the South Wales Branch of the Western Front Association under http://www.powell76.freeserve.co.uk/Rollings.htm

INDEX